Mahatma Gandhi

MAHATMA GANDHI

Dr. C.P. Raj
Dr. Ved Prakash

AMIGA PRESS. INC
Delhi -110051

AMIGA PRESS. INC
H.O :- 28-A, Indra Park, Chander Nagar
Delhi :- 110051 (India)
Tel :- 011-22504028, +91-98736-57000
Email :- amigapress@gmail.com
amigaeditorial@gmail.com
Website :- www.amigapress@co.in

This edition is published by Amiga Press.Inc

ISBN : 978-93-84533-24-3

First Published 2018

PRINTED : THOMSON PRESS INDIA

Preface

Gandhi was born on October 2, 1869, at Porbandar. Mohandas or Mohan was youngest of the three sons of Putlibai and Karamchand Gandhi. In January 1948, before three pistol shots put an end to his life, Gandhi had been on the political stage for more than fifty years. He had inspired two generations of India, patriots, shaken an empire and sparked off a revolution which was to change the face of Africa and Asia. To millions of his own people, he was the Mahatma-the great soul-whose sacred glimpse was a reward in itself. By the end of 1947 he had lived down much of the suspicion, ridicule and opposition which he had to face, when he first raised the banner of revolt against racial exclusiveness and imperial domination. His ideas, once dismissed as quaint and utopian, had begun to strike answering chords in some of the finest minds in the world. "Generations to come, it may be", Einstein had said of Gandhi in July 1944, "will scarcely believe that such one as this ever in flesh and blood walked upon earth."

A hero's welcome awaited Gandhi when he landed on January 9, 1915, at the Apollo Bunder in Bombay. Three days later he was honoured by the people of Bombay at a magnificent reception in the palatial house of a Bombay magnate Jehangir Petit. The Government of India joined with the people of India in showering honours on Gandhi. He received a "Kaiser-I-Hind" gold medal in the King's birthday honours list of 1915. His association with Gokhale was guarantee enough of his being a safe politician. Of course, he had led an extra-constitutional movement in South Africa, defied laws and filled goals, but the cause for which he had fought appeared as much humanitarian as political, dear to all Indian as and all Englishmen whose sense of humanity had not been blunted by racial arrogance or political expediency. Lord Hardinge's open support of the Satyagraha movement had in any case removed the stigma of rebellion from South Africa's Indian movement.

It was the Rowlatt Bill with its denial of civil liberties which finally brought Gandhi into active Indian politics. From 1919 to his death in 1948, he occupied the centre of the Indian stage and was the hero of the great historical drama which culminated in the independence of his country. He changed the entire character of the political scene in India. He only grew. In the thick of the battle he remained a man of God.

Gandhi stayed out of the limelight for most of the 1920s, preferring to resolve the wedge between the Swaraj Party and the Indian National Congress, and expanding initiatives against untouchability, alcoholism, ignorance and poverty. He returned to the fore in 1928. The year before, the British government had appointed a new constitutional reform commission under Sir John Simon, numbering not a single Indian in its ranks. The result was a boycott of the commission by Indian political parties.

World War II broke out in 1939 when Nazi Germany invaded Poland. Initially, Gandhi had favoured offering "non-violent moral support" to the British effort, but other Congress leaders were offended by the unilateral inclusion of India into the war, without consultation of the people's representatives. All Congressmen elected to office resigned en masse.

After Partition in 1947, he continued to work toward peace between Hindus and Muslims. Gandhi was shot to death in Delhi in January 1948 by a Hindu fundamentalist.

In January 1948, Gandhi carried out yet another fast, this time to bring about peace in the city of Delhi. On January 30, 12 days after that fast ended, Gandhi was on his way to an evening prayer meeting in Delhi when he was shot to death by Nathuram Godse, a Hindu fanatic enraged by Mahatma's efforts to negotiate with Jinnah and other Muslims. The next day, roughly 1 million people followed the procession as Gandhi's body was carried in state through the streets of the city and cremated on the banks of the holy Jumna River.

—*Editor*

Contents

1

Biography

Mohandas Karamchand Gandhi was a man considered one of the great sages and prophets. He was held as another Buddha, another Jesus, Indians called him the 'Father of the Nation'. They showered their love, respect and devotion on him in an unprecedented measure. They thronged his way to have a glimpse of him, to hear one world from his lips. They applied on their foreheads the dust on the path he had trodden. For them, he was almost an incarnation of God, who had come to break the chains of their slavery. The whole world bowed to him in reverence. Even his opponents held him in great respect.

Mohandas Gandhi was, however, not a great scholar, nor was he a great warrior. He was not born with exceptional faculties. Neither was he a good orator, nor a great writer. He did not claim anything exclusively divine in him. He did not claim being a prophet or having superhuman powers. He considered himself an average man with average abilities. Born in a middle class Bania family in an obscure princely State in a corner of India, he was a mediocre student, shy and nervous. He could not muster courage to speak in public. His first attempt at legal practice miserably failed.

But he was a humble seeker of Truth. He was a man with exceptional sincerity, honesty and truthfulness. For him, understanding meant action. Once any principle appealed to him, he immediately began to translate that in practice. He did not flinch from taking risks and did not mind confessing mistakes. No opposition, scorn or ridicule could affect him. Truth was his sole guiding star. He was ever-growing; hence he was often found inconsistent. He was not concerned with appearing to be consistent. He preferred to be consistent only with the light within. He sacrificed his all and identified himself with the poorest of the poor. He dressed like them, lived like them. In the oppressed and the depressed people, he saw God. For him, they too were sparks of the divine light. They might not have anything else, but they too had a soul. For Gandhi, soul-force was the source of the greatest power.

He strove to awaken the soul-force within himself and within his fellowmen. He was convinced that the potentialities of the soul-force have no limit. He himself was a living example of this conviction. That is why this tiny and fragile man could mobilise the masses and defeat the mighty British empire. His eleven vows, his technique of Satyagraha, his constructive programme-all were meant to awaken and strengthen the soul-force. He awakened and aroused a nation from semi-consciousness. It was a Herculean task. For, India was not a united country, it was a sub-continent. It was a society divided in different classes, castes and races, in people with different languages, religions and cultures.

It was a society where almost half of the population *i.e.,* women, was behind purdah or confined to the four walls of houses, where one-fourth of the population-the depressed classes-was living marginalised life, where many did not have a single full meal every day. Gandhi made the oppressed sections wake up and break their chains.

He mobilised the people and united them to work for the cause of Swaraj, which gave them a sense of belonging, a sense of purpose. Gandhi wanted to win Swaraj for the masses. For him, Swaraj did not mean replacement of White masters by brown masters. Swaraj meant self-rule by all. He said: "Real Swaraj will come, not by the acquisition of the authority by a few, but by the acquisition of the capacity by all to resist authority when it is abused." He worked to develop such a capacity. Development of such a capacity involved transformation of the individual.

Transformation of the individual and transformation of the society-they were not separate, unrelated things for Gandhi. Revolutionary social philosophies had concentrated on changing the society. On the other hand, spiritual seekers had concentrated on the inner change. Gandhi not only bridged the gap between these extremes, he fused them together. Gandhi was thus both a saint and a social revolutionary. For Gandhi, unity of life was great truth. His principle of nonviolence stemmed from this conviction. Nonviolence was not a matter of policy for him; it was a matter of faith. He applied the doctrine to all the departments of individual and social life and in so doing revolutionized the doctrine, made it dynamic and creative. He believed that a true civilization could be built on the basis of such nonviolence only.

He rejected the modern civilization. For him, it was a disease and a curse. This civilization leads to violence, conflicts, corruption, injustices, exploitation, oppression, mistrust and a process of dehumanisation. It has led the world to a deep crisis. The earth's resources are being cornered by a handful of people without any concern for others and for the coming generations. The conventional energy sources are getting depleted. Forests are being destroyed. Air, water, soil-everything has been polluted.

We are living under the shadow of nuclear war and environmental disasters. Thinking men the world over are looking to Gandhi to find a way out of this crisis and to build an alternative model of sustainable development. Gandhi knew that the earth has enough to satisfy everybody's need but not anybody's greed. He had called for the replacement of greed with love.

Gandhi is, therefore, now a source of inspiration and a reference book for all those fighting against racial discrimination, oppression, domination, wars, nuclear energy, environmental degradation, lack of freedom and human rights-for all those who are fighting for a better world, a better quality of life. Gandhi is, therefore, no longer an individual. He is a symbol of all that is the best and the most enduring in the human tradition. And he is also a symbol of the alternative in all areas of life-agriculture, industry, technology, education, health, economy, political organisations, etc. He is a man of the future-a future that has to be shaped if the human race has to survive and progress on the path of evolution.

BIRTH AND PARENTAGE

Mohandas Karamchand Gandhi was born at Porbandar, a coastal city in Kathiawad (now a part of the Gujarat State) on the 2nd October 1869. He was the youngest child of his parents, Karamchand and Putlibai.

Gandhis belonged to the Modh Bania community. They were originally grocers. However, Uttamchand, Mohan's grandfather, rose to become Dewan of the Porbandar State. Mohan's father. Karamchand, also served as the Dewan of Porbandar, Rajkot and Vankaner States. Kathiawar then had about 300 small States. Court intrigues were the order of the day. At times, Gandhis became their victim. Uttamchand's house was once surrounded and shelled by the State troops. Karamchand was once arrested. However, their courage and wisdom earned them respect. Karamchand even became a member of the Rajashanik Court, a powerful agency to solve disputes among the States.

Karamchand had little education, but had shrewdness of judgment and practical knowledge acquired through experience. He had little inclination to amass wealth and left little for his children. He used to say that "My children are my wealth'. He married four times, had two daughters by the first two marriages and one daughter and three sons by his fourth marriage. Putlibai, his fourth wife, was younger to him by 25 years. She was not much educated but was well-informed about practical matters. Ladies at the palace used to value her advice. She was deeply religious and superstitious and had strong will-power. She used to visit the temple daily and regularly kept difficult vows. Mohan loved his mother. He used to accompany her to the Haveli (Vaishnav temple). Mohan had a great devotion for his father and he often used to be present at the discussions about the State problems. Gandhis had Parsi and Muslim friends and Jain monks used to make regular visit. Mohan thus had occasion to hear discussions about religious matters also. Being the youngest, he was the darling of the household.

CHILDHOOD

Mohan attended Primary School at Porbandar. When he was seven, his family moved to Rajkot. He was a mediocre student, was shy and avoided any company. He read little besides the text books and had no love for outdoor games. He had no love for outdoor games. However, he was truthful, honest, sensitive and was alert about his character. Plays about Shravan and Harishchandra made a deep impression on him. They taught him to be truthful at any cost and to serve his parents with devotion.

He was married along with his brother and cousin for the sake of economy and convenience. He was only 13 then. He enjoyed the festivities of the marriage. Kasturbai, his wife, was of the same age. She was illiterate but strong-willed. His jealousy and immature efforts to make her an ideal wife led to many quarrels. He wanted to teach her but found no time. His experience later made him a strong critic of child-marriages.

Mohan joined High School at Rajkot. He was liked by the teachers and often received prizes. But he neglected physical training and hand-writing. Habit of taking long walks made up for the first neglect, but he had to repent later for the neglect of handwriting. He was devoted to his father and considered it his duty to nurse him during his illness. In the High-School, he made friends with one Sheikh Mehtab, a bad character. He stuck to the friendship despite warnings from family-members. He wanted to reform Mehtab but failed. Mehtab induced him to meat-eating, saying that it made one strong and that the British were ruling India because they were meat-eaters. Mohan was frail and used to be afraid even to go out alone in the dark. The argument appealed to him. Later, he realized that lying to his parents was worse than not eating meat, and abandoned the experiment.

Mehtab once sent him to a brothel, but God's grace saved him. He induced Mohan to smoking. This once led to stealing. But all this became unbearable for Mohan. He confessed his guilt to his father, who did not rebuke him but wept silently. Those tears cleaned Mohan's heart and taught him a lesson in nonviolence.

Mohan's father died when Mohan was 16. He had nursed him daily. But at the time of his death, Mohan was with his wife. He always felt ashamed for this lapse. Mohan passed the matriculation examination in 1887. He attended the College at Bhavnagar, but left after the first term. At that time, the idea of his going to England for studying law came up. Mohan was fascinated. He made up his mind and overcame resistance from the family-members. He took the vow not to touch wine, women and meat at the instance of his mother to remove her fears. He then sailed from Bombay in September 1888, leaving behind his wife and a son. The caste elders were against his going to England. They excommunicated him from the caste.

GANDHI IN ENGLAND

Gandhi reached England by the end of September 1888. Everything was strange to him. He was shy and diffident, could not speak English fluently and was ignorant of British manners. Naturally, loneliness and homesickness gripped him. Gandhi became a vegetarian for life. It was difficult to get vegetarian food. Friends persuaded him to break the vow of vegetarianism but he stuck to it. He began searching vegetarian restaurants and found one ultimately. He purchased Salt's book 'Plea for Vegetarianism', read it and became vegetarian out of conviction. He studied other literature and joined the Vegetarian Society.

He came in contact with the leaders of that radical cult, became a member of the Society's Executive Committee and contributed articles to the Society's paper. He even started a Vegetarian club in his locality and became its Secretary. This experience gave him some training in organising and conducting Institutions. Experiments about diet became a life-long passion for him.

Gandhi Tries to Play the 'English Gentleman'

For a brief period, Gandhi tried to become 'The English Gentleman' to overcome lack of confidence and to make up for the 'fad' of vegetarianism. He wanted to become fit for the British elite society. He got clothes stitched from an expensive and fashionable firm, purchased an expensive hat and an evening suit and learnt to wear the tie. He became very careful about his appearance. He even joined a dancing class, but could not go on for more than three weeks. He purchased a violin and started learning to play it. He engaged a tutor to give lessons in elocution. But all this was for a brief period of three months only. His conscience awakened him. He realised that he was not going to spend his whole life in England; he should rather concentrate on his studies and not waste his brother's money. He then became very careful about his expenses.

Study of Religions

Gandhi also started the study of religions. Before that, he had not even read the Gita. Now he read it in the English translation. He also read Edwin

Arnold's 'The Light of Asia,' Blavatsky's 'Key to Theosophy' and the Bible. Gita and The New Testament made a deep impression on him. The principles of renunciation and nonviolence appealed to him greatly. He continued the study of religions throughout his life.

Gandhi becomes a Barrister

Bar examinations were easy. He therefore studied for and passed the London matriculation examination. Becoming a Barrister meant attending at least six dinners in each of the twelve terms and giving an easy examination. Gandhi, however, studied sincerely, read all the prescribed books, passed his examination and was called to the bar in June 1891. He then sailed for home.

A Period of Turmoil

Gandhi's three year's stay in England was a period of deep turmoil for him. Before that, he knew little of the world. Now he was exposed to the fast-changing world and to several radical movements like Socialism, Anarchism, Atheism etc. through the Vegetarian Society. He started taking part in public work. Many of his ideas germinated during this period.

BIRTH OF SATYAGRAHA

The White rulers were bent on keeping South Africa under their domination. They wanted as few Indians there as possible and that too as slave-labourers. In Transvaal, Indians were required to register themselves. The procedure was humiliating. The registration was proposed to be made stricter in 1906. Gandhi realised that it was a matter of life or death for the Indians. A mammoth meeting was held in September 1906 to oppose the bill. People took oath in the name of God not to submit to the bill at any cost. A new principle had come into being-the principle of Satyagraha. The bill about registration was however passed. Picketing against registration was organised. A wave of courage and enthusiasm swept the Indian community. The Indian community rose as one man for the sake of its survival and dignity.

The agitation was first called 'passive Resistance'. Gandhi, however, did not like that term. It did not convey the true nature of the struggle. It implied that it was the weapon of the weak and the disarmed. It did not denote complete faith in nonviolence. Moreover, Gandhi did not like that the Indian struggle should be known by an English name. The term 'Sadagrah' was suggested. Gandhi changed it to 'Satyagrah' to make it represent fully, the whole idea. Satyagraha means asserting truth through nonviolence. It aims at converting the opponents through self-suffering.

Gandhi was ordered to leave the colony. He disobeyed and was jailed for two months. Indians filled the jails. Repression failed to yield the results.

General Smuts called Gandhi and promised that the law would be withdrawn if the Indians agreed to voluntary registration.

An Attempt of Gandhi's Life

Gandhi agreed. He and his co-workers were set free. Gandhi exhorted Indians to register voluntarily. He was criticized for this by some workers. A Pathan named Mir Alam was unconvinced by Gandhi's arguments and vowed to kill the first man who would register himself. Gandhi came forward to be the first man to register himself. When he was going to the registration office, Mir Alam and his friends assaulted him with lathis. Gandhi fainted with the words 'He Ram' on his lips. It was 10th February 1908. His colleagues tried to save him otherwise it would have been the last day for him. Mir Alam and his friends were caught and handed over to the police. When Gandhi regained consciousness, he inquired about Mir Alam. When told that he had been arrested, Gandhi told that he should be released. Gandhi was taken by his friend Rev. Doke to his house and was nursed there. Rev. Doke later became his first biographer.

Gandhi Betrayed

Smuts however, betrayed Gandhi. The agitation was again resumed. The voluntary registration certificates were publicly burnt. Meanwhile, Transvaal passed Immigration Restriction Act. This too was opposed by the Indians. They crossed Transvaal border illegally and were jailed. Gandhi, too, was arrested and convicted. The fight continued in spite of the repression.

Tolstoy Farm

Gandhi realised that the fight would be a long one. He, therefore, desired to have a center where the Satyagrahis could lead a simple community life and get training for the struggle. Phoenix was at about 30 hours distance from Johannesburg. Gandhi's German friend Kallenbach therefore bought 1100 acres of land at a distance of about 20 miles from Johannesburg, where Tolstoy Farm was established. The community was named after Tolstoy to pay respect to the great Russian writer whose book 'The Kingdom of God is within You' had greatly influenced Gandhi and made him a firm believer in nonviolence.

The inmates numbered about 50-75. It was a heterogeneous group. It was a tribute to Gandhi's leadership that they remained together happily under hard conditions. The inmates erected sheds to accommodate themselves. They did all their work themselves. Drinking, smoking and meat-eating were prohibited. All ate in the community kitchen. Small Cottage Industries were started for self-sufficiency. Gandhi and his colleagues learnt shoe-making. A school was started. Gandhi himself undertook the responsibility of educating the children. The life was simple, hard, but joyful. Experiments at Tolstoy Farm proved to be a source of purification and penance for Gandhi and his co-workers.

The last Phase of Satyagraha

Satyagraha continued for four years. Gandhi discontinued his legal practice in 1910. After many ups and downs, the last phase of Satyagraha began in September 1913. A Black Law imposing three pounds tax on Indians provided occasion for it. Satyagrahis crossed Transvaal border defying the law. Even the women were invited to join. Indian workers in the Natal coal-mines struck work and joined the struggle. Gandhi led a large contingent of these workers. They were about 2200 in number. It was on epic march. It aroused sympathy for Satyagraha and indignation for the South African Government throughout England and India. Indian National Congress supported the Satyagraha. Gandhi was arrested. The Satyagrahis marched to Natal without their leader. There, they were arrested and jailed. Thousands of labourers struck work in sympathy. The public outcry in India forced the Indian Government to express sympathy for the Indian cause. The repression having failed, General Smuts had to bow ultimately. Indian demands were accepted. The fight was over. Gandhi now could return to India where a great work awaited him.

It was South Africa which made Gandhi. He had gone there as a young, shy, Briefless Barrister. He returned as an extraordinary leader who had mobilised masses to an unprecedented extent for a novel fight. In South Africa, Gandhi's ideas were shaped. He was influenced by Ruskin, Tolstoy and Thoreau. He made a deep study of religions there and became a staunch believer in nonviolence. The principle of Satyagraha was born in S. Africa.

MAHATMA AND THE MASSES

It was the Rowlatt Bill with its denial of civil liberties which finally brought Gandhi into active Indian politics. From 1919 to his death in 1948, he occupied the centre of the Indian stage and was the hero of the great historical drama which culminated in the independence of his country. He changed the entire character of the political scene in India. He only grew. In the thick of the battle he remained a man of God. Since the Rowlatt Bill was not a local issue and the struggle was to be launched on an all-India scale, Gandhi pondered deeply what shape it should take.

He had to rouse the people's enthusiasm and yet keep their passions from breaking into violence. Finally, he hit upon the idea of hartal or a national observance of mourning or protest by the closing of shops and places of business.

The hartal was observed all over India, by Hindus and Muslims alike, with an enthusiasm which surprised every one. Even Gandhi had not realized how great was his hold on the imagination of the Indian masses.

The Government's complacency received a rude shock to see the war-time "recruiting sergeant" of the Empire turn a rebel. When Gandhi who was now in demand everywhere left for Delhi and Amritsar, he was served with a notice at Palwal station forbidding him to cross into the Punjab.

On his refusal to obey the order, he was arrested and brought back to Bombay. The news of his arrest spread like wild fire and created great excitement among the people.

Crowds gathered in cities and some violence took place. When Gandhi came to Ahmedabad and found that a police officer had been killed by the mob, he was horrified and felt that "a rapier run through my body could hardly have pained me more". He suspended the Satyagraha movement and undertook a fast for three days as penance for the violence committed by people.

On the very day, April 13, 1919, when Gandhi announced his three-day fast in Ahmedabad, the British General Dyer ordered the massacre of unarmed and peaceful citizens attending a meeting in Jallianwala Bagh at Amritsar.

Later, even the official report admitted that 400 people had been killed and between 1,000 and 2,000 wounded, though the unofficial inquiry conducted by the Gandhi himself estimated 1,200 dead and 3,600 wounded.

This cowardly massacre of the innocent was followed by the declaration of martial law in the Punjab, with wholesale arrests, floggings and the inhuman order by which no Indian could pass a certain street except by crawling on his belly. The events of that day which has been called by Sir Valentine Chirol as "that black day in the annals of British India" mark a turning point in the history of the Indian struggle. The moral prestige of Britain received a fatal blow. Henceforth, Gandhi could not keep away from the battlefield of Indian politics.

It was typical of Gandhi that great as was his concern over the happenings in the Punjab, he shared with equal zeal the Indian Muslim's concern at the rate of the defeated Turkish Sultan who was also the Caliph or the religious head of Islam. In fact, it was at a Muslim Conference held in Delhi in November 1919 that he first advocated noncooperation with the British Government.

It is interesting to recall that four years earlier, when he attended the Lucknow session of the Congress, he was more an observer than a participant and had seemed to Jawaharlal Nehru "very distant and different and unpolitical". In 1920, he dominated the political scene.

In fact, he recreated the Congress and turned talking politicians into active revolutions and anglicized leaders of society into servants of the people who henceforth wore white homespun. He bridged the gulf between the intelligentsia and the masses and widened the concept of Swaraj to include almost every aspect of social and moral regeneration. From now on, the story of life is the story of how Congress fought for and won India's freedom.

Like a magician, Gandhi roused a storm of enthusiasm in the country with his call to non-cooperate. He began the campaign by returning to the Viceroy the medals and decorations he had received from the Government for his war-services and humanitarian work. "I can retain", he wrote to wrong to defend its immorality."

Many Indians renounced their titles and honours, lawyers gave up their practice, students left colleges and schools, and thousand of the city-bred went into the villages to spread the message of nonviolent noncooperation with the "satanic" government and to prepare the masses of defy the law. The somnolent people woke up in a frenzy of courage and self-sacrifice. Bonfires of foreign cloth lit the sky everywhere and the hum of the spinning wheel rose like a sacrificial chant in thousands of homes. Women, secluded for centuries, marched in the streets with men and incidentally freed themselves from age-old shackles. In speech after speech, article after article in his two weeklies, Young India and Navjivan, Gandhi poured forth his passionate utterances which electrified the people. Thousands of people were put in prison and many more thousands were preparing to court arrest.

The anticlimax came suddenly in February 1922. An outbreak of mob violence in Chauri Chaura so shocked and pained Gandhi that he refused to continue the campaign and undertook a fast for five days to atone for a crime committed by others in a state of mob hysteria.

Many of his colleagues protested and though Gandhi admitted that "the drastic reversal of practically the whole of the aggressive programme may be politically unsound and unwise", he maintained that "there is no doubt that it is religiously sound". He felt that "it is a million times better to appear untrue before the world than to be untrue to ourselves".

Where Gandhi's conscience was concerned he was always ready to stand alone. However, the immediate result was that the British Government found this anticlimax a convenient opportunity to arrest him.

He told the English judge at the trial : " I have no personal ill-will against any single administrator, much less can I have any disaffection towards the King's person. But I hold it a virtue to be disaffected towards a government which in its totality has done more harm to Indian than any previous system.

India is less manly under British rule than ever before. Holding such a belief I consider it a sin to have any affection for the system.......... The only course open to you, the judge is either to resign your post and thus dissociate yourself from evil, if you feel that the law you are called upon to administer is an evil and that in reality I am innocent; or to inflict on me the severest penalty if you believe that the system and the law you are assisting to administer are good for the people of this country, and that my activity is therefore, injurious to the public weal."

The judge sentenced him to six years' simple imprisonment and expressed the hope that "if the course of events in India should make it possible for the Government to reduce the period and release you, no one will be better pleased than I."

Prison was for Gandhi more a luxury than a punishment. He could devote more time to prayer, study and spinning than he could outside. But in January 1924 he fell seriously ill with acute appendicitis.

He was removed to a hospital in Poona where a British surgeon performed the operation. While he was convalescing he was released by the Government. What he saw of India as a free man greatly pained him. At the time of his arrest he had left his people on the wave of a great moral upsurge which had united Hindus and Muslims as never before.

But in the meanwhile the Khilafat issue had been killed by Kamal Ataturk. The Muslims no longer needed Hindu support; the two communities had drifted apart. There were communal riots in several places.

Not knowing how to stem this tide of frustration, he undertook a fast if twenty-one days a to atone once again for the sins of his people. "It seems as if God has been dethroned," he said, announcing the fast. "Let us reinstate Him in our hearts." The fast caused considerable heart-searching, and long before it was over, pledges of amity poured in upon him from men of various communities.

For the next five years Gandhi seemingly retired from active agitational politics and devoted himself to the propagation of what he regarded as the basic national needs, namely, Hindu-Muslim unity, removal of untouchability, equality of women, popularization of hand-spinning and the reconstruction of village economy in general.

"I am not interested". He wrote in June 1923, "freeing India merely from the English yoke. I am bent upon freeing and social and economic freedom, must go together.

There was also the fact that Gandhi, on his release from prison, had found the Congress divided. By 1929, however, the various groups had once more rallied under his leadership, and when on the last day of that year he himself moved the Resolution in the Congress session declaring complete Independence as the goal of Congress policy, it was obvious that he was again ready to lead the nation in an open challenge which was taken by millions throughout the country on January 26, 1930, which day has been celebrated as Independence as the goal of Congress policy, it was obvious that he was again ready to lead the nation in an open challenge to British rule.

He drew up a pledge of "Purna Swaraj" or complete independence which was taken by millions throughout the country on January 26, 1930, which day has been celebrated as Independence Day ever since.

All eyes were now turned to Sabarmati. What will the wizard of nonviolence do next? On March 12, 1930, after having duly informed the Viceroy, Gandhi, followed by seventy-eight members of his ashram, both men and women, began his historic 24-day march to the sea beach at Dandi to break the law which had deprived the poor man of his right to make his own salt. This seemed a small issue, but the dramatic manner in which he announced and executed the plan, the march on foot of this unarmed man of God for 241 miles, with villagers flocking from miles around to kneel by the roadside, set the imagination of the nation aflame and roused enthusiasm such as no one had anticipated.

Early in the morning of April 6, after prayers, he went to the beach and picked up a little lump of salt left by the waves. This simple act was immediately followed by a nationwide defiance of the law.

Men and women, simple villagers and sophisticated city folk, marched in thousands to invite arrest, police lathi charges and even shooting in many cases. Gandhi himself was arrested on May 4, soon after midnight. Within a few weeks about a hundred thousand men and women were in jail, throwing mighty machinery of the British Government out of gear.

When the First Round Table Conference met in November 1930, the Labour Government was faced with an embarrassing situation.

At the closing session of the Conference, on January 19, 1931, Ramsay MacDonald expressed the hope that the Congress would be represented at the Second Round Table Conference. Gandhi and some other Congress leaders were therefore unconditionally released on January 26, exactly a year after the first independence pledge had been taken.

Soon after, on February 14, the Gandhi-Irwin talks began to the disgust of Winston Churchill, who was scandalized at "the nauseating and humiliating spectacle of this one-time Inner Temple Lawyer, now seditious fakir, striding half-naked up the steps of the Viceroy's palace, there to negotiate a parley on equal terms with the representative of the King-Emperor."

POLITICIAN LIFE AND IMPORTANT WORK OF GANDHI

In April 1893, Gandhi had sailed for South Africa, a young and inexperienced barrister in search of fortune. In January 1915 he finally returned to India, a Mahatma, with no possessions and with only one ambition-to serve his people. Though the intelligentsia had heard of his exploits in South Africa, he was not much known in India and Indians in general did not realize that "the Great Soul in beggar's garb", as the poet Tagore called him called him later, had reached her shores. Nor did he know his shores. Nor did he know his India well. He therefore readily promised his "political guru", Gokhale, that he would spend the first year in India studying the country, with "his ears open but his mouth shut". At the end of his year's wanderings, Gandhi settled down on the bank of the river Sabarmati, on the outskirts of Ahmedabad, where he founded an ashram in May 1915. He called it the Satyagraha Ashram. The inmates about twenty-five men and women, took the vows of truth, ahimsa, celibacy, non-stealing, non-possession and control of the palate, and dedicated themselves to the service of the people.

Gandhi's first public address in India was on the occasion of the opening ceremony of the Benares Hindu University in February 1916, which was distinguished by the presence of many magnets and princes and of the Viceroy himself. Speaking in English he shocked them all by expressing his "deep humiliation and shame" at being compelled "to address my countrymen in a language that is foreign to me". He shocked them more when turning to the bejewelled princes he said: "There is no salvation for India unless you strip yourselves of this jewellery and hold it in trust for your countrymen in India." Many princes walked out.

His first Satyagraha in India was in Champaran, in Bihar, where he went in 1917 at the request of a poor peasants to inquire into the grievances of the much exploited peasants of that district, who were compelled by British indigo planters to grow indigo on 15 percent of their land and part with the whole crop for rent. The news that a Mahatma had arrived to inquire into their sufferings spread like wild fire and thousands of peasants left their villages to have his darshan and to tell him of their woes. The vested interests were up in arms and the police superintendent ordered Gandhi to leave district. Gandhi refused and was summoned to appear in court the next day. Thousand of peasants followed him there. The embarrassed magistrate postponed the trial and released him without bail, for Gandhi refused to furnish any.

Later, the case was withdrawn and Gandhi proceeded with his inquiry. Along with the inquiry, he educated the peasants in the principles of Satyagraha and taught them that the first condition of freedom was freedom from fear. He sent for volunteers who helped to instruct the illiterate and ignorant peasants in elementary hygiene and ran schools for their children. This kind of activity was typical of Gandhi. Even as he taught people to fight for their rights, he taught them to fulfil their obligations. A free people must learn to stand on their feet. But the more he worked for the people the less was his presence welcome to the Government who were at last obliged to set up a committee of inquiry. The report of the committee of which Gandhi was a member went in favour of the tenant farmers. The success of his first experiment in Satyagraha in India greatly enhanced Gandhi's reputation in this country.

Hardly had his work in Champaran been done when Gandhi was called to his ashram at Sabarmati by an urgent appeal from the textile workers of Ahmedabad whose dispute with the mill-owners was taking a serious turn. Having satisfied himself that the workers' demands were legitimate and mill-owners' refusal to submit the dispute to arbitration unreasonable, Gandhi asked the workers to strike, on condition that they took a pledge to remain nonviolent. They agreed, but after a few days their zeal began to flag and Gandhi feared that they might break the pledge and resort to violence. Since it was the fear of starvation which drove the workers to desperation, Gandhi decided to starve himself. He declared that he would not touch food until a settlement had been reached. At the end of three days, both parties agreed on an arbitration amid general rejoicing.

Almost immediately after came the agrarian trouble in the Kheda district of Gujarat. The peasants who were on the verge of starvation were being forced by the Government to pay the usual tax. Gandhi advised Satyagraha and persuade all the peasants, the well-to-do as well as the poor, to take a pledge not to pay any tax until those who could not pay were granted remission. The no-tax campaign lasted for about four months at the end of which the Government suspended the assessment for the poor peasants.

Now there took place an event which still baffles the pacifists in the West. In 1917, the Viceroy Lord Chelmsford invited Gandhi to a War conference convened in Delhi to enlist the support of Indian leaders for the recruitment campaign. At that time Gandhi believed that the British Empire was by and large a power for good, and that since India had on the whole benefited by British connection, it was the duty of every Indian to help the Empire in the hour of its need. Gandhi not only supported the resolution of the War Conference but actually toured the Kheda district (where previously he had led the peasants in Satyagraha) to persuade people to enlist.

RETURN TO INDIA

A hero's welcome awaited Gandhi when he landed on January 9, 1915, at the Apollo Bunder in Bombay. Three days later he was honoured by the people of Bombay at a magnificent reception in the palatial house of a Bombay magnate Jehangir Petit. The Government of India joined with the people of

India in showering honours on Gandhi. He received a "Kaiser-I-Hind" gold medal in the King's birthday honours list of 1915. His association with Gokhale was guarantee enough of his being a safe politician.

Of course, he had led an extra-constitutional movement in South Africa, defied laws and filled goals, but the cause for which he had fought appeared as much humanitarian as political, dear to all Indian as and all Englishmen whose sense of humanity had not been blunted by racial arrogance or political expediency. Lord Hardinge's open support of the Satyagraha movement had in any case removed the stigma of rebellion from South Africa's Indian movement. Gandhi was in no hurry to plunge into politics. His political mentor on the Indian scene was Gokhale. One of the first things Gokhale did was to extract a promise from Gandhi that he would not express himself upon public questions for a year, which was to be a "year of probation". Gokhale was very keen that Gandhi should join the Servants of India Society in Poona. Gandhi was only too willing to fall in with the wishes of Gokhale, but several members of the Society feared that there was too great a gap between the ideals and methods of the Society and those of Gandhi. While the question of his admission as a 'Servant of India' was being debated, Gandhi visited his home towns of Porbandar and Rajkot and went on to Shantiniketan in West Bengal, the cosmopolitan University of the Poet Rabindranath Tagore.

WORLD WAR I

When World War I broke out, Gandhi was on the high seas, he was homeward bound, though he hoped to spend a few weeks in England. On August 6, 1914, he landed on English soil and lost no time in calling a meeting of his Indian friends to raise an ambulance unit. The argument that the Empire's crisis was India's chance did not impress him: "I knew the difference of status between an Indian and an Englishman," he wrote later, "but I did not believe that we had been quite reduced to slavery. I felt then that it was more the fault of individual officials than of the British system, and that we could convert them by love. If we would improve our status through the help and cooperation of the British, it was our duty to win their help by standing by them in their hour of need." Were it not for an attack of pleurisy, Gandhi may have continued to serve in the ambulance unit he had raised, and his return to India may have been indefinitely delayed.

When he arrived in India he found that nationalist opinion was opposed to unconditional support for the war effort. Only those who were politically backward or flourished on official patronage were for loyalty at all costs. Gandhi did not favour a bargain with the government by offering cooperation at a price and said: "That we have been loyal at a time of stress is no test of fitness for Swaraj (self-government). Loyalty is no merit. It is a necessity of citizenship all the world over."

During the years 1916-18, Gandhi did not take active part in politics. His ideals and methods did not quite fit in with those of the two dominant groups in the Indian National Congress. The Moderates did not like his extra-constitutional methods of Satyagraha, the Extremists did not like his studied tenderness to the British Government during the war. He did not participate in the Home Rule agitation nor in the negotiations which led to the Lucknow pact between the Indian National Congress and the All India Muslim League. He seemed to be isolated from the main currents of Indian politics. It was not Gandhi, but the Annie Besant-Tilak combination which dominated the national scene and impressed the Government. Edwin Montague, a member of the British Cabinet, who visited India in 1917, recorded in his diary that Tilak was "at the moment probably the most powerful man in India." Gandhi seemed to Montague "a social reformer with a real desire to find grievances and to cure them not for any reasons of self advertisement, but to improve the conditions of his fellowmen. He dresses like a coolie, forswears all personal advancement, lives practically on the air and is a pure visionary." The fact that he was committed to abstention from political agitation during the war did not prevent Gandhi from championing just grievances which could not brook delay. In the summer of 1917, he went to the indigo-growing district of Champaran and took up the cause of the tenants against the European planters. The same year he led the textile workers of Ahmedabad in a strike against the mill-owners. The following year, he agitated for reduction of land tax in Kaira district where crops had suffered from the failure of rains. The local officers were perturbed by Gandhi's activities but the Government was anxious not to precipitate a showdown. Gandhi himself took care to localize these conflicts and sought solutions which secured a modicum of justice to the workers and peasants without creating a national crisis.

Early in 1918, the war seemed to be going badly for the Allies; a German thrust was expected on the western front, and the Viceroy summoned prominent leaders of Indian opinion to a War Conference in Delhi. Gandhi supported the resolution on recruitment with a single sentence in Hindi: "With a full sense of my responsibility, I beg to support the resolution." After the War Conference, Gandhi threw himself heart and soul into a recruiting campaign There was something comic in this votary of nonviolence touring the villages of his home province of Gujarat to secure recruits for the British Indian army to fight in the battle fronts of Europe.

Not infrequently, unable to get bullock-carts for their journeys in the interior of the Gujarat countryside, Gandhi and his colleagues had to march on foot twenty miles a day. The strain was too much for him and at last a severe attack of dysentery laid him low.

Meanwhile the war came to end, and Gandhi learnt that the Sedition Committee Report had been published and the Government of India proposed to introduce legislation to curb civil liberties. He had been almost alone among Indian leaders who had argued for unconditional support to Britain in her hour of need in the hope of a worthy gesture at the end of he war. He felt that he had received stone for bread. He had done his best to keep out of political agitation during the war. Now he felt an irresistible call to fight a wrong perpetrated in peace.

ROWLATT BILLS

The Government of India rushed the Rowlatt Bills, through the Imperial Legislative Council in March 1919 in the teeth of the opposition of all the elected Indian members. Gandhi heard the debate in the Imperial Legislative Council and saw how the eloquent logic of Indian councillors had been wasted on the official benches. "You can wake a man," he wrote later, "only if he is really asleep; no effort that you may make will produce any effect upon him if he is merely pretending sleep". The conviction grew upon him that the Government of India was impervious to popular feeling. A Government which really cared for public opinion would not have enacted a measure-whatever its merits-which had been opposed by every shade of public opinion.

NONVIOLENT NON-COOPERATION

The programme of "nonviolent noncooperation" included the boycott of councils, courts and schools, set up by the British and of all foreign cloth. With some naivete Gandhi claimed that his movement was not unconstitutional: In his dictionary, constitutional and moral were synonymous terms. The British saw that the success of "noncooperation" would paralyse their administration. Lord Chelmsford, the Viceroy, tried to kill with ridicule "the most foolish of all foolish schemes", which would "bring ruin to those who had any stake in the country". A number of eminent "moderate" politicians joined official critics in underlining the risks of mass noncooperation as proposed by Gandhi.

That a political programme had no chance of success without an adequate organization to implement it, Gandhi had realized at the age of twenty-five, when he had founded the Natal Indian Congress to fight for the rights of Indians in Natal. The Indian National Congress, had, therefore, to be refashioned, if it was to prove an efficient instrument of nonviolent noncooperation. Gandhi saw that what the country needed was not a forum for an annual pageant and feast of oratory, but a militant organization in touch with the masses. Under the new constitution, the Congress was given a broad-based pyramidal structure by formation of village, taluka, district and provincial committees, with the All India Congress Committee and the Working Committee at the apex. The Congress was thus reorganized not only on a more representative basis, but in such a way that it could function efficiently between its annual sessions. It ceased to be a preserve of the upper and middle classes; its doors were opened to the masses in the small towns and villages whose political consciousness Gandhi himself was quickening.

Gandhi was swept to the top of Indian politics in 1919-20 because he had caught the imagination of the people. He was loved and respected as the Mahatma, the great soul; with voluntary poverty, simplicity, humility and saintliness, he seemed a rishi (sage) of old who had stepped from the pages of an ancient epic to bring about the liberation of his country. Nay, to millions he was the incarnation of God. It was not only for his message that people came to him, but for the merit of seeing him. The sacred sight of the Mahatma-his darshan-was almost equivalent to a pilgrimage to holy Benares. The unthinking adoration of the multitude sometimes made Gandhi feel sick. "The woes of the Mahatma", he wrote, "are known only to the Mahatma". But this adoration was the mainspring from which was drawn the immense influence he exercised over Indian public life.

Gandhi had struck some of the inner chords of Indian humanity; his appeal for courage and sacrifice evoked a ready response because he was himself the epitome of these qualities. It was because he was, to use Churchill's epithet, a "naked fakir", because his life was one of austerity and self-sacrifice that a great emotional bond grew between him and the Indian people. The number of such "fakirs" was to multiply fast. Among those who gave up their lucrative careers and queued up for prison under Gandhi's leadership were Motilal Nehru, Rajendra Prasad, C.R. Das, Vallabhbhai Patel, and C. Rajagopalachari. Life acquired a new meaning for them. Abbas Tyabji, a former Chief Justice of Baroda, wrote from a village that he was feeling twenty years younger. "God?" he exclaimed, "what an experience !

I have so much love and affection for the common folk to whom it is now an honour to belong. It is the fakir's dress that has broken down all barriers." It is of this period that Jawaharlal Nehru has written in his autobiography that the movement absorbed him so wholly that he "gave up all other associations and contacts, old friends, books, even newspapers except in so far as they dealt with the work in hand.... I almost forgot my family, my wife, my daughter."

From the autumn of 1920, the noncooperation movement gathered momentum. The attitude of the Government at first was one of caution. It was reluctant to launch a drastic repression, as it did not want to alienate moderate Indian opinion. Soon after his arrival in India in April, 1921, Lord Reading, the new Viceroy, met Gandhi. In a private letter to his son, the Viceroy confessed to a feeling of excitement, almost a thrill, in meeting his unusual visitor and described his religious and moral views as admirable, though he found it difficult to understand his practice of them in politics.

Throughout 1921, the tension between the Congress and the Government was steadily mounting. There was no meeting of minds between Gandhi and Reading. The Ali Brothers, the principal leaders of the Khilafat, were arrested in September 1921 on a charge of inciting the army to disloyalty; their offence was repeated by a number of Indian leaders including Gandhi. This was a challenge which was difficult for the Government not to accept. The official optimism that the movement would melt away by internal differences or popular apathy proved to be misplaced. Nearly thirty thousand non-cooperators were arrested.

The Government was reluctant to touch Gandhi until a favourable opportunity came. Indeed as late as December 1921, Lord Reading seemed willing to hold a round table conference with Gandhi and other Indian leaders to reach an understanding and to avoid unseemly scenes during the visit to India of the Prince of Wales. Lord Reading was, however, hardly in a position to make any substantial political concessions. Meanwhile, Gandhi was under increasing pressure from his adherents to launch a civil disobedience campaign. The Ahmedabad Congress in December 1921 invested him with authority to launch a mass movement. Mass civil disobedience was, in the words of Gandhi, "an earthquake, a sort of general upheaval on the political plane-the Government ceases to function... the police stations, the courts, offices, etc., all cease to be Government property and shall be taken charge of by the people." He proposed to proceed cautiously. His plan was to launch civil disobedience in one district; if it succeeded he proposed to extend it to the adjacent districts, and so on, until the whole of India was liberated. But he gave a clear warning that if violence broke out in any form in any part of the country, the movement would lose its character as a movement of peace, "even as a lute would begin to emit notes of discord the moment a single string snaps."

A riot which disfigured Bombay during the visit of Prince of Wales in November 1921 had led Gandhi to postpone civil disobedience. Nevertheless, two months later, under growing pressure from his colleagues, he decided to launch a no-tax campaign in Bardoli taluka in Gujarat. He communicated the step he contemplated, with his reasons for it, in a letter to the Viceroy. This was taken by the Government of India as an ultimatum. A head-on collision between the Government on the one hand and the nationalist forces on the other seemed imminent. Gandhi's letter to the Viceroy was dated February 1,1922. Three days later, there was a clash between a procession and the police at Chauri Chaura, a small village in the United Province, in which the police station was set on fire and 22 policemen were killed.

Gandhi viewed the Chauri Chaura tragedy as a red signal, a warning that the atmosphere in the country was too explosive for a mass movement. He decided to retrace his steps, to cancel the plans for civil disobedience in Bardoli, to suspend the aggressive part of the noncooperation campaign, and to shift the emphasis to the 'constructive' programme of hand-spinning, communal unity, abolition of untouchability, etc. His action shocked and bewildered his closest colleagues. Their reaction is best expressed in Romain Rolland's words: "It was dangerous to assemble all the forces of a nation and to hold the nation panting before a prescribed movement, to lift one's arm to give the final command, then at the last moment, let one's arm drop and thrice call a halt just as the formidable machinery has been set in motion. One risks ruining the brakes and paralysing the impetus." The Viceroy, Lord Reading, cheerfully confided to his son that Gandhi "had pretty well run himself to the last ditch as a politician by extraordinary manifestation in the last month or six weeks before his arrest".

1947-1952: TRANSFORMATION

Constitution

The last series of political issues that the Congress Party of the Independence era contributed to was the creation of the Constitution of India and working the Constituent Assembly of India. In the Assembly and Constitution debates, the Congress attitude was marked by inclusiveness and liberalism. The Government appointed some prominent Indians who were Raj loyalists and liberals to important offices, and did not adopt any punitive control over the Indian civil servants who had aided the Raj in its governance of India and suppression of nationalist activities.

A Congress-dominated Assembly adopted B.R. Ambedkar, a fierce Congress critic as the chairman of the Constitution draft committee. Syama Prasad Mookerjee, a Hindu Mahasabha leader became the Minister for Industry. The Congress stood firm on its fundamental promises and delivered a Constitution that abolished untouchability and discrimination based on caste, religion or gender. Primary education was made a right, and Congress governments made the zamindar system illegal, created minimum wages and authorized the right to strike and form labour unions.

Leadership Change

In 1947, the Congress presidency passed upon Jivatram Kripalani, a veteran Gandhian and ally of both Nehru and Patel. India's duumvirate expressed neutrality and full support to the elected winner of the 1947, 1948 and 1949 presidential races.

However, a tug of war began between Nehru and his socialist wing, and Patel and Congress traditionalists broke out in 1950's race. Nehru lobbied intensely to oppose the candidacy of Purushottam Das Tandon, whom he perceived as a Hindu revivalist with problematic views on Hindu-Muslim relations. Nehru openly backed Kripalani to oppose Tandon, but neglected courtesy to Patel upon the question.

With Patel's tacit support (especially in Patel's home state of Gujarat, where due to Patel's work, Kripalani received not one vote) Tandon won a tight contest, and Nehru threatened to resign. With Patel's convincing, Nehru did not quit. However, with Patel's death in 1950, the balance shifted permanently in Nehru's favour. Kripalani, C. Rajagopalachari and Tandon were marginalized, and the Congress Party's election fortunes began depending solely on Nehru's charismatic popularity. With the 1952 election sweep, the Congress became India's main political party.

GANDHI'S DEATH

It was January 1948. Communal feelings were high due to the partition of the country. Hindu communalists thought that Gandhi was pro-Muslim. His fast for communal amity which resulted in the Government of India honouring its obligation of giving Rs. 50 Crores to Pakistan had further angered them. Gandhi was staying at the Birla house in New Delhi. He used to hold evening prayer meetings regularly. He used to speak on various issues. Once a bomb was thrown during his prayer meeting. Still, Gandhi did not permit security checks.

On 30th of January 1948, about 500 people had gathered for the prayer meeting on the lawns of the Birla House. Gandhi was a bit late as Sardar Patel had come to see him.

At 5.10 p.m. he left the room and walked to the prayer ground. He was supporting himself on the shoulders of Abha and Manu, his grand daughter-in-law and granddaughter respectively. People rushed forward to get his darshan and to touch his feet.

Gandhi folded his hands to greet them. When he was a few yards away from the prayer platform, a young man came forward. He saluted Gandhi, suddenly took out a small pistol and fired three shots. The bullets hit Gandhi on and below the chest. He fell to the ground with the words. 'Hey Ram' on his lips. He died within minutes. The crowd was shocked. The assassin was Nathuram Godse,' a worker of Hindu Mahasabha. He was caught and handed over to the Police.

Gandhi's body was taken to Birla House. People thronged the place and wept bitterly. The whole world was plunged in sorrow. The next morning, Gandhi's body was placed on a gun-carriage and taken to Rajghat. Millions of people joined the procession to have the last darshan (glimpse) of the Mahatma. His son Ramdas lit the funeral pyre. The Mahatma had become a martyr for communal unity.

2

Gandhi as a Politician

Gandhi returned to India in January 1915. He was welcomed and honoured as a hero. He spent a year touring the country at the instance of Gokhale, his guru. He travelled mostly in third class railway compartments. He saw the conditions in the country first-hand. He founded the Satyagraha Ashram in May 1915 and started getting involved in the social and political life of the country. The Champaran Satyagraha was his first major struggle.

Champaran Satyagraha

Champaran was a district in Northern Bihar. When Gandhi was called there, it was virtually under the rule of European indigo planters. They cruelly exploited and terrorised the tenants. Under the 'tinkathia' system, the tenants had to cultivate indigo in 3/20th part of the land. The tenants were oppressed and fear-stricken. The British administration supported the planters.

Gandhi was invited to visit Champaran by Rajkumar Shukla, a peasant from the area, in December 1916. Gandhi was first reluctant. But Shukla's persistent requests made him change his mind. He went to Champaran in April 1917 to know the conditions there and the grievances of the peasants. Before visiting the district, Gandhi visited Muzaffarpur and Patna. He discussed the matter with lawyers and social workers. Gandhi declined to seek legal remedies as he felt that law courts were useless when the people were fear-stricken. For him, removal of fear was most important. He made request to the lawyers for clerical assistance. Many of them gladly offered the same. Gandhi first met the planters and the District Commissioner. They were hostile. Gandhi was ordered to leave the area. He ignored the order. He was then summoned to the court.

The news electrified the area. Crowds gathered at the court. Gandhi pleaded guilty, saying that he was obeying a higher law, the voice of conscience. The case against him was later dropped. Gandhi and his co-workers met thousands of the peasants. They recorded about 8000 statements. Efforts were made to ensure that they were true. Recording was done in the presence of police officials. Undue publicity and exaggeration were avoided. Planters' campaign of slander was ignored. The masses in Champaran overcame their fear. Public opinion in the country was aroused. The Government ultimately appointed an enquiry committee in June 1917, with Gandhi as a member. The committee recommended abolition of tinkathia system and partial refund of money taken illegal by the planters. The Satyagraha was thus successful. Champaran Satyagraha was the first Satyagraha on the Indian soil. It was Gandhi's first major political work in India. It was carried out strictly in accordance with the principles of Satyagraha. Attention was paid to constructive work like sanitation, education and primary health-care.

Kheda Satyagraha

Kheda was a district in Gujarat. In 1917, there was a crop failure due to famine. Peasants were unable to pay the land revenue. The rules permitted suspension of revenue collection when the crops were less than four annas. According to the peasants' estimate, the crops were less than four annas. Gandhi's inquiries, as well as inquiries by independent observers, showed that the peasants were right.

The Government, however, thought otherwise. It even turned down a suggestion of an impartial enquiry. It started coercing the peasants to collect revenue. Petitions etc. were of no avail. Satyagraha was therefore started on the 22nd March 1918.

Gandhi advised the peasants to withhold payment to revenue. Satyagrahis took a pledge not to pay the same and resolved to be ready to face the consequences. Volunteers went to villages to keep up the morale of the peasants. As in Champaran, Gandhi's main concern was to remove the fear from the peasants' minds. The officials started attaching the property of the peasants including cattle and even standing crops. Notices were sent for attachment of the land. An occasion for civil disobedience arose when standing onion crop was attached at one place. Gandhi advised one Mohanlal Pandya and a few volunteers to remove the crop. This was done. The volunteers were arrested. Pandya earned the nickname 'Onion Thief.'

The struggle went on for about four months till July 1918. It tested the people's patience. The Government discontinued coercive measures. It advised that if the well-to-do peasants paid up, the poor ones would be granted suspension. In one sense, the Satyagraha was thus successful. The peasants' demand was not, however, fully met. Gandhi was not satisfied. He wanted people to come out stronger after Satyagraha. However, the Satyagraha resulted in awakening the peasants. It educated them politically. It was the first peasant struggle under Gandhi's leadership, the first nonviolent mass civil disobedience campaign organised by Gandhi in India. The peasants became aware of their rights and learnt to suffer for them.

Rowlatt Act

British Government appointed a Committee in 1917 under the chairmanship of Justice Rowlatt, (1) to enquire and report to the Government about the nature and extent of anti-government activities, and (2) to suggest legal remedies to enable the Government to suppress those activities. The Committee submitted its report in April 1918. Its work was carried out in secrecy. The Committee's recommendations were embodied in two bills.

The first bill sought to make a permanent change in the Criminal Law. The second bill intended to deal with the situation arising out of the expiry of Defence of India Rules. The first bill made punishable the possession of an antigovernment document with mere intention to circulate it. The second bill also gave sweeping powers to the officers. There were other harsh provisions also. The bills shocked the entire country. All the leaders considered the bills unjust, unwarranted and destructive of elementary human rights and dignity. The second bill was eventually dropped and the first one passed as a Law in March 1919.

Ahmedabad Satyagraha

A dispute between the textile mill-owners and the labourers at Ahmedabad arose in 1918, about the grant of bonus and dearness allowance. The labourers wanted 50% increase allowance due to steep rise in prices. The mill-owners were ready to give only 20% increase. Gandhi was approached to find a solution. He persuaded both the parties to agree to arbitration. But after a few days, some misunderstanding led to a strike.

The mill-owners seized the opportunity and declared lock-out. Gandhi studied the case. He thought that 35% increase would be reasonable. He advised the labourers to demand the same. Regular strike began on the 26th February 1918. Thousands of labourers struck work. They took a pledge not to resume work till their demand was met or arbitration was agreed upon. They also decided to observe nonviolence and maintain peace. Gandhi had friends in both the camps.

The mill-owners being led by Shri Ambalal Sarabhai. His sister Ansuyaben was leading the labourers. During the struggle, Gandhi's co-workers regularly visited the labourers' quarters to solve their problems and to keep high their morale. Daily meetings and prayers were held. Bulletins were issued. Gandhi did not like charity. Efforts were made to find alternative employments for the workers. However, after a fortnight, the workers started getting tired. It was difficult to face starvation. It was unbearable for Gandhi that they should break the vow. He then decided to undertake an indefinite fast. This strengthened the workers. It brought moral pressure on the mill-owners. They consented to arbitration after three days. Gandhi broke his fast. The Satyagraha was successful. The arbitrator studied the case for three months and recommended 35% increase in dearness allowance. The workers' demand was thus fully met. However, Gandhi's fast did involve in an element of coercion. But it was a spontaneous decision. The situation demanded some drastic action. The Satyagraha was significant in many respects. It was the first Satyagraha by industrial workers. It was wholly peaceful. It showed how workers could fight nonviolently. It also gave rise to a strong Gandhian Labour Union.

Satyagraha against the Rowlatt Act

India had helped the British in the World War. She expected substantial political rights. Instead, she received the Black Rowlatt bills. Gandhi had decided to help the British war efforts during the war. He undertook a recruiting campaign and worked hard which ruined his health. While he was recovering, he heard about Rowlatt bills. He was shocked. He took up the matter and started propaganda against the bill. Gandhi carried out propaganda against the bill. A separate body called Satyagraha Sabha was formed. A Satyagraha pledge was drafted and signed by selected leaders. The Government was, however, adamant. It then suddenly it occurred to Gandhi that a call for nationwide hartal should be given. Everybody in the country should suspend his business and spend the day in fasting and prayers. Public meetings should be held everywhere and resolutions passed for withdrawal of the Act.

The programme was taken up. 30 March was fixed as the day of the hartal, but it was later postponed to 6th April. The notice was very short. Still the masses rose to the occasion. The country rose like one man. Hartal was observed throughout India. Communal prejudices were forgotten. All fear disappeared. In Delhi, Swami Shraddhanand, the Hindu sanyasi was invited to Jama Masjid. It was also decided that civil disobedience should be offered to selected laws which could easily be disobeyed by the people. Gandhi suggested breaking of the Salt law and the sale of the banned literature. The civil disobedience was a great success. Throughout India, meetings were held and processions taken out.

The public awakening was unprecedented. It startled the British. Repression was let loose. Processions were broken up by mounted police and firing was done at several places. Many persons were killed. At some places, people lost balance in the face of repression. In such a situation, Gandhi thought it fit to suspend the Civil Disobedience Campaign. It was done on the 18th April. Satyagraha against the Rowlatt Act was historic. It was the first nationwide struggle, in which crores of people participated and showed exemplary courage. The Indian freedom movement was transformed into a truly people's movement. The period also witnessed Hindu-Muslim friendship to an extent that was never surpassed thereafter.

Jallianwala Bagh

Satyagraha in Punjab was also quite successful. Its leaders Dr. Satyapal and Dr. Kitchlew were arrested. People observed hartal and took out a procession in Amritsar to demand their release. It was fired upon, and many persons were killed. The crowd therefore became violent and killed 5-6 Englishmen. Some public buildings were burnt. Army troops were rushed in to stop the violence. This was on April 10th 1919. On April 11, a peaceful funeral procession was taken out.

General Dyer then took command of the troops. Meetings and gatherings were prohibited. Still a large meeting was held on April 12th at Jallianwala Bagh. General Dyer took no steps to prevent the meeting. But when the meeting was taking place, he surrounded the place and without any warning, gave orders of firing. The crowd of nearly 10,000 men and women was peaceful and unarmed.

They had no idea that they would be fired upon. When the firing started the people became panicky. There was only one exit. Bullets were showered on the trapped people. 1650 rounds were fired. About 400 persons were killed and 1200 injured. General Dyer did this deliberately to teach the Indians a lesson. Jallianwala Bagh massacre shocked the country. It showed how brutal the British power could get. It was followed by many more atrocities. They turned Gandhi fully against the British Empire.

Amritsar Congress

The annual session of the Indian National Congress was held at Amritsar in Punjab in December 1919. Most of the leaders in jails were released before or during the session. The session was attended by 8000 delegates including 1500 peasants. It was the last Congress session attended by Lokmanya Tilak. The Moderates, however, did not attend it. Pandit Motilal Nehru was in the Chair. The Congress was now acquiring a mass character. The proceedings were conducted mainly in Hindustani.

The Congress passed a resolution for removal of General Dyer, the butcher of Jallianwala Bagh. Recall of the Punjab Governor and the Viceroy was also demanded. It was decided to erect a memorial for the Jallianwala Bagh martyrs. Gandhi moved a resolution condemning violence on the part of the people and got it passed. It was a very significant event. The resolution also urged the people to remain peaceful. The Congress also reiterated the demand for responsible Government. The Montague Reforms were considered inadequate, disappointing and unsatisfactory. But it was decided to work the reforms. Revival of hand-spinning and hand-weaving was recommended. The Congress appointed a subcommittee for reconsideration of the Congress Constitution with Gandhi as the Chairman. It was the first Congress session in which Gandhi took an active part. His leadership was strengthened in Amritsar Congress.

The Khilafat Question

During the First World Way, Turkey sided with Germany against the British. The Sultan of Turkey was the Khalifa, the religious head of the Muslim world. The future of Khalifa, therefore, became a matter of concern for Indian Muslims. The British Government promised them that the Khilafat would not be violated and favourable peace terms would be offered to Turkey. But when Turkey was defeated in the war, the promises were forgotten. Turkish Empire was broken. Indian Muslims felt agitated over this. Gandhi sympathised with the Khilafat cause. He felt that Hindus should help the Muslim in their need. For him, it was an excellent opportunity to forge communal unity, bring Muslims in the freedom movement and form a common front against the British. The Khilafat Committee was formed. It demanded that terms of treaty with Turkey should be changed to satisfy the Indian Muslims. Gandhi suggested the programme of Non-Cooperation with the British Government. This programme was adopted by the Committee in May 1920.

The Non Cooperation Movement

The redressal of injustice of Punjab and Khilafat and the attainment of Swaraj became the key issue. The masses were getting awakened. Gandhi announced the inauguration of Nonviolent Noncooperation Movement on the 1st August 1920. A special session of Congress in September accepted the programme. The Nagpur Congress in December 1920 endorsed it enthusiastically.

The programme consisted of the following points:

Surrender of titles and honours given by the British Government

Boycott of law-courts

Boycott of educational institutions

Boycott of councils and elections

Boycott of foreign cloth

Boycott of Government functions

Picketing of liquor shops

Refusal to get recruited in the army

The programme was not just negative. It included the building of new institutions. National Education was encouraged. Stress was laid on Khadi. Charkha became the symbol of freedom.

The Congress was completely reorganised and a new constitution drafted by Gandhi was adopted to make it a mass organisation and a useful tool for the struggle. The movement started with hartal, fasting and prayers. It soon spread like wildfire. The freedom movement had become a mass movement. Gandhi declared the Swaraj could be won within one year if the programme was fully implemented. People showed great unity, determination and courage. Hundreds of National schools were established. Tilak Swaraj Fund was over-subscribed. About 20 lakh charkhas began to be plied in the country. The boycott shook the Government. 1921 was the year of the rise of Indian Nationalism Gandhi became a Mahatma, the most loved and revered figure in the country. Masses looked to him as a saint, as an incarnation of God who had come to free them from slavery and poverty.

The Government started repression. Arrests were made. Firing took place at some places. The country boycotted the visit of Prince of Wales, the British Prince in November 1921. Disturbances broke out at Bombay and Gandhi had to fast to control the situation. By the end of 1921, the number of prisoners had risen to 30,000. Processions and meetings were being broken up. The masses were getting impatient. Call was given for Civil Disobedience. Gandhi wanted to start the campaign step-by-step. He chose Bardoli in Gujarat for starting the campaign. Notice was given to Government on the 1st February 1922. However, the movement had to be called off within a few days. On the 5th February, a mob including Congressmen set fire to a police station at Chauri Chaura in U.P., killing about 22 policemen. Gandhi was shocked. He realised that people had not fully accepted nonviolence. He persuaded the Congress to suspend the agitation. Gandhi was arrested in March and was sentenced to 6 years' imprisonment. He was kept in the Yeravda jail near Pune.

YOUNG POLITICIAN

The first experience of political agitation into which Gandhi had been pitch forked cured him of what once had seemed an incorrigible self-consciousness. Not that he had a sudden attack of egotism; he was conscious of his limitations, and in a letter dated July 5, 1894 to Dadabhai Naoroji, the eminent leader of the Indian National Congress, wrote: "A word for myself and I have done. I am inexperienced and young and, therefore, quite liable to make mistakes.

The responsibility undertaken is quite out of proportion to my ability. So, you will see that I have not taken the matter up, which is beyond my ability, in order to enrich myself at the expense of the Indians. I am the only available person who can handle the question." The concept of inferiority is a relative one; in a community looking to him for leadership, Gandhi forgot his own limitations. As the only available person, he undertook a task from which elsewhere he would have shrunk.

Gandhi had come to South Africa in 1893 for a year. He could hardly have imagined that he would have to stay on for the best part of two decades. The struggle of the Indian immigrants for elementary civic rights was to be long and hard The disfranchising of the Indians which had been the immediate cause of Gandhi's intervention in the politics of Natal was only a symptom of the racial malaise that had begun to afflict the Dark Continent.

"The Asiatics", wrote Lord Milner, "are strangers forcing themselves upon a community reluctant to receive them." In fact, the Indian emigration to South Africa in the eighteen-sixties started at the instance of the European settlers who were in possession of vast virgin lands ideal for tea, coffee and sugar plantations, but lacked man-power.

The Negro could not be compelled to work after the abolition of slavery. Recruiting agents of the European planters toured some of the poorest and most congested districts of India and painted rosy prospects of work in Natal. Free passage, board and lodging; a wage of ten shillings a month for the first year rising by one shilling every year; and the right to a free return passage to India after five years' 'indenture' (or alternatively, the option to settle in the land of their adoption) drew thousands of poor and illiterate Indians to distant Natal.

The European planters and merchants did not relish the idea of Indian Labourers settling down as free citizens at the end of the five year' 'indenture'. A tax of £3 was therefore levied on every member of the family of an ex-indentured labourer even though he was merely exercising his right to settle in Natal in terms of the agreement which had governed his emigration from India. It was a crippling tax for the poor wretches whose wages ranged between ten and twelve shillings month. The Indian merchant who had followed the Indian labourer to Natal had disabilities of his own. No one could trade without a licence, which a European could have for the asking and Indian only after much effort and expense, if at all. And since an educational test in a European language was made a sine quanon for an immigrant from India, except of course the semi-slave indentured labourers who continued to be imported.

The legal disabilities on Indians were bad enough, but the daily humiliations they suffered were worse. They were commonly described as "Asian dirt to be heartily curse, chokeful of vice, that live upon rice and the black vermin". They were not allowed to walk on footpaths. First and second class tickets were not issued to them. If a white passenger objected, they could be unceremoniously bundled out of a railway compartment; they had sometimes to travel on footboards of trains. European hotels would not admit them.

Gandhi realized that what the India urgently needed was a permanent organization to look after their interests. Out of deference to Dadabhai Naoroji, Who had presided over the Indian National Congress in 1893, he called the new organization Natal Indian Congress. He was not conversant with the constitution and functions of the Indian National Congress. This ignorance proved an asset, as he fashioned the Natal Congress in his own way to suit the needs of the Natal Indians, as a live body functioning throughout the year and dedicated not only to politics but to the moral and social uplift of its members. Though it served a community which had very little political experience, it was not a one-man show. An indefatigable secretary though he was, Gandhi enlisted popular interest and enthusiasm at every step. He made the enrolment of members and the collection of subscriptions into something more than a routine. He employed a gently but irresistible technique for exerting moral pressure on halfhearted supporters. Once in a small village, he sat through the night and refused to take his dinner until at dawn his host, an Indian merchant, agreed to raise his subscription for the Natal Indian Congress from three to six pounds.

In these early years of his politics apprenticeship, Gandhi formulated his own code of conduct for a politician. He did not accept the popular view that in politics one must fight for one's; arty, right or wrong. He avoided exaggeration and discouraged it in his colleagues. The Natal Indian Congress was not merely an instrument for the defence of political and economic rights for the Indian minority, but also a lever for its internal reform and unity. He did not spare his own people and roundly criticized them for their shortcomings. He was not only the stoutest champion of the Natal Indians, but also their severest critic.

Under his leadership, the Indian community in Natal endeavoured to secure the repeal of discriminatory laws and vexatious regulations and stave off further oppressive measures. Gandhi was in touch with Naoroji and other members of the British committee of the Indian National Congress in London. He sought their advice and support in representing the South African Indian Indian's case to the Secretary of State for India, and British Colonial Secretary.

He was an indefatigable correspondent, bombarding his friends, opponents, newspaper editors and men in authority in three continents, with telegrams, letters and memoranda on the grievances of the India in South

Africa. It is a measure of Gandhi's success as a publicist that the Indian National Congress Recorded its protest against the disabilities imposed upon the Indian settlers in South Africa, and the London Times devoted several leading articles to this problem.

In 1896 he paid a brief visit to India to canvass public support for the cause he had made his own. On return to Natal from this trip on January 10,1897, he was nearly lynched in the streets Durban by a mob of Europeans who had been infuriated by Press reports of Gandhi's advocacy of the Indian cause in his native land.

On the outbreak of the Boer War in 1899, Gandhi organized an Indian Ambulance Corps of 1100 men. Vere Stent, the editor of the Pretoria News, has left a fascinating pen-portrait of Gandhi in the battlefield: "After a night's work which had shattered men with much bigger frames, I came across Gandhi in the early morning sitting by the roadside-eating a regulation biscuit. Every man in (General) Buller's force was dull and depressed, and damnation was heartily invoked on everything. But Gandhi was stoic in his bearing, cheerful and confident in his conversation and had a kindly eye."

It must be recognised that Gandhi's ideas on non-violence had not yet fully matured. His argument at this time was that Indian settlers in British colonies, while demanding all the privileges of citizenship must also accept all its obligations, which included participation in the defence of the country of adoption. Gandhi's gesture in raising an ambulance corps on behalf of a minority which was denied elementary rights was a fine one, but it was wasted. The end of the Boer War brought no relief to the Indians. Their grievances remained unredressed. Indeed, new chains were forged for them in the former Boer Colonies.

BARDOLI SATYAGRAHA

Bardoli was a tehsil in Gujarat. Government increased the land revenue assessment there by 30%. Protests brought it down to 22%. The peasants thought it unjust. Vallabhbhai Patel studied the case. He was convinced that the peasants were right. The peasants decided to withhold the payment until the enhancement was cancelled or an impartial tribunal appointed for setting the case. Gandhi blessed the Satyagraha. It started in February 1928.

Vallabhbhai Patel led the struggle. He organised sixteen camps under the charge of 250 volunteers. His organisation was superb. It earned him the title 'Sardar'. The government tried its best to terrorise the people and extract the payment. It tried flattery, bribery, fines, imprisonment and lathi-charge. Pathans were brought in to threaten the people. The cattle was taken away and lands auctioned at several places. Patel kept up the people's morale.

His volunteers were arrested. People imposed a social boycott on the Government officials and against those who bought auctioned property. Seven members of the Legislative Council resigned in protest against the Government repression. Several village officials, too, resigned their posts.

1) The Government issued an ultimatum for payment. Patel demanded that
2) The Satyagrahi prisoners should be released.
3) The lands sold and forfeited, should be returned.
4) The cost of seized movables should be refunded.

All the dismissals and punishments should be undone. Gandhi and Patel promised to call off the agitation if these demands were met and an inquiry ordered. The Government ultimately yielded. An Inquiry Committee was appointed. The Committee recommended an increase of 5.7% only. The Satyagraha was thus successful. The Bardoli struggle was very well organised one. The peasants remained united against all odds. Women took part in the struggle on a large scale. The struggle became a symbol of hope, strength and victory for the peasants in the country.

Rising Discontent

The discontent against the British Government was increasing. The Government appointed Simon Commission to decide about the grant of political rights of India. Indian leaders had not been consulted. There was no Indian Member in the Commission. The country boycotted Simon Commission.

Gandhi had regarded himself as a 'Prisoner' and refrained from political activities till 1928, when his jail term was to expire. He thereafter took the reins of Congress in his hands. Congress resolved in 1929 to fight for complete independence. Confrontation with the Government became imminent. Gandhi launched Civil Disobedience Campaign-the famous Salt Satyagraha.

THE SALT SATYAGRAHA

Gandhi wrote to the Viceroy, listing eleven demands which, according to him, formed the substance of self-government. They were rejected. Gandhi then decided to start Civil Disobedience by breaking the Salt Law, which heavily taxed the salt, an article of daily consumption for the poorest of the poor.

He started his epic Dandi March on the 12 March 1930 from Ahmedabad. A carefully selected band of 78 Satyagrahis accompanied Gandhi in this March to Dandi, a deserted village on the sea-coat, at about 240 miles from Ahmedabad. As the March progressed, the atmosphere in the country was electrified.

Several village officials resigned their posts. Gandhi declared that he would not return to Sabarmati Ashram till Independence was won. Congress Committee met on the 21st March to plan the strategy. Gandhi reached Dandi on the 6th April and broke the Salt law symbolically by picking up a pinch of salt. It was signal for the nation.

Civil Disobedience campaign was started throughout the country. Salt Law broken at many places by illegal production of salt and its sale. Gandhi went to the surrounding places and started a campaign to cut toddy trees. Picketing of liquor and foreign cloth shops was started. Women were on the forefront in picketing the liquor shops. The whole country was stirred. Some other laws like Forest Laws were also taken up for disobedience at some places.

Government intensified the repression. Most of the important leaders including Gandhi were arrested. But the agitation grew in strength. People bravely faced police brutalities and even firing at many places. A wave of strikes and hartals swept the country. At Peshawar, soldiers of Garhwali regiment refused to fire on the unarmed people. They were court-martialled. Before his arrest, Gandhi hit upon a novel idea to raid salt depots. The Dharasana raid, in which several nonviolent Satyagrahis were mercilessly beaten, sent shock-waves throughout the world. It lowered the British prestige. The movement progressed till January 1931. The boycott of foreign cloth, liquor and British goods was almost complete.

Gandhi and other leaders were subsequently released from jail. Government started negotiations. Gandhi-Irvin Pact was signed in March. The Satyagraha was discontinued. This was a major Satyagraha, during which 111 Satyagrahis died in firings and about one lakh persons went to jail.

A Phase of Repression

Gandhi took part in the Round Table Conference in England in 1931 as the representative of the Congress. It was a frustrating experience for him. The British were bent on prolonging their rule by following the policy of Divide and Rule'. Gandhi stayed in London in a poor locality. He even met the unemployed textile mill-workers who had lost the jobs due to Gandhi's movement of Swadeshi and Boycott. He explained to them the rationale behind Khadi. The workers showered love on him.

The Round Table Conference yielded nothing. Gandhi returned in December 1931. He was arrested and the Civil Disobedience Campaign was resumed. The Congress was declared illegal. The Government was determined to crush the movement. The leaders and a large number of workers were arrested. Ordinances were issued to arm the Government with wide powers. Gandhi was lodged in the Yervada jail.

Yeravda Pact

While Gandhi was in Yeravda jail the British Prime Minister Ramsay MacDonald announced the provisional scheme of minority representation, known as the Communal Award. The depressed classes (now known as Scheduled Castes) were recognised as a minority community and given separate electorates. Gandhi was shocked. It was an attempt to divide and destroy the Hindu Society and the Nation and in turn to perpetuate India's slavery. It was not good for the depressed also. Gandhi announced his decision to fast unto death from the 20th September 1932. He was fully for the representation to the depressed classes, but he was against their being considered as a minority community and given separate electorates.

Gandhi's decision stirred the country. Indian leaders began hectic efforts to save Gandhi's life. But Dr. Ambedkar described the fast as a political Stunt. Gandhi's decision awakened the Hindu Society. It dealt a blow to the orthodoxy. Hindu leaders resolved to fight untouchability. Several temples were thrown open to the Harijans. The fast began on 20th September. Attempts to evolve an alternative scheme were continuing. Gandhi's health started deteriorating. He had several rounds of discussions with Dr. Ambedkar. At last, an agreement was reached on the 24th September.

The Government was urged to accept the same. The British Government ultimately gave its consent. Gandhi broke his fast on 26th September. The agreement is known as the Yeravda Pact or the Poona Pact. It provided for doubling the number of representatives of depressed classes. Separate electorates were however, done away with. It was decided that for every reserved seat, members of the depressed classes would elect four candidates and the representative would be elected from them by joint electorate. The system of primary election was to be for ten years.

Anti-untouchability Campaign

Yeravda Pact gave a great boost to the anti-untouchability work. Harijan Sevak Sangh was established. 'Harijan' Weekly was started. After his release, Gandhi put aside political activities and devoted himself to Harijan service and other constructive work. All-India Village Industries Association was also formed. Gandhi gave the Sabarmati Ashram to the Harijan Sevak Sangh and later settled at Wardha. He toured the entire country and collected Harijan Fund. The massive anti-untouchability propaganda launched by him had spectacular results. He had, of course, of face opposition. Even a bomb was once thrown at him. The campaign destroyed the legitimacy of untouchability. It cleared the way for legal ban. In 1936, Gandhi settled down at Sevagram, a village near Wardha. In 1937, he presided over the Educational Conference, which gave rise to the scheme of Basic Education.

India and the War

While Gandhi was busy in the constructive work, elections to the provincial assemblies were held in 1937. Congress Ministers were formed in several provinces. The Second World War began in 1939. The British Government dragged India into the War without consulting Indian leaders. Congress Ministries resigned in protest.

The Congress expressed sympathy for the Allied powers' fight against Nazism and Fascism and offered cooperation provided responsible Self-Government was granted. Gandhi was however against any cooperation in war efforts on the ground of Nonviolence. When the Government turned down the Congress demand, Gandhi was requested to resume the leadership. Gandhi decided to launch Anti-War individual Satyagraha against curtailment of freedom. It was inaugurated by Vinoba in October 1940. Pandit Nehru was the Second Satyagrahi. The Satyagrahis were arrested. By May 1941, the number of Satyagrahi prisoners had crossed 25000.

Cripps Mission

The War was approaching India's borders with the advance of Japan. England was in difficulties. It could not afford any agitation in India. There were various other pressures on the British Government to make political concessions. As a result, Sir Stafford Cripps was sent to India in March 1942. Cripps discussed the matter with the Indian leaders. He proposed Dominion Status with power to the States and the provinces to secede and convening of a constitution-making body after the War. But the adherence to the constitution drafted by that body was not to be obligatory.

Indian leaders including Gandhi found the Cripps Proposals disappointing. They were aptly termed as post dated cheque on a crashing bank. The Muslim League wanted a definite pronouncement about Pakistan and therefore criticised the Cripps proposals. Congress rejected the Cripps scheme because it did not provide for the participation of the people of the states and the principles of non-accession was against Indian unity. The Cripps Mission failed.

'QUIT INDIA' MOVEMENT

The country wanted nothing but Complete Independence. The Congress passed the historic 'Quit India' resolution on 8th August 1942. Gandhi and other leaders were arrested. The country now rose in revolt. With most of the leaders in jail, it fought in the way it thought fit. Railway lines and telegraphic communications were interfered with. Government property was burnt or destroyed in several places. The people displayed unprecedented courage and heroism. Unarmed people faced police lathis and bullets. Young boys suffered flogging without flinching. Government machinery was paralysed and parallel Government was set up at some places. Many workers went underground. About 1000 people died in firings during the movement. About 1600 were injured and 60000 people were arrested. It was noteworthy that violence was done to Government property only. Englishmen were safe throughout the Movement. There was little personal violence. Thus, while the masses rose to great heights of heroism, they also displayed remarkable restraint. It was surely Gandhi's contribution. The rebellion was, however, gradually put down.

Gandhi was in Agakhan Palace jail. He was blamed by the British for the disturbances. He could not tolerate questioning of his faith and honesty and fasted for 21 days. Gandhi lost his wife Kasturba and his Secretary Mahadev Desai in the Agakhan Palace. It was a great blow to him. His health was not in a good condition. He was finally released in May 1944 on health grounds. He then started efforts to break the political stalemate.

Background of the Partition

The Hindu-Muslim unity, forged at the time of the Khilafat agitation, collapsed thereafter. The country witnessed a wave of communal riots. The British encouraged Muslim communalism and used it to obstruct the path of the Freedom Movement. M. A. Jinnah, an erstwhile liberal leader, who had been sidelined when the Congress became a mass organisation, assumed the leadership of Muslim communalism.

The Muslim League under his leadership became more aggressive, unreasonable and violent. The two-nation theory-that Hindus and Muslims were two separate Muslim homeland called 'Pakistan,' consisting of the Muslim-majority provinces. Jinnah's shrewdness, ambition and ruthlessness, communalisation of large sections of society and the British support for Jinnah, brought about such a situation that the Muslim demands became an obstacle in the way of India's Independence. Jinnah kept the demands fluid and utilised every opportunity to frustrate the Nationalist Movement and further his end with the support of the British rulers.

The two-nation theory was an untruth. The Hindus and Muslims had lived together in India for centuries. Gandhi fought this untruth with all his might. He did everything possible, including meeting Jinnah several times. But he failed. Jinnah wanted recognition of the League as the sole representative of the Muslims. It was not acceptable to the Congress.

Cabinet Mission

The War ended in 1945. After an election, Labour Party's Government came to power in England. England had been extremely weakened financially and militarily. The Azad Hind Sena had shown that even the army was not untouched by nationalism. Mutiny of the naval ratings in February 1946 gave the same indication. The people were in an agitated mood. The British rule had lost legitimacy in the eyes of the people. The British, therefore, decided to withdraw from India.

Cabinet Mission was sent to India to help in the formation of Interim Government and to purpose a scheme regarding the transfer of power. The mission proposed that the provinces be divided in three groups, in one of which Hindus were in the majority while in the other two Muslims. Subjects like defence, foreign affairs, communications etc., were to be with the Central Authority and the groups were to be free to frame constitutions about other subjects. Gandhi found the proposals defective. Muslim League declared 'Direct Action' to get Pakistan. 'Direct Action' meant unleashing of violence. The Hindus retaliated. In Calcutta alone, over 6000 people were killed 4 days. The Hindu communalism too became stronger.

The Noakhali Massacre

In the Noakhali area of East Bengal, where Muslims formed 82% of the population, a reign of terror was let loose in a planned and systematic way in October 1946. The Hindus were killed and beaten, their property was burnt, thousands of Hindus were forcibly converted and thousands of Hindu women were abducted and raped. Temples were defiled and destroyed.

The League Government in Bengal aided the goondas. Even ex-serviceman joined in committing the atrocities. In Noakhali, about three-fourth of the land belonged to the Hindu landlords and the tenants were mostly Muslims. The peasant unrest was naturally there. It was now turned along communal channels. The Noakhali massacre had few parallels in the history. It showed to what level communal politics could stop to. It was meant to terrorise, kill, convert or drive away the Hindus from Muslim-majority areas so that Pakistan could become a reality.

Gandhi's Noakhali March

Gandhi was deeply shocked. He could not bear the defeat of his long-cherished principles. On 6th November 1946, he rushed to Noakhali. It was to be his final and perhaps the most glorious battle.

Gandhi reached Shrirampur and camped there for a few days. He sent his associates including Pyarelal and Sushila Nayyar to different villages which were mostly deserted by the Hindus. He did all his personal work himself. He worked like a possessed man. He walked barefooted, went from house to house, talked to Hindus and Muslims, heard their points of view, and reasoned with them and addressed meetings. He wanted to instill fearlessness into the Hindus. He exhorted them to die nonviolently, if need be, but not to submit to terror. He did not appease the Muslim. He told the truth bluntly. He wanted to win their confidence and make them see reason and earn the confidence of the Hindus. He did not only preach, he served the village poor.

He was testing his Nonviolence. It was very difficult to establish mutual trust. The League had made poisonous propaganda against him. But Gandhi's mission began to yield results. It boosted the morale of Hindus. Passions began to subside. Some evacuees started returning home. Some even returned to their original faith. Gandhi gradually succeeded in earning the love and confidence of even the Muslims.

INDIA WINS INDEPENDENCE

Noakhali had its reaction in Bihar, where Hindus resorted to violence. The country was seized by communal madness. Gandhi went to Bihar and brought the situation under control.

The situation in the country was explosive. Civil War was imminent. The Congress ultimately consented to the partition of India. Despite Gandhi's bitter opposition, he could not do anything to prevent the partition.

While the country was celebrating the Independence. Day on 15th August 1947, Gandhi was in Bengal to fight communal madness. Partition was followed by riots, a massacre of unparalleled dimensions. It witnessed movement of about one crore persons and killing of at least six lakh persons. Calcutta was once more on the verge of riots. Gandhi under-took a fast which had a magical effect. Lord Mountbatten described him as 'one-man peace army'. Gandhi continued to plead for sanity in those turbulent days.

3

Freedom Movements of Gandhi

KHILAFAT MOVEMENT

The Khilafat movement (1919-1924) was a political campaign launched mainly by Muslims in British India to influence the British government and to protect the Ottoman Empire during the aftermath of World War I. The position of Caliph after the Armistice of Mudros of October 1918 with the military occupation of Istanbul and Treaty of Versailles (1919) fell into a disambiguation along with the Ottoman Empire's existence. The movement gained force after the Treaty of Sèvres (August 1920) which solidified the partitioning of the Ottoman Empire.

In India, although mainly a Muslim religious movement, the movement became a part of the wider Indian independence movement. The movement was a topic in Conference of London (February 1920).

History

The Caliphate is an Islamic system of governance in which the state rules under Islamic law. Caliph literally means "successor" or "representative" and emphasizes religious authority for the head of state. It was adopted as a title by the Ummayad Caliphs and then by the Abbasid Caliphs, as well as by the Fatimid Caliphs of North Africa, the Almohad Caliphs of North Africa and Spain and the Ottoman Dynasty. Most historical Muslim rulers were sultans or amirs, and gave token obedience to a caliph who often had very little real authority. Moreover, the Muslim clergy, the ulema and the various Sufi orders, exercised more religious influence than the Caliph.

Ottoman Caliphate

Ottoman emperor Abdul Hamid II (1876-1909) had launched his Pan-Islamic program in a bid to protect the Ottoman empire from Western attack and dismemberment, and to crush the Westernizing democratic opposition in Turkey. He sent an emissary, Jamaluddin Afghani, to India in the late 19th century. The cause of the Ottoman monarch evoked religious passion and sympathy amongst Indian Muslims. Being a Caliph, the Ottoman emperor was the supreme religious and political leader of all Sunni Muslims across the world (although this authority was titular in practice).

A large number of Muslim religious leaders began working to spread awareness and develop Muslim participation on behalf of the Caliphate. Muslim religious leader Maulana Mehmud Hasan attempted to organise a national war of independence against the British with support from the Ottoman Empire. He was overthrown by a secretive nationalist group called the 'Young Turks.' Abdulhamid was succeeded by his brother Mehmed VI (1844-1918) but real power lay with the nationalists.

Partitioning

The Ottoman empire, having sided with the Central Powers during World War I, suffered a major military defeat. The Treaty of Versailles (1919) reduced its territorial extent and diminished its political influence but the victorious European powers promised to protect the Ottoman emperor's status as the Caliph. However, under the Treaty of Sèvres (1920), territories such as Palestine, Syria, Lebanon, Iraq, Egypt severed from the empire.

Within Turkey, a pro-Western nationalist movement arose, Turkish national movement. During the Turkish War of Independence (1919-1924) led by one of the Turkish revolutionaries, Mustafa Kemal Atatürk, abolished the Treaty of Sèvres with the Treaty of Lausanne (1923). Pursuant to Atatürk's Reforms, the Republic of Turkey abolished the position of Caliphate in 1924 and transferred its powers within Turkey to the Grand National Assembly of Turkey.

EVENTS IN TURKEY

An attempt was made towards inaugurating a Pan-Islamic movement i.e. the Aligarh movement during the last quarter of the 19th century. It did not succeed but the sentiment never died out altogether. It is proved by the active sympathy of the Indian Muslims (M) towards the Turks in their fight against Italy and the Balkhan powers.

Turkey's entry into the war as an ally of Germany put the Indian M into a quandary. Their natural sympathy lie with the Sultan of Turkey as their Caliph or religious head but as British subjects they were to be loyal to the British throne. Realizing their predicament the British PM, Lloyd George declared on 05/01/1918, that the allies "were not fighting to deprive Turkey of the rich and renowned lands of Asia Minor and Thrace which are predominantly Turkish in race".

These assurances led the Indian M to believe that whatever happened, the territorial integrity and independence of Turkey, so far as her Asiatic dominions would be maintained. However, what happened was different.

Thrace was presented to Greece while the Asiatic portions of Turkey passed to England and France. Thus Turkey was dispossessed of her homelands and the Sultan deprived of all real authority. Indian M regarded this as a great betrayal and carried on agitations through out 1919 but to no effect.

At the same time, Mustufa Kemal Pasha a highly gifted leader rose in Turkey brushed aside the weak regime of the Caliph and resolved to make a new, powerful Turkey on modern nationalistic lines. Aware that the Caliph was the religious leader of the Arab world he decided to get rid his country of Arabism and liberate it from the stronghold of the maulvis and mullahs. (Something that Pakistan needs to do today). He was helped by Jamaluddin Afghani, an Arab born in Afghanistan in 1838. The rise of a powerful state in Turkey did not suit the Brits. They prodded Aga Khan to join hands with the Caliph. Aga Khan and Amir Ali went to Kemal Pasha and begged him to save the Caliph, Abdul Majid. Kemal treated them with contempt and derided Aga Khan (a Shia) and Amir Ali (a Khoja) as heretics of Islam who had no business to advise the Sunni Turkish Muslims.

Kemal said that it was ironical that two men who were the pillars of the Brit rule in India had come to advise Turkey on their national policy. He exposed these two men, dethroned Islam from the pedestal of the official state religion and transformed Turkey into a secular state.

But the Khilafat leaders in India would not give up. Under the leadership of the Ali brothers they approached King Abdul Azeez of Arabia to become the new Caliph. The King had the Indians in a corner by asking them "If it is Islam that you are zealous about, why do not you join hands with Gandhi and free India of the Brit rule. That's what Islam teaches. You come to me as a slave of the Brits and it seems to me that you have come to lead me into a Brit trap". Next the leaders approached Reza Shah, the ruler of Iran. But Shah proud of his Aryan tradition, evinced little interest.

In 1921, Muhammad Ali had written a letter to the Amir of Afghanistan inviting him to invade India. The Brits got scent of this and arrested the Ali brothers. On his written assurance that he was no opponent of the Brits he was released. In 1921, when the Khilafat agitation was at its peak, Ali again sent a wire to the Amir urging him not to enter into any agreement with the Brits. When Ali was taken to task by the Congress leaders he showed Swami Shraddananada (renowned Arya Samaj leader) a hand written draft of the wire.

The Swami writes "What was my astonishment when I saw the draft of the same self-same telegram in the peculiar handwriting of the Father of the nonviolent non-cooperation movement". Writing in the Young India in May 1921 Gandhi said, "I would, in a sense, certainly assist the Amir of Afghanistan if he waged war against the British Govt.. It is no part of the duty of a nonviolent non-cooperator to assist the Govt. against war made upon it by others. I would rather see India perish at the hands of the Afghans than purchase freedom from Afghan invasion at the cost of her honour. To have India defended by an unrepentant Govt. that keeps the Khilafat and Punjab wounds still bleeding is to sell India's honour". Gandhi was criticized by Lala Lajpat Rai and B C Pal for his statements. Thus it is interesting to note that the Hindu Congress leaders took up the case of the Caliph when the Muslim world itself had refused to do so.

Khilafat Movement (1919-1924) was a Pan-Islamic movement influenced by Indian nationalism. The Ottoman Emperor Abdul Hamid II (1876-1909) had launched a Pan-Islamic programme to use his position as the Sultan-Khalifa of the global Muslim community with a view to saving his disintegrating empire from foreign attacks and to crush the nationalistic democratic movement at home.

The visit of his emissary, Jamaluddin Afghani, to India in the late nineteenth century to propagate Pan-Islamic ideas received a favourable response from some Indian Muslim leaders.

These sentiments intensified early in the twentieth century with the revocation in 1911 of the 1905 partition of bengal, the Italian (1911) and Balkan (1911-1912) attacks on Turkey, and Great Britain's participation in the First World War (1914-18) against Turkey.

The defeat of Turkey in the First World War and the division of its territories under the Treaty of Sevres (10 August 1920) among European powers caused apprehensions in India over the Khalifa's custodianship of the Holy places of Islam. Accordingly, the Khilafat Movement was launched in September 1919 as an orthodox communal movement to protect the Turkish Khalifa and save his empire from dismemberment by Great Britain and other European powers.

The Movement was initiated by the Ali brothers, Muhammad Ali and Shawkat Ali, Maulana Abul Kalam Azad, Dr. MA Ansari, and Hasrat Mohani. Khilafat Conferences were organised in several cities in northern India. A Central Khilafat Committee, with provisions for provincial branches, was constituted at Bombay with Seth Chotani, a wealthy merchant, as its President, and Shawkat Ali as its Secretary. In 1920 the Ali Brothers produced the Khilafat Manifesto. The Central Khilafat Committee started a Fund to help the Nationalist Movement in Turkey and to organise the Khilafat Movement at home.

KHILAFAT IN SOUTH ASIA

Although political activities and popular outcry on behalf of the caliphate emerged across the Muslim world, the most prominent activities took place in India. A prominent Muslim cleric and journalist, Maulana Mohammad Ali Jouhar had spent four years in prison for preaching resistance to the British and support for the caliphate. At the onset of the Turkish war of independence, Muslim religious leaders feared for the caliphate, which the European powers were reluctant to protect.

Ali and his brother Maulana Shaukat Ali joined with other Muslim leaders such as Sheikh Shaukat Ali Siddiqui, Dr. Mukhtar Ahmed Ansari, Raees-Ul-Muhajireen Barrister Jan Muhammad Junejo, Hasrat Mohani, Maulana Abul Kalam Azad and Dr. Hakim Ajmal Khan to form the All India Khilafat Committee.

The organization was based in Lucknow, India at Hathe Shaukat Ali, the compound of Landlord Shaukat Ali Siddiqui. They aimed to build political unity amongst Muslims and use their influence to protect the caliphate. In 1920, they published the Khilafat Manifesto, which called upon the British to protect the caliphate and for Indian Muslims to unite and hold the British accountable for this purpose.

In 1920 an alliance was made between Khilafat leaders and the Indian National Congress, the largest political party in India and of the nationalist movement. Congress leader Mohandas Gandhi and the Khilafat leaders promised to work and fight together for the causes of Khilafat and *Swaraj*.

Seeking to increase pressure on the British, the Khilafatists became a major part of the Non-cooperation movement — a nationwide campaign of mass, peaceful civil disobedience. The support of the Khilafatists helped Gandhi and the Congress ensure Hindu-Muslim unity during the struggle. Khilafat leaders such as Dr. Ansari, Maulana Azad and Hakim Ajmal Khan also grew personally close to Gandhi. These leaders founded the Jamia Millia Islamia in 1920 to promote independent education and social rejuvenation for Muslims.

The non-cooperation campaign was at first successful. Massive protests, strikes and acts of civil disobedience spread across India. Hindus and Muslims collectively offered resistance, which was largely peaceful. Gandhi, the Ali brothers and others were imprisoned by the British. However, the Congress-Khilafat alliance began withering soon. The Khilafat campaign had been opposed by other political parties such as the Muslim League and the Hindu Mahasabha. Many Hindu religious and political leaders identified the Khilafat cause as Islamic fundamentalism based on a pan-Islamic agenda.

Collapse

In wake of these disturbances, the Ali brothers began distancing themselves from Gandhi and the Congress. The Ali brothers criticised Gandhi's commitment to non-violence and severed their ties with them after he suspended all non-cooperation movement after the killing of 22 policemen at Chauri Chaura in 1922. Although holding talks with the British and continuing their activities, the Khilafat struggle weakened as Muslims were divided between working for the Congress, the Khilafat cause and the Muslim League.

The final blow came with the victory of Mustafa Kemal's forces, who overthrew the Ottoman rule to establish a pro-Western, secular republic in independent Turkey. The Khilafat leadership fragmented on different political lines. Leaders such as Dr. Ansari, Maulana Azad and Hakim Ajmal Khan remained strong supporters of Gandhi and the Congress. The Ali brothers joined the Muslim League. They would play a major role in the growth of the League's popular appeal and the subsequent Pakistan movement. There was, however, a Caliphate Conference in Jerusalem in 1931 following Turkey's abolition of the Khilafat, to determine what should be done about the caliphate.

Legacy

The Khilafat struggle evokes controversy and strong opinions. It is regarded as a political agitation based on a pan-Islamic, fundamentalist platform and being largely indifferent to the cause of Indian independence.

Critics of the Khilafat see its alliance with the Congress as a marriage of convenience. Proponents of the Khilafat see it as a major milestone in improving Hindu-Muslim relations, while advocates of Pakistan and Muslim separatism see it as a major step towards establishing the separate Muslim state. The Ali brothers are regarded as founding-fathers of Pakistan, while Azad, Dr. Ansari and Hakim Ajmal Khan are widely celebrated as national heroes in India.

The cause of establishing an Islamic State by reviving the caliphate system has been adopted by organisations such as the Muslim Brotherhood, Jamaat-e-Islami umbrella groups in South Asia, founded in 1941 by Maulana Maududi and most of all Hizb ut Tahrir.

CHAURI CHAURA

Chauri Chaura is a town near Gorakhpur, Uttar Pradesh, India. The town is famous for an event that took place on 22 February 1922 during British rule when a police *chowki* (pron.-chau key) (station) was set on fire by a nationalist mob, killing 22 of the police occupants.

In the years 1920 and 1921, Indians launched a nationwide revolt now recognized as the Non-Cooperation Movement, which protested authoritarian laws like the Rowlatt Acts of 1919, and lack of human freedom and self-government for Indians in their own country.

Mahatma Gandhi was the leader of the nationwide revolts organised by the Indian National Congress based upon civil disobedience, or *Satyagraha* by peaceful means alone.

The Incident

On February 4, 1922, around 2,000 protesters gathered for picketing of the liquor shop at the local market in Chauri Chaura. Sensing the trouble, armed policemen were sent to the city police station to control the situation. The crowd marched towards the market and started shouting anti-government slogans.

The policemen fired into the air as a warning signal. However, it had the reverse effect on the crowd who were in no mood to retreat and started pelting stones at the armed policemen. Seeing the situation was getting out of control, the sub inspector ordered the policemen to commence firing on the advancing crowd.

Three protesters were killed on the spot and several others were injured. Seeing this, the crowd became violent and attacked the police from all the sides. The armed policemen lost their courage to fire, seeing thousands of protesters marching towards them. They retreated to the shelter of the police station. The crowd decided to take revenge for their dead comrades and set fire to the building from all the sides. Twenty-three policemen were burnt alive, including the station sub inspector.

Consequences

Mahatma Gandhi asked all Indians to end the Non-cooperation movement, and went on a five-day fast to absolve himself of what he perceived as his role in inciting the attacks. Gandhi felt that he had acted too hastily in encouraging a revolt against the British Raj, while not emphasizing the importance of ahinsa (non-violence) and not training the resisters enough. Due to his fast and the exhortation of Congress leaders, Indians gave up civil resistance.

Other consequences is a Birth of INA, Opposing the step towards endof Non-cooperation movement, Subash Chandra Bose formed INA and belived army struggle is the only way to get freedom from British rule faster.

Limelight of Lengendary freedom fighters Bhagath Singh and Chandershekhar Azad, Opposing the decision of endof Non-cooperation movement they both joined HRA (Hindustan republic association) formed in the year 1923 to fight against British rule. Incidents like Chauri Chaura (1922) contributed in getting faster independence for India. Its one of the greatest and historical incident which always to be discussed.

The Trial and the Judgement

The British government was furious after this incident and imposed martial law in the city of Chauri Chaura and surrounding areas. All the areas were raided and hundreds of people were arrested. 172 people were charged and put on the trial. On April 20, 1923 Allahabad high court awarded death sentence to 19, various jail terms including life imprisonment to 2 years jail to 113 accused, and acquitted 38 due to lack of evidence, whereas 3 accused died during the course of the trial.

Modern Assessment

Many modern historians view the Chauri Chaura incident as a minor episode of violence, which while regrettable, did not merit the cancellation of a nation's demand for political freedom.

Supporters of Gandhi's point of view agree with his decision, as it was feared by Gandhi that Chauri Chaura was not an isolated incident, but a shocking episode in a rising trend of violence between protesters and police, which could have degenerated into an orgy of mob violence, which would justify martial law and police suppression of even more civil liberties.

Thus (in Gandhi's view) the spiral of violence would have wrecked the wider agenda and organization, while maligning India's patriots as bloodthirsty murderers in the eyes of the world.

The nationalist version of historiography in India has linked it with the larger conscious call of Gandhi in Non-cooperation movement. However, the recent subaltern scholarship has tried to dug more substantive meanings of the incidence. The metaphor of Gandhi in the consciousness of masses, the way he moved in masses and his symbolic gestures had a myriad 'meanings' to the masses. Shahid Amin in his book *Event, Metaphor, Memory* has portrayed the chain of events that were occurring in Gorakhpur in that time. He had tried to argue that the nationalist meta-narrative of Indian National Congress has failed to bring out the history from below. The reason of the masses to act in a manner they did in Gorakhpur was as diverse as caste tensions, belief as Gandhi as liberator that enabled them to defy authority of local zamindars or the British.

Therefore, there can be alternative versions of history. The over-arching explanation of event like Chauri Chaura in the Nationalist historiography can be concealing if not read with other accounts.

AHAMADABAD MILL WORKER

There exists in India a powerfully organised Labour movement. The secretary of the Indian Labour Federation, or "Standing Committee of the All-India Trade Union Congress," as it is called, is Mr. Chiman Lal, who claimed that under this federation are combined 97 unions, with 1,500,000 members. These unions embrace nearly all the industries of the country. The leading organisation is the Railwaymen's Union, which has organised 50 per cent of those employed, which is about 325,000 workers. The second in importance is the Textile Workers' Union, and the third is the Miners' Union.

Trade Unionism is a new thing in India. Before 1918 it did not exist except for a few unions for white workers. It was out of the strike movement of 1918 that the unions came into existence.

The first one was organised at Madras by Mr. B. P. Wadia. Since then the progress of the movement has been both rapid and successful. The amount of success can be determined from the huge number of organised members, representing about 25 per cent of the total number of the factory-going workers. This growth indicates that the Indian labourers are speedily realising the need for their own organisations.

It is important to observe that the Indian Labour movement is rapidly becoming revolutionary. To illustrate this, take, for example, the number of strikes that have taken place in India since 1918, the history of which are written in blood. Strikes were common in the Indian factories, but they were never of a country-wide nature, and did not demonstrate any solidarity among the workers. The first instance of such a strike took place in Bombay, known as the General Strike, in which 120,000 workers, mostly textile operators, took part.

The solidarity of the masses on that occasion was shown by sympathetic strikes in other parts of the country. The strike was practically lost. About 200 workers were shot down by the soldiers. There were no proletarian leaders at that time, and the Nationalist middle-class politicians who took the lead utilised the strike for demonstration purposes. Similarly, another strike of several hundred thousand plantation workers took place in Assam, about 2,000 miles from Bombay, three years after the general strike, and it, too, was lost, due to the Nationalist leaders exploiting it for political purposes. Once again strikers were killed. According to the report of the Government Commission appointed to inquire into the reason for labour unrest in India it was shown that in nine months, from July, 1920, to March, 1921, in the province of Bengal, 137 strikes took place, reacting on all branches of industry. 244,180 workers took part in these strikes, and 2,631,488 working days were lost.

Of these strikes 110 were for higher wages and 13 were for the continuation of former strikes. A note issued by the labour officer of Bombay states that in three months, from April to June, 1921, 33 strikes took place in that town alone, involving 240,000 workers, with a loss of 500,000 working days. About the middle of the same year a strike of 20,000 workers took place in the town of Madras. To suppress the labour movement in Madras, the Government, with the help of the capitalists, tried by all means to subdue the labourers. They imprisoned strikers, burnt their houses, and fined the unions, but the labourers were very determined in their demands. The strike ended in a compromise due to the reformist character of the leaders.

This strike movement was country wide. In the north, in 1920, a strike of over 60,000 railway workers took place; the printers struck work to show their sympathy with their railroad comrades. Out of this strike was organised the Punjab Labour Union. The strike of the Cawnpore leather and textile workers, altogether about 30,000 men, is also noteworthy. They organised themselves and put forward 21 demands, including increased wages, unemployment insurance, and a share in profits. In short, in the year 1920, altogether 2,500,000 workers were involved in the strike movement, and in many cases it ended in bloodshed. It is estimated that altogether there were 1,000 workers wounded and killed.

An important fact is that this strike agitation was not a class-conscious revolutionary movement, but it does mark the beginning of the class struggle in India. To illustrate the growth of capitalism in India I quote the following figures from the 15 volumes of official statistics for the year 1917. In the year 1917 there were 8,000 mills and workshops, of which 67 per cent. were driven by mechanical power. The railway and tramways amount to 38,000 miles. The total industrial production was valued at £261,000,000. This is excluding handicraft work and including railways. The persons taking part in this production numbered 3,500,000; thus the production per person employed was £74 for the year. In the United Kingdom in 1907 the production per person amounted to £100. Of these workers 327,000 formed the bureaucracy, both native and Europeans; the rest were wage earners.

The sum paid as wages amounted only to £27,000,000, or little over 10 per cent. of the production, as against 53 per cent. in the United Kingdom and 50 per cent. in the United States in 1907. The salaries paid amounted to £33,000,000, or £6,000,000 more than the wages of the proletarians. These salaries are due to the existence of about 28,000 European workers, whom the capitalists have to bribe with high wages in order to keep them on their side and to keep them out of the Labour movement and away from the Indian native workers. Deducting 33 per cent. of the total production as cost of material and 23 per cent. from wages and salary, we can fix the profit at 44 per cent. on an average.

To support this the following figures from the Labour Review of November last may prove interesting. In one year the Indian cotton textile mills profited 100 per cent. of its outlayed capital. One factory in 1920 declared a dividend of 160 per cent. on an inflated capital of £300,000, while the dividend declared becomes 500 per cent. when the original capital invested by the shareholders is taken into account, which was only £100,000. Another mill, the Ring Mills, declared a dividend of 365 per cent. in the same year. Over a dozen mills have given dividends between 100 per cent. and 300 per cent., and quite a number between 50 per cent. and 100 per cent.

The coal mining industry in that year produced £4,512,000. Deducting from this one and a half per cent. to cover the cost of material, which is the rate in the United Kingdom, Germany and France, we get the income of the mines at £3,902,880; of this 25 per cent. or £978,036 was paid as wages against 56 per cent. in France and 59 per cent. in Germany before the war. The salaries amounted to £350,000, and the rest was profit. The coal mines show dividends which rise to 120 per cent. In one case the average dividend for 15 years was 95 per cent. The cheapness of woman labour has already caused their wholesale introduction into all industrial spheres. In one year 43 per cent. of the coal mine workers were women. No less than 40,030 women and 665 children were employed underground, and 18,872 women and 2,283 children worked on the top. The earnings of the miners were £10 8s. per year as against £55 in France and £57 in Germany before the war. The average wages of the mine workers were £6 in 1917, which was raised to £7 5s. in 1918, or 6d. per working-day. The cheapness of labour in India has kept the modern improved machines out of the Indian mines; as a result of obsolete methods 30 per cent. of the labour is wasted.

Again, in the tea gardens, the output amounted to £12,400,000, and putting 20 per cent. aside as cost of material, we get £9,920,000 as the income. The workers numbered 703,585, of whom 640,267 are women. The wages paid amounted to £3,579,952, or 35 per cent. of the income. The salaries paid amounted to 60 per cent. of the amount paid in wages, and two-thirds of these salaries were drawn by a few European supervisors. The average wage of a woman worker in the tea plantations was £5 per year. Eighty per cent. of the factory capital, 30 per cent. of the plantation capital, 40 per cent. of the mining capital, and 2 per cent. of the railway capital is Indian. Three-fourths of the rest is British and the rest international, mostly American. The following figures will show the increase of the Indian industry since 1917:—"The average total capital of the new companies registered in India year by year was approximately £12,000,000 per year for the years 1910-14. In the first three years of the war the average fell to £6,000,000 per year. After the war it rose to the enormous figure of £183,000,000, and in 1920, to March, 1921, owing to the extraordinary ordinary disturbances in the exchange rate, it went up to £100,000,000."

On the face of these figures it is needless to argue about the class struggle in India. These figures prove that the struggle between labour and capital in India is a struggle of a twofold character—it is both a class struggle against native capitalists and a fight against British imperialism. This explains why the class war sometimes appears in a national form. There is an idea that the Indian workers are semi-proletarian; and that they have connection with their native villages, where they can take refuge in case of long trouble. To disprove this I quote the following written by a Indian trade union secretary who inquired into the matter after the plantation workers' strike of last year. He writes:

"The nationalists repatriated the workers in their villages, with the result that all of them returned to the gardens and the strike was lost. I found that the repatriation of the coolies had practically resulted in sending them to death. Most of the returning emigrants had no homes, no lands. Many of them had been born in the gardens and did not even know the names of their villages. The village people absolutely refuse to have anything to do with them. The villagers find it difficult to keep themselves from starvation, and therefore feeding the returned coolies is an impossibility. In the villages there are no industries in which these men might be employed, nor any kind of work can be found for the day labourers. It is futile to bring away the coolies from the gardens and send them to the villages, because 50 or 60 men are leaving daily for the gardens owing to the famine conditions prevailing there."

Indian labour can be divided into five groups: (1) The land labourers, who are the largest in number—about 30,000,000. Their chronic poverty, continual semi-starvation, are well known; it is bitterly illustrated by the fact that their earnings, including unemployed days, are between £4 and £6 per year. (2) The plantation workers, whom I have already described. The planters are organised, and consequently their misery is not growing. (3) The mine workers. In the mining districts rice is the main food of the miners. The price of clothing has gone up three times, but the wages have remained the same since 1918; the average wage is 6d. per day, and 300 working days a year. (4) The handicraft workers, numbering about 2,500,000 hand weavers and 8,700,000 metal wood, ceramic, and other hand labourers. Their income, according to the calculation of the India Industrial Commission of 1916-18, was, weavers

£2 7s. per year, and others £4 a year. (5) The factory going workers, who stand as the advance guard of the labour movement. To a certain extent the second and third groups are still the mainstay of the Nationalist leaders, whose opportunism is forcing the workers towards class-consciousness, as was proven during the plantation strikes of last year.

The main principles of the Indian Trade Unions are as follow:—(1) The status of labour as a labourer, his relation to his employer, and effect on the economic and industrial life of the country. (2) The status of the labourer as a citizen, as related to the political movements and its result. (3) The status of the labourer in the industrial world, which has been rising ever since the Russian Revolution.

These extracts are from the Madras Labour Union's programme. It is said that the Union started with the first principle. "It was when the work of education was begun, when several questions were submitted by the Union men, that the second factor emerged.... In dealing with the second we were face to face with the necessity of recognising the third factor." It is further given out that in formulating these principles very little help was received from the educated class. "The workpeople themselves, with a culture of their own, vaguely felt, but were unable to express what was passing in their mind, and what was bound up in the three factors described above."

The value of solidarity has already been realised by the Indian workers. The president of the Madras Union, Mr. Wadia, writes "Indian labour understands that men working on the railway in Punjab, in the mills of Bombay, in the engineering shops of Bengal, are no better off than those working in the mills of Messrs. Binney & Co., Madras. The distance of a few hundred miles makes no difference in their solidarity, which alone will lead them to the final victory, the destruction of wage slavery."

About the International he says: "The fate of the International is in the balance, what with the activities of the Second and Third, but as soon as a properly constituted International begins to work the Indian labourers will naturally ally themselves with the movement.

The labourers, by themselves, are not sufficiently organised; they are not educated in the modern method of political struggle, and, therefore, if a long, weary fight between labour and capital, between landlordism and peasantry, is to be avoided, the Indian labourer must gain moral and other support from his comrades and brothers in other parts of the world."

The Unions in India were not recognised by the capitalists at the beginning, and the government backed their attitude. But the strength of the movement has forced recognition upon both of them. In November, when the Second Congress was to have taken place, the Mine Owners' Association opposed it and requested the Government to send the military to disperse it, but the Government refused. Consequently the conference went on unhampered, and the clever bourgeoisie, finding it not possible to fight labour face to face, adopted the diplomatic method and sent a deputation to make friendly relations with the workers, but not with the labour leaders. This capitalist deputation apologised for its former opposition and agreed to adopt 44 hours a week instead of 72, in addition to some other minor concessions.

The direction of this potential revolutionary labour movement in India is in the hands of people who can be classed into four groups (1) The Nationalists; (2) The Reformists; (3) The Government and capitalist agents; and (4) the leaders who have come out from the ranks of the labouring class. The foremost of the Nationalist politicians interested in labour is Mr. Lajpat Rai. He is the veteran centrist leader, a rich advocate, a journalist and landowner, but very orthodox. The same Mr. Rai in the year 1920 shamelessly condemned the printers' strike of Lahore because it touched his pocket. Despite this, in 1921, a year afterwards, he was elected as president of the First All-Indian Trade Union Congress.

The union leaders who elected him to preside, by this action alone, demonstrated their real character. Another Nationalist labour leader is Mr. B. K. Chakrabarty, an advocate, landowner, and multimillionaire. He was the president of the Calcutta Tramway Workers' Union, one of the most virile groups of Indian workers. Dr. R. K. Mukherji, a bourgeoisie economist and professor, is a leader of a small national centrist group.

He was delegated from the Bengal Unions to the First Congress of the Trade Unions. Some dozen other such advocates and professors can be shown to be interested in trade unionism; it is the fashion, at present, to become a labour leader in India. This is due to the fact that the nationalists understand the power of the industrial labour movement and want to control it; besides, it wants to frighten the Government with the organised force of the unions for political purpose.

Mr. Gandhi, the now imprisoned leader of the Indian nationalists, also tried his hand on the trade unions, but without much success. He left the labour field after the workers of the textile mills of Ahmedabad, Gandhi's native town, refused to break the strike on terms agreed between himself and the nationalist mill owners. He said: "We must not tamper with the labourers. It is dangerous to make political use of the factory proletariat" (*The Times*, May, 1921).

The most prominent leader of the labour movement is Mr. B. P. Wadia. It was he who first started the labour unions in India. Wadia is an ex-member of the Indian Home Rule League (a moderate political organisation with a programme to achieve self-government by gradual concessional process) and a well-known theosophist. He is president of five virile unions in Madras. He says that the economic aim of the Indian labour movement is not only to get higher wages, etc., but the ultimate destruction of wage slavery. In his opinion the international labour movement is too materialistic, and lacks a soul. This spiritual task, he contends, is a special one left for the Indian workers to develop. His reformist attitude became most marked in his evidence on labour reform, given before the Joint Parliamentary Committee, which collected material to find the best means of introducing political reforms into India. He said: "It is my considered opinion that Indian Ministers are better fitted to carry out adequate factory reforms than the Official Executive."

The next leader in importance is the reformist Indian Labour leader, Mr. Joseph Baptista. He was president of the Second Congress of the Indian Trade Union Congress. Four months before the Congress, on the 29th July, he addressed a mass meeting requesting them to follow the pacificism preached by Gandhi. He was met with cries of "Shame." The chairman of this meeting was Mr. Jamnadas Dwarkadas, a well known member of the Bombay Mill Owners' Association, and among those present on the platform was Mr. R. Williams, chief Publicity Bureau officer of the Government of Bombay. This bureau was specially created to fight the revolutionary tendency of the masses. Mr. Baptista came to the forefront after Colonel Wedgewood's visit to India, and though we do not know of any relation or agreement between them we know that Mr. Baptista is following the policy of the very moderate I.L.P. Labour M.P., and is introducing Fabian Socialism to India. In his presidential speech he declared that: "The political policy of the Congress must steer clear of extreme Individualism and Bolshevism and follow the golden path of Fabian Socialism."

The Government and capitalist agent types of labour leaders are Mr. Lokhande, of Bombay; Dr. Nair, of Madras, and Mr. Jones, of Calcutta. Jones was the general secretary of the All-Indian Railwaymen's union. He was the J. H. Thomas of India, and he had to resign because his treachery became too well known. The charges against the first two are so well known that Comrade Saklatvala had to warn everybody against them recently in the *Labour Monthly*. Regarding these types of labour leaders, there are very few Indians amongst them; they are mostly Europeans residing in India. We want European assistance, but we do not desire moderate Labourism of the I.L.P. brand. It is here that the British Communist Party can and ought to help us directly.

The labour leaders who have come from the masses themselves are not very well known. One who has become prominent is Comrade Viswanandda, leader of the miners of Bihar. At the Second Congress he declared that "If the present misery of the workers of India is allowed to continue nothing will stop Bolshevism. Let them take due warning, because the Indian workers are determined to become the rightful owners and rulers of the wealth produced by their labour." These mass leaders lack a definite viewpoint. They have picked up, here and there, some news of the Russian revolution from the bourgeoisie newspapers, and a few Communist ideas have influenced them. But they are our men, and we ought to gather them together for the Indian Communist Party and then push them to take leadership of the unions. This is the immediate task of the Party.

But in India there is no strong Communist Party, and it will take some time to create an effective one. The Internationals are not yet in touch with India, and at the present rate no one knows how long it will take them to reach the native masses. On the other hand, as I have shown, the Indian Fabians and moderates are spending all their energy to capture the masses. That they are somewhat successful may be seen in the growing timidity of the strike movement. The Indian workers have been flattered by the moderate labour leaders, and have been urged to be contented with the little increases in wages, etc., which were won during the time of the great strikes. The British Labour Party is also busy with the Indian workers and their unions. These British leaders must understand, however, that the industrial victories of the English workers can only be maintained by cooperation with the Indian masses. For their own interests, therefore, the British workers must stand on common ground with their coloured comrades of India. The tie of economic interests that binds them is very close. The British Labour Party, which expects to control the governing power very soon, must stop fooling the Indian masses by pushing the Baptista moderate type of labour leader. On the other hand the organising radical societies in England for helping the Indian workers must show the International comrades that the real driving force in Indian emancipation rests in the organised power of the native masses.

CHAMPARAN AND KHEDA SATYAGRAHA

The first Satyagraha revolutions inspired by Mahatma Gandhi in the Indian Independence Movement occurred in Kheda district of Gujarat and the Champaran district of Bihar between the years of 1918 and 1919. Champaran Satyagraha was the first to be started but the word Satyagraha was used for the first time in Anti Rowlatt agitation.

Champaran, Bihar

In Champaran, a district in state of Bihar, tens of thousands of landless serfs, indentured labourers and poor farmers were forced to grow indigo and other cash crops instead of the food crops necessary for their survival. These goods were bought from them at a very low price. Suppressed by the ruthless militias of the landlords (mostly British), they were given measly compensation, leaving them mired in extreme poverty. The villages were kept extremely dirty and unhygienic, and alcoholism, untouchability and purdah were rampant. Now in the throes of a devastating famine, the British levied an oppressive tax which they insisted on increasing in rate. Without food and without money, the situation was growing progressively unlivable and the Bhumihar Brahmins in Champaran revolted against indigo cultivation in 1914 (at Pipra) and 1916 (Turkaulia) and Pandit Raj Kumar Shukla took Mahatma Gandhi to Champaran and the Champaran Satyagraha began.

Kheda, Gujarat

In Kheda, a district of villages and small towns in Gujarat, the peasants mostly owned their own lands, and were economically better-off than their compatriots in Bihar, although on the whole, the district was plagued by poverty, scant resources, the social evils of alcoholism and untouchability, and overall British indifference and hegemony. However, a terrible famine had struck the district and a large part of Gujarat, and virtually destroyed the agrarian economy. The poor peasants had barely enough to feed themselves, but the British government of the Bombay Presidency insisted that the farmers not only pay full taxes, but also pay the 23% increase stated to take effect that very year.

Gandhi's Solution

While many civic groups sent petitions and published editorials, Gandhi proposed *satyagraha*-non-violence, mass civil disobedience. While it was strictly nonviolent, Gandhi was proposing real action, a real revolt that the oppressed peoples of India were dying to undertake. Gandhi also insisted that neither the protestors in Bihar nor in Gujarat allude to or try to propagate the concept of *Swaraj*, or *Independence*. This was not about political freedom, but a revolt against abject tyranny amidst a terrible humanitarian disaster. While accepting participants and help from other parts of India, Gandhi insisted that no other district or province revolt against the Government, and that the Indian National Congress not get involved apart from issuing resolutions of support, to prevent the British from giving it cause to use extensive suppressive measures and brand the revolts as treason.

In Champaran

Gandhiji established an ashram in Champaran, organizing scores of his veteran supporters and fresh volunteers from the region. He organized a detailed study and survey of the villages, accounting the atrocities and terrible episodes of suffering, including the general state of degenerate living. Building on the confidence of villagers, he began leading the clean-up of villages, building of schools and hospitals and encouraging the village leadership to undo purdah, untouchability and the suppression of women. He was joined by many young nationalists from all over India, including Dr. Sri Krishna Sinha, Ramarshi Deo Trivedi "Rishi Ji", Brajkishore Prasad, Dr. Rajendra Prasad, Dr. Anugrah Narayan Sinha and Jawaharlal Nehru.

But his main assault came as he was arrested by police on the charge of creating unrest and was ordered to leave the province. Hundreds of thousands of people protested and rallied outside the jail, police stations and courts demanding his release, which the court unwillingly did. Gandhi led organized protests and strike against the landlords, who with the guidance of the British government, signed an agreement granting more compensation and control over farming for the poor farmers of the region, and cancellation of revenue hikes and collection until the famine ended. It was during this agitation, that Gandhi was addressed by the people as *Bapu* (*Father*) and *Mahatma* (*Great Soul*).

In Kheda

In Gujarat, Gandhi was only the spiritual head of the struggle. His chief lieutenant, Sardar Vallabhbhai Patel and a close coterie of devoted Gandhians, namely Narhari Parikh, Mohanlal Pandya and Ravi Shankar Vyas toured the countryside, organized the villagers and gave them political leadership and direction. Many aroused Gujaratis from the cities of Ahmedabad and Vadodara joined the organizers of the revolt, but Gandhi and Patel resisted the involvement of Indians from other provinces, seeking to keep it a purely Gujarati struggle.

Patel and his colleagues organized a major tax revolt, and all the different ethnic and caste communities of Kheda rallied around it. The peasants of Kheda signed a petition calling for the tax for this year to be scrapped in wake of the famine. The government in Bombay rejected the charter. They warned that if the peasants did not pay, the lands and property would be confiscated and many arrested. And once confiscated, they would not be returned even if most complied. None of the villages flinched. The tax withheld, the government's collectors and inspectors sent in thugs to seize property and cattle, while the police forfeited the lands and all agrarian property. The farmers did not resist arrest, nor retaliate to the force employed with violence. Instead, they used their cash and valuables to donate to the *Gujarat Sabha* which was officially organizing the protest. The revolt was astounding in terms of discipline and unity. Even when all their personal property, land and livelihood were seized, a vast majority of Kheda's farmers remained firmly united in the support of Patel. Gujaratis sympathetic to the revolt in other parts resisted the government machinery, and helped the shelter the relatives and property of the protesting peasants. Those Indians who sought to buy the confiscated lands were ostracized from society. Although nationalists like Sardul Singh Caveeshar called for sympathetic revolts in other parts, Gandhi and Patel firmly rejected the idea. The Government finally sought to foster an honourable agreement for both parties. The tax for the year in question, and the next would be suspended, and the increase in rate reduced, while all confiscated property would be returned. Gujaratis also worked in cohesion to return the confiscated lands to their rightful owners. The ones who had bought the lands seized were influenced to return them, even though the British had officially said it would stand by the buyers.

Success and Legacy

Gandhi's resulting fame spread like fire all over the nation. He had become a defining influence on Indian Nationalism. People in Gujarat still revere Gandhi and Sardar Patel, and their role in the freedom struggle. Gujarat is the most industrialized and progressive state in India today. In Bihar, poverty and social conflict pervades what was the founding of the Satyagraha movement. The Naxalite insurgency is centred around the same age-old problem of class struggle between poor farmers and rich landlords, now involving terrorism.

NON-COOPERATION MOVEMENT

Contemporaneously, Mohandas Karamchand Gandhi led his nonviolent nationalist movement satyagraha, as a protest against government repression evidenced, for example, in the Rowlatt Act of 1919, and the Jallianwalla Bagh Massacres of April 1919. To enlist Muslim support in his movement, Gandhi supported the Khilafat cause and became a member of the Central Khilafat Committee. At the Nagpur Session (1920) of the Indiana national congress Gandhi linked the issue of Swaraj (Self-Government) with the Khilafat demands and adopted the non-cooperation plan to attain the twin objectives.

By mid-1920 the Khilafat leaders had made common cause with Gandhi's non-cooperation movement promising non-violence in return for Gandhi's support of the Khilafat Movement whereby Hindus and Muslims formed a united front against British rule in India. Support was received also of Muslim theologians through the Jamiyat-al Ulama-i-Hind (The Indian Association of Muslim Theologians). Maulana Mohammed Akram Khan of Bengal was a member of its Central Executive and Constitution Committee. However, the movement's objectives of communal harmony and nonviolence suffered a setback because of the Hijrat (Exodus) to Afghanistan in 1920 of about 18,000 Muslim peasants, mostly from Sindh and North Western Provinces, the excesses of Muslims who felt that India was Dar-ul-Harb (Apostate land), the Moplah rebellion in South India in August 1921, and the Chauri-Chaura incident in February 1922 in the United Provinces where a violent mob set fire to a police station killing twenty-two policemen. Soon after Gandhi called off the Non-cooperation movement, leaving Khilafat leaders with a feeling of betrayal.

The extra-territorial loyalty of Khilafat leaders received a final and deadly blow from the Turks themselves. The charismatic Turkish nationalist leader Mustafa Kemal's startling secular renaissance, his victories over invading Greek forces culminating in the abolition of the Sultanate in November 1922, and the transformation of Turkey into a Republic in October 1923, followed by the abolition of the Khilafat in March 1924, took the Khilafatists unaware. By 1924 the Khilafat Movement, had become devoid of any relevance and significance and met its end.

The first stirrings in favour of the Khilafat Movement in Bengal was seen on 30 December 1918 at the 11th Session of the All India Muslim league held in Delhi. In his presidential address, AK Fazlul Huq voiced concern over the attitude of Britain and her allies engaged in dividing and distributing the territories of the defeated Ottoman Empire. When the Paris Peace Conference (1919) confirmed these apprehensions, Bengali Khilafat leaders such as Maulana Akram Khan, Abul Kasem, and Mujibur Rahman Khan held a Public meeting in Calcutta on 9 February 1919 to enlist public support in favour of preserving the integrity of the Ottoman Empire and saving the institution of Khilafat.

In Bengal, the Khilafat-Non-Cooperation Movement (1918 to 1924) became a mass movement in which both Muslims and Hindus participated. The Bengal movement benefited from coordinated action by and between the Central and Provincial Khilafat leaders. Maulana Abul Kalam Azad propagated Khilafat ideas in rural Bengal. In the initial stage, the movement was popularised by Bengali leaders such as Maulana Akram Khan, maniruzzaman islamabadi, Mujibur Rahman Khan, the brothers Maulana Abdullahil Kafi and Maulana Abdullahil Baqi, Ismail Hossain Shiraji, Abul Kasem and AK Fazlul Huq.

Maulana Akram Khan and Maniruzzaman Islambadi toured Bengal and organised Khilafat meetings, particularly in Dhaka and Chittagong. In an article Asahojogita-o-Amader Kartabya, Maniruzzaman Islambadi declared that to protect Khilafat and to acquire Swaraj were the twin aims of the movement and that it was the sacred duty of every Indian to support these ideas.

During the observance of the first Khilafat Day on 17 October 1919, most Indian-owned shops remained closed in Calcutta, prayers were offered at different mosques, and public meetings were held all over Bengal. On 23-24 November 1919 the first All-India Khilafat Conference held in Delhi was presided over by AK Fazlul Huq from Bengal.

It was resolved that pending a resolution of the Khilafat problem there would be no participation in the proposed peace celebrations, that British goods should be boycotted, and that a policy of non-cooperation with the government would be adopted. In early 1920 the Bengal Provincial Khilafat Committee was organised with Maulana Abdur Rauf as President, Maniruzzaman Islambadi as Vice President, Maulana Akram Khan as General Secretary, and Mujibur Rahman and Majid Baksh as Joint Secretaries respectively. The office of the organisation was located at Hiron Bari Lane of Kolutola Street in Calcutta.

The first Bengal Provincial Khilafat Conference was held at the Calcutta Town Hall on 28-29 February 1920. Several members of the Central Khilafat Committee attended.

Prominent Bengali Khilafat leaders such as A K Fazlul Huq, Abul Kasem, Mujibur Rahman participated in the conference and reiterated the view that unless their demands on the Khilafat problem were met non-cooperation and boycott would continue. The conference decided to observe 19 March 1920 as the Second Khilafat Day.

In March 1920 a Khilafat delegation led by Maulana Muhammad Ali went to England to plead for the Khilafat cause. Abul Kasem represented Bengal in this delegation. Local Khilafat Committees were also constituted. Maulana Abul Kalam Azad and Maulvi Abdur Rahman became President and Secretary respectively of the Calcutta Khilafat Committee. On 20 December 1919 the Dhaka Committee was founded at the ahsan manzil with Nawab khwaja habibullah as President, Syed Abdul Hafez as alternate President, and Gholam Quddus as Secretary. In response to the demands of the citizens of Dhaka, a "Sadar Khilafat Committee" was formed; Khwaja Sulaiman Kadar was its President, Maulana Abdul Jabbar Ansari, Hafez Abdur Razzak, Hafez Abdul Hakim its Vice-Presidents, and Maulvi Shamsul Huda its Secretary.

On 19 March 1920 the Second Khilafat Day was observed in Bengal. In Calcutta life almost came to a standstill and numerous Khilafat meetings were held in Dhaka, Chittagong and Mymensingh. The largest meeting was held in Tangail and was presided over by Abdul Halim ghaznavi, the liberal nationalist Muslim zamindar. At this meeting, Maniruzzaman Islambadi urged the public to adopt Satyagraha as the symbol of the Khilafat movement.

Most districts of Bengal witnessed a mushroom growth of Khilafat Committees alongside existing Congress Committees, often with common membership. This was the first significant anti-British mass movement in which Hindus and Muslims participated with equal conviction.

The media, both Muslim and Hindu, played a vital role in popularising the movement. 'Mohammadi', 'Al-Eslam' and 'The Mussalman' were publications, which deserve mention. The Khilafat Movement engendered a Muslim political consciousness that reverberated throughout Bengal under the leadership of Maulana Azad, Akram Khan, Maniruzzaman Islambadi, Bipin Chandra Pal and Chitta Ranjan das.

Though the Khilafat movement was orthodox in origin, it did manage to generate liberal ideas among Muslims because of the interaction and close understanding between Hindus and Muslims. Following the example of Calcutta, volunteer organisations were set up in rural Bengal to train volunteers to enforce boycott of foreign goods, courts, and government offices.

They were also engaged in spinning, popularising items of necessity, and raising contributions for the Khilafat cause. In some areas in Dhaka, Muslim zamindars extracted 'Khilafat Salami' from Muslim tenants by declaring themselves the representatives of the Sultan of Turkey. Ironically, due to the ignorance of these tenants this custom continued long after the Khilafat was abolished.

Visibly shaken by the popularity of the Movement, through a Notification on 19 November 1921 the Government of Bengal declared the activities of the Khilafat and Congress volunteers illegal. Government officers raided Khilafat offices, confiscated documents and papers, banned meetings, and arrested office bearers. About a hundred and fifty personalities including Maulana Azad, CR Das, Akram Khan, and Ambika Prashad Bajpai were arrested in Calcutta on 10 December 1921.

At this critical juncture, a rift arose between Khilafat and Non-cooperation leaders on the issue of boycotting educational institutions and legislative councils. Some Muslim leaders believed that such boycott would be suicidal for Muslims. They were in favour of participating in the elections under the India Act of 1919 that assured self-governing institutions in India.

Prominent among this group of Swarajist leaders were CR Das, Bipin Chandra Pal, Motilal Nehru, Surendranath Banerjea, Ashutosh Chowdhury, Asutosh Mookerjee and Sarat Chandra Bose. Notable Muslims subscribing to the same ideas were AK Fazlul Huq, Abul Kasem, Khwaja Muhammad Azam, Khwaja Afzal, Nawab Khwaja Habibullah, Hakim Habibur Rahman, Syed Nawab Ali Chowdhury, Sir Syed Shamsul Huda, Sir Abdullah al-Mamun Suhrawardi, Maulana Abu Bakr Siddiky (Pir of Furfura), Shah Ahsanullah, Kazem Ali and Huseyn Shaheed Suhrawardy. Indian National Congress and the Muslim nationalists were strongly opposed to the idea of joining the councils. Eminent Hindu personalities in Bengal who supported the Khilafat movement were Bipin Chandra Pal, Shrish Chandra Chattopadhya, Kaminikumar Bandyopadhaya, Dr. Rai Kumar Chakravarty, PC Ghosh, Basanta Kumar Majumdar, Aswini Kumar Dutta, Pyarilal Roy, Gurucharan Aich, Sarat Kumar Gupta, Poet Mukunda Das, Haranath Ghosh, Nagendra Bhattacharya, Satindra Sen, Dr. Tarini Gupta, Sarol Kumar Dutta, Nishi Kanta Ganguly, Monoranjan Gupta, Sarat Kumar Ghosh, Nagendra Bijoy Bhattacharya, Nalini Das, Sailendra Nath Das, Khitish Chandra Roy Chowdhury and many others.

In addition to the front-rank leaders of the Khilafat movement, a new class of Muslim leaders emerged during this period from urban as well as from distant parts of Bengal.

They gained experience in organizing and mobilizing the public. The Khilafat movement provided an opportunity to throw up a new Mofassil based leadership, which played a key role in introducing a coherent self-assertive political identity for Bengali Muslims. After the 1947 Partition, these personalities played effective roles in their respective areas of activity.

Non-Cooperation Movement was initiated by Mahatma Gandhi. To advance the Indian nationalist cause, the Indiana national congress under the leadership of of Gandhi decided in 1920 to follow a policy of passive resistance to British rule.

The Rowlatt Act, the Jalliwanwala Bagh massacre and martial law in Punjab had belied the generous war time promises of the British.

The montagu-chelmsford report with its ill-considered scheme of dyarchy satisfied few. Gandhi, so far believing in the justice and fair play of the government, now felt that Non-Cooperation with the government must be started.

At the same time, the harsh terms of the Treaty of Sevres between the Allies and Turkey was resented by the Muslims in India. The Muslims started the khilafat movement and Gandhi decided to identify himself with them. Gandhi's 'skilful top level political game' secured in winning over the Muslim support in the coming Non-Cooperation Movement in India.

The movement was launched formally on 1st August 1920, after the expiry of the notice that Gandhi had given to the Viceroy in his letter of 22 June, in which he had asserted the right recognised 'from time immemorial of the subject to refuse to assist a ruler who misrules'.

At the Calcutta Session (September 1920) the programme of the movement was clearly stated. It involved the surrender of the titles and offices and resignation from nominated posts in the local bodies. The Non-Cooperators were not to attend Government duties, *Durbar*s and other functions and they were to withdraw their children from schools and colleges and establish national schools and colleges. They were to boycott the British courts and establish private arbitration courts; they were to use *swadeshi* cloth. Truth and non-violence were to be strictly observed by Non-Cooperators.

The Calcutta decision was endorsed at the Nagpur Session of the Congress (December 1920). There the betterment of party organisation was emphasised. Congress membership was thrown open to all adult men and women on payment of 4 annas as subscription. The adoption of the Non-Cooperation resolution by the Congress gave it a new energy and from January 1921, it began to register considerable success all over India. Gandhi along with Ali Brothers undertook a nation-wide tour during which he addressed hundreds of meetings.

In the first month, 9,000 students left schools and colleges and joined more than 800 national institutions that had sprung up all over the country. The educational boycott was particularly successful in Bengal under the leadership of Chitta Ranjan das and Subhas Chandra Bose. Punjab, too, responded to the educational boycott and Lala Lajpat Rai played the leading role. Other areas that were active were Bombay, UP, Bihar, Orissa and Assam; Madras remained lukewarm.

The boycott of law courts by lawyers was not as successful as the educational boycott. Many leading lawyers, like, CR Das, Motilal Nehru, Mr. Jayakar, S Kitchlew, V Patel. Asaf Ali Khan and others gave up lucrative practices, and their sacrifice became a source of inspiration for many. In number again, Bengal led followed by Andhra, U P, Karnataka and Punjab. But perhaps, the most successful item of the programme was the boycott of foreign cloth. The value of imports of foreign cloth fell from Rs. 102 crore in 1920-21 to 57 crore in 1921-22.

In July 1921, a new challenge was thrown to the government. Mohammad Ali along with other leaders was arrested for holding the view that it was 'religiously unlawful for the Muslims to continue in the British army'. Gandhi as well as the Congress supported Mohammad Ali and issued a manifesto. The next dramatic event was the visit of the Prince of Wales that began on 17 November 1921.

The day the Prince landed in Bombay was observed as a day of *hartal* all over India.

He was greeted with empty streets and downed shutters wherever he went. Emboldened by their successful defiance of the government, Non-Cooperators became more and more aggressive. The Congress volunteer corps emerged as a powerful parallel police, and the sight of its members marching in formation and dressed in uniform was hardly one that warmed the government heart.

The Congress had already granted permission to the Provincial Congress Committees to sanction mass civil disobedience including the non-payment of taxes wherever they thought that the people were ready.

The Non-Cooperation Movement had other indirect effects as well. In UP it became difficult to distinguish between a Non-Cooperation meeting and a peasant meeting. In Malabar in Kerala it helped to rouse Muslim tenants against their landlords. In Assam, labourers on tea plantations went on strike. In Punjab, the Akali movement was a part of the general movement of Non-Cooperation.

In Bengal, particularly, it acquired considerable strength. Not only in Kolkata, but also in rural Bengal an elemental awakening was observed. It reached a major climax following the Gurkha assault on coolies at the river port of Chandpur (20-21 May). Under the leadership of JM Sengupta the whole of Eastern Bengal was in ferment. But the best organised of the village movements was the anti-Union Board agitation in Midnapur led by Birendranath Sasmal.

As the Non-Cooperation Movement continued it became clear that the women of Bengal were willing to play an active role in the protest movement. The women nationalists here organised themselves under the *Mahila Karma Samaj* or the Ladies Organisation Board of the Bengal Pradesh Congress Committee. Women of the Samaj organised meetings and propagated the spirit of Non-Cooperation.

Women volunteers were enlisted. Basanti Devi and Urmila Devi, wife and sister respectively of CR Das, Nellie Sengupta, wife of JM Sengupta, along with others like Mohini Devi, Labanya Prabha Chanda played a prominent role in this movement.

Picketing of foreign wine and cloth shops and selling of *Khaddar* on the streets happened to be the main areas of their activities.

The government promulgated Sections 108 and 144 of the Code of Criminal Procedure at various centres of the agitation. Volunteers' Corps was declared illegal and by December, over 30,000 people were arrested from all over India. Among prominent leaders, only Gandhi remained out of jail.

In mid-December there was an abortive attempt at negotiations, initiated by Malaviya, but the conditions offered were such that it meant sacrificing the Khilafat leaders, a course that Gandhi would hardly accept. At that time he had been also under considerable pressure from the Congress rank and file to start the phase of mass civil disobedience. Gandhi presented an ultimatum to the government but as the government did not respond he started to initiate the civil disobedience movement in Bardoli taluqa of Surat district. Unfortunately at this time the tragedy of Chauri Chaura occurred which changed the course of the movement. A mob of 3,000 killed twenty-five policemen and one inspector. This was too much for Gandhi who stood for complete non-violence. The result was that he gave order for the suspension of the movement at once. Thus on 12 February 1922, the Non-Cooperation Movement came to an end.

As regards the limitations and achievements of the Non-Cooperation Movement, it apparently failed to achieve its object of securing the Khilafat and making good of the Punjab wrongs. The Swaraj was not attained in a year as promised. Still, the retreat that was ordered on 12 February 1922 was only a temporary one. The battle was over, but the war would continue.

4

Gandhi and Dandi March

INTRODUCTION

One of the momentous events in the history of Indian struggle for independence was the Dandi Salt March, launched under the unparalleled leadership of M K Gandhi. With this historic event, The Civil Disobedience Movement was formally introduced on a nation-wide basis. Within the context of the Indian freedom struggle, the Dandi Salt March holds a place of paramount importance. The entire nation coalesced under the call of a single man, internalizing the cherished doctrines of ahimsa or non violence, and satyagraha or passive resistance. With an awakened political consciousness, all segments of the Indian community plunged into a battle, which till date is an instance of the indefatigable power of civilian resistance.

THE IMPACT OF DANDI MARCH

The immediate repercussion of the Dandi march was the arrest of Nehru and several other delegates of the Congress. On 5th May, midnight, Gandhi was arrested from Karadi. The wider impact of Dandi march on all sections of the society was simply insurmountable. The entire nation joined forces with Mahatma Gandhi. Salt was being made and bought illegally throughout the country. Gandhi's popularity reached an all time high, with several new followers joining the troop of his satyagrahis. The Dandi episode unfolded a new chapter in the history of Indian nationalism. The large scale participation of the masses in India's struggle for freedom commenced with the Dandi march.

The event of Dandi March assumed a much wider significance as it not only remained a landmark incident in India's pre independence history, but took a symbolic significance that eternally appealed to the political and social scenario of the world. Dandi March has come to epitomize the inherent potential of any form of passive civilian resistance. It affirmed the halo of

Gandhi as the Mahatma, for he proved to the world that the victory of a guide is in practicing what he preaches. His ideologies of satyagraha and ahimsa found physical manifestation in his simple gesture of picking up a stick and walking a distance of two hundred miles, as an expression of his denial and violation of British laws.

HISTORY OF DANDI MARCH

The march on foot undertaken by Gandhi and seventy-eight Congress volunteers was the most significant event in the history of the breach of salt law in our country. It was commenced in accordance with a fixed schedule to be carried on by them during the long journey ending at Dandi. Undoubtedly, it was a disciplined band of nonviolent satyagrahis who were to present a new model of Satyagraha which later on converted into a bigger movement at all-India level. On 12 March 1930 at 6-10 A.M. Gandhi came out of his room, calm and composed, accompanied by Prabhashankar Patani, Mahadev Desai and Pyarelal, his secretary. He offered prayers, looked at his watch and exactly at 6.30 A.M. commenced his march with seventy-eight volunteers.

With his usual gentle smile, betokening his unifying faith in the justice of the cause he was pursuing and in the success of the great campaign he had embarked upon, he headed the procession with quick and unfaltering steps. 'Like the historic march of Ram Chandra to Lanka, the march of Dandi would be memorable' exclaimed Motilal Nehru in a message. P.C. Ray called it the 'exodus of Israelites under Moses? Jawaharlal Nehru called Gandhi, '.... the pilgrim on his quest of truth, quiet, peaceful, determined and fearless who would continue that quiet pilgrimage regardless of consequences.' The satyagrahis were to face a fatiguing journey through heat and dust of the Kheda villages. Thousands of men, women and children accompanied the marching column for a few miles and thousands lined the route and showered flowers, coins, currency notes and kum kum at the satyagrahis.

Following the commencement of his epic Dandi March, a tremendous wave of enthusiasm swept over the entire country. The historic day was celebrated all over India. Calcutta woke that morning amidst sounds of conch shells and shouts of 'Gandhiji ki Jai'. At a conference of the Congress leaders of Bengal a decision was taken to appoint immediately an ad hoc council to be called the Bengal Civil Disobedience Council, with the object of carrying out the programme outlined by Gandhiji. J. M. Sen Gupta appealed to all men and women of the province to enrol themselves as volunteers for the Civil Disobedience Movement. He said, 'Bengal is on trial. She had always been in the vanguard of the country's battle for freedom and cannot lag behind. Let us plunge head-long in the fight and regain the rights which are ours.'

In Bombay, a public meeting was held under the presidentship of K. F. Nariman. He exhorted the audience to get ready for the fight. The 'War Council' of the Bombay Provincial Congress Committee announced a Iit of 'iron-sides' to join the first detachment of volunteers from the town. In Madras, at a public meeting at Tilak Ghat, prayers were offered for the success of Civil Disobedience campaign by the Madras District Congress Committee, Andhra Congress Committee, the Triplicate Congress Sabha and the political section of the Youth League. The meeting reiterated India's resolve to achieve Swaraj by nonviolent means under Gandhi's leadership by following his path.'

In Lahore, a band of Congress volunteers paraded the streets and raised shouts of 'Mahatma Gandhi Ki Jai'. In a mammoth meeting of the citizens of the town, held under the auspices of the City Congress Committee, Maulana Abdul Qadir, in opening the proceedings, said, 'The 12th of March would be a red letter day and it would figure in letters of gold in the future history of India'. He hoped that the people of India, from that day onward would give practical demonstration of their determination to win freedom. He believed that as soon as the people of the Punjab would receive the news of Gandhi's arrest, they would suspend their business and work out the plan of the movement.

In Peshawar, the 'Satyagraha Day' was observed by taking out a procession and holding a public meeting. Resolutions reiterating the pledge of independence and wishing Godspeed to the soldiers of freedom and congratulating Vallabhbhai Patel on his imprisonment were unanimously passed. Besides, a large number of volunteers were enlisted for the Satyagraha. Civil Disobedience Day was celebrated in Delhi in a meeting attended by about 10,000 persons, including a large number of ladies. Devdas Gandhi gave the detailed history of the salt tax and called it the most 'barbarous' tax which effected the poor classes, and pleaded for its abolition immediately. He also exhorted the people to observe complete but peaceful hartal if Mahatma Gandhi was arrested.

Allahabad, the nerve centre of U. P. politics, witnessed scenes of enthusiasm in connection with the celebration of the commencement of the Satyagraha campaign. Jawaharlal Nehru hoisted the national flag over the building occupied by the offices of the A.I.C.C., the City Congress Committee and the All-India Spinners' Association, U.P. branch. A large gathering participated in the ceremony. While addressing the audience, Nehru said that the pledge of Satyagraha laid stress on nonviolence which was the very basis of the Civil Disobedience campaign. He warned that only those who were convinced of the efficacy of that method either as a creed or as a policy in the present circumstances of the country, should take the pledge. He opined that nonviolence was not a convenient shelter either for cowards or for those who wanted to prepare for violence. He asked the non-believers in nonviolence to withdraw from the movement to give others a chance. In Ahmedabad, a meeting of the Youth League was held in which a resolution was passed empowering the secretaries to enlist volunteers for Civil Disobedience Movement. About twenty-five names were enlisted on the spot including two secretaries and Miss Mridula Ambalal, daughter of a local mill-magnate. The 'Dandi March Day' was observed in Nagpur by hoisting the national flag. A procession passed through the main bazaars of the town, and, thereafter, a public meeting was also held. Gandhi's letter to the Viceroy was read out and explained to the audience. An appeal for the enlistment of volunteers was also made. While exhorting the people to give the moment their whole-hearted support M. V. Abhyankar said, 'I shall perish in the struggle for Independence or live to enjoy freedom after its achievement?

Similar celebrations were held all over the country and considerable enthusiasm was aroused with people for participating in the Civil disobedience Movement. For the first time, a new spirit for Swaraj-full and complete-was found bubbling everywhere. The Viceroy informed the Secretary of State on 13 March 1930, 'Most of my thought at the moment is concentrated upon Gandhi. I wish I felt sure what the right way to deal with him is.' The same day Gandhi and his satyagrahis reached a small village, Aslali, where they were received well by the villagers. Gandhi emphasised the importance of salt and criticised the salt tax levied by the government. He stated, 'The poor destitute villagers do not have the strength to get this tax repealed. We want to develop this strength... We should make a resolve that we shall prepare salt, eat it, sell if to the people and, while doing so, court imprisonment, if necessary. If, out of Gujarat's Population of 90 lakhs, we leave out women and children, and the remaining 30 lakhs et ready to violate the salt tax, the Government does not have enough accommodation in jails to house so many people.'

Next day, Gandhi, who was apprehensive of his arrest, informed Jawaharlal Nehru, 'The news given to me of my impending arrest was said to be absolutely authentic. But we have reached the second stage. We take the third tonight' The second halt of the Dandi marchers was at Bareja, a village with a Population of 2,500. He emphasised the importance of Khadi, its production and use by the villagers. 'Khadi is the foundation of our freedom struggle.... I request you to renounce luxuries and buy Khadi from this heap before you.

'We have come forward to win our freedom from this tyrannical and oppressive Government. If we cannot put our own house in order in an organized manner, how shall we run the country's Government? I ask you, therefore, to learn order and organization.... This struggle against the Government on which we have embarked is not going to reach its conclusion with five, or twenty-five, or even millions of men getting killed. We have to look after other things also simultaneously.' 18 As Gandhi entered the Kheda district, memories-some sweet, some bitter-filled his mind. It was while working in this district that he became one with the lives of people. He had seen nearly all the villages of the district and had covered many of them on foot. He stated, 'I have come to Navagam in the middle of a battle... The Government found some pretext or other to arrest Vallabhbhai... Pressure was brought to hear on the Magistrate some how to serve a notice on Sardar and he was arrested. What could a poor Magistrate do where the entire atmosphere is vitiated?

When some headmen and matadars of Kheda district submitted their resignations as a protest against the oppressive policy of the government, Gandhi advised them, 'Remember that in the resignations, you have handed in I see God's hand. The Kheda District has made an auspicious beginning.' At Vasana, where the villagers had gathered to accord reception to the marchers and listen to their leader, Gandhi explained that abolition of the salt-tax or remission of some taxes would not mean Swaraj for them. Winning of Swaraj was not going to be so easy as they might think. It was only a way to it and by following it they would reach the goal of freedom. He had a word of praise for the headmen of Navagam, Vavdi, Agam, Mahelaj and other villages who had tendered their resignations. 'Why should they stick to Headmanship for the mere five rupees a month that the government pays them? If the Collector summons a Headman, let him say, 'Give us back our Sardar. Grant us a remission in land revenue.' At Nadiad, a town with a population of thirty-one thousand, Gandhi reminded the people, 'Bound by the chains of slavery, we are being crushed at present and we want to shake them off.' He wished all government servants to give up their jobs. A government job gave them the power to tyrannize over others. Finally, be asked them to enlist themselves as volunteers. And as soon as he got behind the bars or as soon as the All-India Congress Committee gave a call, they should come forward to offer themselves for being jailed. 'Then alone shall I believe that Nadiad has made its contribution to our struggle'.

In a letter to Jayaprakash Narayan which Gandhi wrote from Anand on 17 March, he explained, 'No where else have I observed such zeal for sacrifice as has been displayed by the Ashram women. At present the women are to a great extent managing the internal affairs of the Ashram. The chance of acquiring such experience will never be repeated. I would therefore advise you to send Prabhavati there. After my arrest the Ashram women too will court imprisonment. I think Prabhavati should join them. She is worthy in every respect.'

At Anand, an educational centre of Patidars, Gandhi demanded, 'In your hands lies the honour of the Patidars of Charotar. You are like salt in the sea of Patidars. If the salt loses its savour, wherewith shall it be salted ? Salt is more sapid than either sugar or juggery. The latter may even cause jaundice, whereas a pinch of salt adds flavour to the meal. If Anand gives up its savour if courage and such other virtues which have been attributed to the Patidars are not displayed in Anand at this juncture, where else can one see them?.' The students' services to the national cause were also applauded. They were advised to suspend their studies for as long as this struggle continued. Formerly, Gandhi had asked his students to leave schools and to set up national schools.

But this time he asked them to leave schools and come out on the 'battle-field' and become 'mendicants' for the sake of the country. But he did not ask them to give up their studies for good, but only to give up book-learning so long as the struggle lasted. At Borsad, the reception of Gandhi and his satyagrahis was celebrated with the immediate announcement of the resignations of headmen, matadars and ravanias of twenty villages of the taluka. Over one hundred village officers of twenty-five villages submitted their resignations.

The government sources commented, 'Gandhi's attention is directed on two points *i.e.* resignations of patels and enrolling volunteers. Under his instructions local workers are trying to get more resignations under the threat of social boycott. They were warmly received by the village folk. They were keen to listen to Gandhi's discourse· He explained to them, 'Our patience has been severely tried. We must free ourselves from the yoke of this Government and we are prepared to undergo any hardships that we may have to suffer in order to secure Swaraj, it is our duty as well as our right to secure Swaraj.

'Today we are defying the salt law. Tomorrow we shall have to consign other laws to the wastepaper basket. Doing so we shall practise such severe noncooperation that finally it will not be possible for the administration to be carried on at all. Let the Government then, to carry on its rule, use guns against us, send us to prison, hang us. But how many can be given such punishment? Try and calculate how much time it will take a lakh of Britishers to hang thirty crores of persons.'

Gandhi once again exhorted the students to leave their institutions and join the struggle for independence. He desired that all students studying in the local high school and who were above the age of fifteen, and all teachers too, should enrol themselves. He pleaded that wherever revolutions had taken place, that is, in Japan, China, Egypt, Ireland and in England, students and teachers had played a prominent role. In Europe, war broke out on 4 August 1914, and when Gandhi reached England on the 6th of the same month, he found that students had left colleges and marched out with arms. Gandhi further explained that his prostrating himself on the ground for the sake of removing the hardships of crores of people was of no avail. He had spared no efforts in drafting appeals.

He became a revolutionary when politeness and persuasion proved infructious. He indeed found peace in describing himself as a revolutionary and appealed that in a revolution of that nature which was calm, peaceful and truthful, people should get themselves enrolled regardless of the religious faith to which they belonged. He was confident that if they enlisted themselves with sincerity and if they could keep up their courage, the salt tax would have been abolished, this administration would have come to an end and all the hardships enumerated in the letter to the Viceroy as well as those which had not been enumerated would have to cease. On 19 March, the party of satyagrahis reached Ras Taluka where Sardar Patel was arrested and sentenced to prison and in which he had carried on such a vigorous struggle in 1924 that the Government had finally to admit its 'error and mete out justice that should not have required a struggle. It is as if Sardar was sentenced to prison as a reward for having served you'.

During the short stay of Gandhi, some of the headmen and matadars had handed in their resignations. But Gandhi expressed unhappiness on the small number of resignations at Ras. In fact, the headman, talati and revania were the representatives of the government in the villages and it was through these persons that the latter carried on its administration. A village which was afraid of a handful of men and continued to act in a manner contrary to its own wishes, neither enhanced the prestige of the headman, the talati or the revania nor that of the villagers themselves. Sardar Patel had been making great effort to end this indignity. Gandhi praised the services rendered by Sardar Patel. He also apprised the villagers of his mission. He explained 'Sardar neither made speeches nor came here to foment trouble. Neither the Magistrate nor you had acted any sort of trouble. The task for which Sardar had approached you was not a secret to anyone. A satyagrahi has no secrets....... What secret can a satyagrahi like Sardar have?' He had come there to clear the way for Gandhi and he had not come there to convey the message regarding salt. Gandhi was at a loss to know about the offence committed by Sardar Patel and wondered that a man of his stature should have been awarded a sentence of three months' jail and labelled it a matter of shame to the Sardar and to the government. Gandhi wished that a person like Sardar Patel should be sentenced to a term of seven years' imprisonment or be exiled. 'It would not befit the Government to sentence me to three months' imprisonment. Exile for life or hanging would be a punishment fit for a person like me. I am guility of sedition. It is my dharma to commit sedition against the Government. I am teaching this dharma to the people. A regime under which tyranny is being perpetrated, under which the rich and the poor are made to pay the same amount of tax on an item like salt under which exorbitant sums are being spent on watchmen, the police and the army under which the highest executive receives a salary which is five thousand times the income of the cultivator, under which an annual revenue of 25 crores of rupees is derived from narcotics and liquor, under which foreign cloth of the value of Rs. 60 cores is imported every year, and under which crores of persons continue to remain unemployed, it is one's dharma to rise against and destroy such a regime, to pray that fire may consume its policies.

Meanwhile, the A.I.C.C. held a meeting on the banks of the Sabarmati on 20 March. Besides the president Jawaharlal Nehru, it was attended by other prominent leaders like Maulana Azad, Sarojini Naidu, P. D. Tandon, Abbas Tyabji, Darbar Gopaldas, J. B. Kripalani, N.C. Kalelkar, Kasturba Gandhi, Ansuyabehn and Mrs. Ambalal.

Many members excused themselves from attendance on the plea that they were busy with preparations for Civil Disobedience Movement, in their own areas. The leaders met under a sense of 'heavy' responsibility and the result was foregone conclusion. By its principal resolution, the A.I.C.C. confirmed the Working Committee's resolution authorising Gandhi to launch Civil Disobedience Movement. It laid down the conditions under which the various provinces should start Satyagraha on a mass scale.

The Provincial Congress Committees were given wide discretion about the manner, the form and the place of Civil Disobedience. It was open to them, to prepare their provinces for any form of Satyagraha, best suited to them. But it was clearly laid down that the salt Satyagraha should be undertaken in every province when it was possible. Other forms of Satyagraha might be prepared for, but should be reserved for the second stage of the campaign. In case Gandhi was arrested, the Provincial Congress Committees should immediately determine to start Civil Disobedience, and if he was not arrested, they should await instructions which he might issue on reaching his destination. He would give the necessary signal and the Provincial Congress Committees would be informed immediately through the A.I.C.C. Office.

The Government of India felt much concern over the resolution of Congress. The Home Member suggested, 'it is essential that we should able to give timely warning owing to local Governments'. He also suggested that the correspondence of the members of the Working Committee; the correspondence of the head office of the Congress and of all provincial Congress offices and provincial Congress Presidents and of any particular individual whose correspondence in local government concerned might regard as likely to yield 'specially important' information, should be censured.

It was barely ten days ago that Gandhi had begun his historic march and the actual campaign was yet to be started. The whole country was already in a state of forewent for a parallel to which one might recollect the 'hottest days' of the Noncooperation Movement of 1920-22. People in the provinces were planning to start the movement, and in some cases preliminary steps had already been initiated. In Bengal, for instance, which had for the moment, lost both its outstanding leaders, a 'War Council' had been formed. In the United Provinces, the Provincial Congress Committee had started a Satyagraha committee consisting of prominent leaders, including the President of the Congress himself. Judging from the signs, the whole country appeared in the throes of an agitation of unprecedented magnitude.

The Civil Disobedience plans of Gandhi and the Congress leaders. As the march proceeded, so the pressure of publicity and social boycott was built up and resignations began to occur in large numbers. By 22 March, approximate number of resignations were four from Ahmedabad district: twenty-seven from Kaita (of whom sixteen were from Borsad taluka) seventeen from Broach, and two from Surat. But Surat soon became the most affected district by 5 April. One hundred and forty headmen had resigned and ten clays later, the figure had risen to two hundred and twenty seven. Gandhi warned them, 'It will be regarded as cowardice to hand in one's resignation and then to withdraw it. There is no compulsion to resign. It is advisable to give up the post of Headman, looking upon it as something base, dirty and filthy.'

The speech delivered by Gandhi at Broach on 26 March dealt with the communal question. He explained that he had never dreamt that he could win Swaraj merely through his effort or assisted only by the Hindus. He sought the assistance of Muslims, Parsis, Christians, Sikhs, Jews and all other Indians. He needed the assistance even of Englishmen. 'But I know too that all this combined assistance is worthless if I have not one other assistance, that is, from God. All is vain without His help. And if he is With this struggle, no other' help is necessary.

In a letter to Jawaharlal Nehru on 31 March Gandhi expressed his optimism about he forthcoming movement. 'Things seem to be shaping very well indeed in Gujarat... I feel you are right in attention to the salt tax for the time being. What more we can or should do. Unless you hear from me to the contrary, please take 6th April as the date for simultaneous beginning.'

At Jambusar, Kamaladevi Chattopadhyaya arrived to see Gandhi to remove the general impression that had gone abroad that as he had not included women in his first batch of volunteers, they might not be taken up at all. Gandhiji told her, 'If impatient mothers will be a little patient they will find ample scope for their zeal and sacrifice in this national struggle for freedom'. She asked Gandhi what women with children should do. He said that he neither desired nor expected women to neglect their children. They might have to wait and bide their time, and thus be of use in some ways. Those women, however, who could make some satisfactory arrangements to have the children well looked after, should join the struggle.

At Surat where Gandhi and the satyagrahis reached on I April, they received a big welcome. He called the salt tax as beastly, inhuman and a Satanic Law. 'I have not heard of such justice anywhere in the world where it prevails... To bow to an empire which dispenses such justice is not dharma but adharma. A man who prays to God every morning at dawn cannot, must not, pray for the good of such an empire. On the contrary while praying or saying the namaaz he should ask God to encompass the destruction of such a Satanic empire, such an inhuman government. To do so is dharma.' In a message to the nation in the issue of Young India dated 3 April 1930, Gandhi exhorted the people 'Remember 5th April', and scart mass Civil Disobedience regarding the salt laws. He advised them to observe nonviolence in the fullest sense of the term. This was to be the spontaneous action. The workers were required to merely guide the masses in initial stages. Later, the masses would regulate the movement themselves.

The congress volunteers would render aid wherever needed. They, however, would be expected to be in the forefront. They were advised not to take sides in any communal quarrel. Wherever, there was a violent eruption, volunteers were expected to die in the attempt to quell violence. Those who were to be engaged in Civil Disobedience were occupy themselves and induce others to be engaged in some national service, such as Khadi work, liquor and opium picketing, foreign-cloth shops, village sanitation, assisting the families of civil resistance prisoners in a variety of ways. Gandhi also expected that if there was a real response about civil resistance regarding the salt tax, people should by proper organisation secure boycott of foreign cloth through Khadi and secure total prohibition. This would mean a saving of 91 crores per year, and supplementary work for the millions of unemployed. 'If we secure these things, we cannot be far from independence. And not one of these things is beyond our capacity.

Thus at each village, where the party stopped, Gandhi spoke briefly, telling the villagers that a great ordeal was at hand. He filled his political appeal with exhortation relevant to village life, such as Khadi, cow-protection, cleanliness and untouchability. His appeal was not for money but for change of attitudes: he called on village officials to resign their posts which buttressed the exploitive regime. As he journeyed, he continued to give press interviews and to write to Navajivan and Young India, spreading his massage of Swaraj and giving instructions for the conduct of the campaign during the days ahead. Out of twenty-five days, which the journey took, the party of satyagrahis had walked for twenty-two days, excluding three days of Gandhi's silence. On his way, Gandhi passed by forty villages and towns and everywhere he addressed the audience. The whole countryside was awake to the call of the Mahatma.

At least fifty thousand persons heard his stirring message to the nation: his speeches were generally impassioned and always brave and there was a tone of pathos which had gone home to the hearts of the listeners. Despite all the fatigue and other hardships of the journey, he never allowed himself any comfort that was denied to the last man of his 'army'.

The satyagrahis reached Dandi on 5 April. Sarojini Naidu had already arrived there to welcome them. When interviewed by special correspondent of The Bombay Chronicle, Gandhi said, ' Government, perhaps, deserves congratulations for their policy of non-interference which is not exactly in keeping with their proved capacity for provoking popular sentiment.'

Next day he was to break the salt tax law. If the Civil Disobedience Movement become widespread in the country and the government tolerated it, the salt law, Gandhi declared, might be taken as abolished. He indeed had no doubt in his mind that the salt tax stood abolished the very moment that the decision to break that salt laws was reached. 'If they arrest me or my companions tomorrow, I shall not be surprised. I shall certainly not be pained. It would be absurd to be pained if we get something that we have invited on ourselves.'

Gandhi advised the people to make salt freely in every home, as our ancestors used to, and sell it from place to place, and they should continue doing so wherever possible till the government yielded, so much so that the salt in government stocks would become superfluous. 'If the awakening of the people in the country is true and real, the salt law is as good as abolished'.

Gandhi highlighted the importance of Dandi and praised the efforts of the people of the taluka. He explained,' Dandi was chosen not by a man but by God. How otherwise could we have chosen for the battlefield of Satyagraha such an out-of-the-way place-a place where no food grains are to be had, where there is scarcity of water, where thousands can assemble only with difficulty, walking ten miles from the railway station, and where if you are travelling on foot, you have to negotiate creeks full of slush and mud? The truth is that in this struggle we have to put up with suffering. You have made the road from Navsari to Dandi famous throughout the world by arranging for free drinking-water at frequent intervals all along it... Dandi should be a sacred ground for us, where we should utter no untruth, commit so sin. Everyone coming here should come with this devout feeling in his heart.' 'If you have not yet gone out to remove salt, let the whole village get together and go. Hold the salt in your fist and think that you are carrying in your hand salt worth Rs. 6 Crores. Every year the Government has been taking away from us Rs. 6 Crores through its monopoly of salt.'

Gandhi and his volunteers broke the salt laws at 8-30 A.M. on 6 April 1930 by taking a lump of natural salt which was deposited in a small pit. Hundreds of persons witnessed this scene. Sarojini Naidu stood by Gandhiji's side, and, as the symbolic gesture was made, she cried, 'Hail Deliverer'.

Gandhi, while picking up a lump of salt in his hand, said, 'With this, I am shaking the foundation of the British Empire.' Not a single policeman or excise officer was present there. While talking to the representative of the free press, Gandhi said, 'Now that the technical or ceremonial breach of the Salt Law has been committed it is open to any one who would take the risk of prosecution' under the Salt Law to manufacture salt wherever he wishes and wherever it is convenient. My advice is that the workers should everywhere manufacture salt to make use of it and to instruct the villagers to do so.'

'Thus the war against the salt tax should be continued during the national week. Those who are not engaged in this sacred work should devote themselves to a vigorous propaganda for the boycott of foreign cloth and the use of Khadar. They should also endeavour to manufacture as much Khadar as possible.' After Gandhi had addressed the meeting on 6 April about two tolas of salt which was taken by him in the morning and also cleaned by him, was auctioned for Rs. 525/-to Seth Ranchhod Shodhan, a mill-owner of Ahmedabad. Gandhi's march on foot, form village to village through Gujarat which was his home and where his influence was greatest, aroused considerable interest and excitement. It has in fact appealed to the imagination of multitudes of people who were emotionally swayed by the dramatic turn of events. Throughout the march, Gandhiji went on preaching his cult of truth and nonviolence to the multitudes that gathered from far and near and he did not hesitate to impose the strictest discipline on the satyagrahis that flocked to his banner. The salt became the symbol of India's will to freedom. The same day the salt laws were broken throughout India at least by five million people at over 5,000 meetings. The entire countryside became acutely conscious of the struggle for Swaraj which was intensifying. The Dandi march received worldwide publicity. Soon the Civil Disobedience Movement spread simultaneously in western, northern, central, eastern and southern regions of India.

CIRCUMSTANCES LEADING TO THE DANDI MARCH

The political and social milieu of India was in turmoil following the formation of the Simon Commission for drawing up a constitution for India and the subsequent rejection of the Nehru Report. Gandhi requested the Viceroy, Lord Irwin, to mellow his stance in dealing with the constitutional crisis. On March 2nd 1930, Gandhi wrote a letter to the Viceroy wherein he highlighted an 11 point Charter of Demands. This included a considerable reduction in the Pound-Sterling-Rupee exchange rate, curtailing of military budget, a fifty percent reduction in land revenue, preservation of indigenous textile machinery, abolition of Salt Tax and releasing political prisoners. The British government did not react favorably to any of the propositions made by the Congress. The political segment of the country took no time to realize that the British government would not relent to any kind of persuasions. Anti British sentiments flared up as never before and the launch of a civil disobedience movement became inevitable. On February 15th, the Congress Working committee gave the authority to Gandhi and his followers to initiate the civil disobedience. The first step in this direction was the Dandi March.

Violation of British laws constituted an integral part of civil disobedience. The British salt tax law captured the attention of Gandhi and soon became the center of his anti British agendas. According to the British salt tax law, the sale or manufacture of salt by any other source barring the British government would be adjudged as a criminal offence, liable for punishment by law. Salt was extremely essential for the people of India, particularly for its temperate climate. The low-lying coastal regions of the country had extensive reserves of the mineral that were easily available to the laborers. The new salt tax law, however, impelled them to purchase the mineral that could be collected free of cost. In Gandhi's words; "There is no article like salt, outside water, by taxing which the sate can reach even the starving millions, the sick, the maimed and the utterly helpless. The tax constitutes, therefore, the most in human poll tax, the ingenuity of man can devise." Moreover, the issue of salt cut across class, caste, regional and ethnic distinctions and Gandhi could unite the entire country bound by a single cause. This oppressive salt tax law thus became the pivot around which the program of civil disobedience was designed. The British salt tax law provided the apt background against which a massive satyagraha struggle could be launched, throughout the country.

The Commencement of the Dandi March

When the Viceroy turned a deaf ear to the pleas of Gandhi, a disheartened Mahatma said; "On bended knees I asked for bread and I have received stone instead". In the letter to Lord Irwin, Gandhi had mentioned; "If my letter makes no appeal to your heart, on the eleventh day of his month I shall proceed with such co-workers of the Ashram as I can take, to disregard the provision of the Salt Laws." To give effect to this promise made by Gandhi in his letter to Lord Irwin, on the historic day of March 12th, he embarked on his Dandi March. Gandhi's entourage consisted of seventy nine members of his Sabarmati Ashram, who were well trained in the principles of satyagraha. As part of the preparation of this massive satyagraha campaign, Gandhi addressed a mass meeting on 10th March attended by the inmates of the Sabarmati ashram. At the prayer meeting on 11th March at Sabarmati Ashram, Gandhi invoked the inner strength of the satyagrahis and resolved to continue their non violent means of passive resistance until swaraj could be achieved in India. Finally, on 12th March at 6.30 a.m., Gandhi set out on his two hundred miles long journey, from Sabarmati Ashram to Dandi in the company of his few chosen followers. In this journey to Dandi, Gandhi's trail increased in size as thousands of inspired followers joined him in his march.

On 13th March Gandhi delivered a speech at Bareja, where he invited the villagers among whom there was a considerable number of Christians and Muslims, to join hands in supporting the cause of India's freedom. In his 14th March speech at Vasana, Gandhi asked the amassed audience whether they would believe him, if he made a prediction that a day would dawn when the British would apologize to the Indians. Gandhi addressed to the people of Dabhan on March 15th. In this speech he appealed to the people that if they have the armor of inner strength, they should boycott Government jobs, endorse Khadi, reject foreign made goods and abandon alcohol. Armed with an innate commitment to the eternal spirit of truth and self righteousness, they should join the army of salt satyagrahis.

On 17th March Gandhi delivered a speech at Anand, wherein he urged the students to withdraw from their academic pursuits, until the salt satyagraha campaign achieved its goal. On 23rd March, he challenged the British government's capability to arrest him although he had embarked on a mission to disobey British laws. In the speech delivered on 25th March, Gandhi declared that he had decided to stay at the residence of a Muslim friend, from where he would undertake his satyagraha struggle. In his way Gandhi sought to garner the support of the Muslim community as well in his satyagraha campaign against the unjust British salt tax law. On 26th March, 28th March and 29th March, Gandhi delivered speeches at Ankleshwar, the bank of River Keem and Bhatgam respectively. In Bhatgam, Gandhi condemned indulgence and extravagance and said that there is no place for these in a satyagraha campaign. Addressing the cloth merchants of Bombay who attended his speech at Sandihiyer on March 30th, Gandhi said that the involvement of the merchant class in the satyagraha struggle signifies their commitment to the cause of Indian's struggle for freedom.

On April 5th, Gandhi addressed the associated press at Dandi. He appreciated the government for resorting to absolute non interference, while he was on his march to Dandi. With the blessings of God, he communicated his noble intention to initiate civil disobedience in the company of his followers on 6th April. Since the incident of Jallianwallah Bagh massacre, 6th April had come to symbolize a day of self abasement and purging of the soul. The day, declared Gandhi would begin with fasting and prayer. On 6th March, Gandhi, on the Dandi beach, breached the British salt laws. He picked up a fistful of salt and mud and manufactured salt by boiling it in sea water. He urged his followers to violate the British Salt Tax law by manufacturing salt all along the sea coast. It was decided that the crusade against the salt tax would be carried on till April 13th that mark the National Week.

SALT SATYAGRAHA

The Satyagraha was a campaign of nonviolent protest against the British salt tax in colonial India which began with the Salt March to Dandi on March 12, 1930. It was the first act of organized opposition to British rule after *Purna Swaraj*, the declaration of independence by the Indian National Congress. Mahatma Gandhi led the Dandi march from his Sabarmati Ashram to Dandi, Gujarat to produce salt without paying the tax, with growing numbers of Indians joining him along the way. When Gandhi broke the salt laws in Dandi at the conclusion of the march on April 6, 1930, it sparked large scale acts of civil disobedience against the British Raj salt laws by millions of Indians.

Gandhi was arrested on May 5, 1930, just days before his planned raid on the Dharasana Salt Works. The Dandi March and the ensuing Dharasana Satyagraha drew worldwide attention to the Indian independence movement through extensive newspaper and newsreel coverage. The satyagraha against the salt tax continued for almost a year, ending with Gandhi's release from jail and negotiations with Viceroy Lord Irwin at the Second Round Table Conference. Over 80,000 Indians were jailed as a result of the Salt Satyagraha. The campaign had a significant effect on changing world and British attitudes toward Indian independence, and caused large numbers of Indians to actively join the fight for the first time, but failed to win major concessions from the British.

The Salt Satyagraha campaign was based upon Gandhi's principles of nonviolent protest called *satyagraha*, which he loosely translated as "truth-force." In early 1930 the Indian National Congress chose satyagraha as their main tactic for winning Indian independence from British rule and appointed

Gandhi to organize the campaign. Gandhi chose the 1882 British Salt Act as the first target of satyagraha. The Salt March to Dandi, and the beating of hundreds of nonviolent protesters in Dharasana, demonstrated the effective use of civil disobedience as a technique for fighting social and political injustice. The satyagraha teachings of Gandhi and the March to Dandi had a significant influence on American civil rights activist Martin Luther King, Jr., and his fight for civil rights for blacks and other minority groups in the 1960s.

Declaration of Independence

At midnight on December 31, 1929, the Indian National Congress raised the tricolour flag of India on the banks of the Ravi at Lahore. The Indian National Congress, led by Gandhi and Jawaharlal Nehru, publicly issued the Declaration of Independence, or *Purna Swaraj*, on January 26, 1930. The declaration included the readiness to withhold taxes, and the statement:

We believe that it is the inalienable right of the Indian people, as of any other people, to have freedom and to enjoy the fruits of their toil and have the necessities of life, so that they may have full opportunities of growth. We believe also that if any government deprives a people of these rights and oppresses them the people have a further right to alter it or abolish it. The British government in India has not only deprived the Indian people of their freedom but has based itself on the exploitation of the masses, and has ruined India economically, politically, culturally and spiritually. We believe therefore, that India must sever the British connection and attain *Purna Swaraj* or complete independence.

The Congress Working Committee gave Gandhi the responsibility for organizing the first act of civil disobedience, with Congress itself ready to take charge after Gandhi's expected arrest. Gandhi's plan was to begin civil disobedience with a satyagraha aimed at the British salt tax. The 1882 Salt Act gave the British a monopoly on the collection and manufacture of salt, limiting its handling to government salt depots and levying a salt tax. Violation of the Salt Act was a criminal offence. Even though salt was freely available to those living on the coast (by evaporation of sea water), Indians were forced to purchase it from the colonial government.

Gandhi's choice of the salt tax was met with incredulity by the Working Committee of the Congress, though Gandhi had his reasons for choosing the salt tax. The salt tax was a deeply symbolic choice, since salt was used by nearly everyone in India. It represented 8.2% of the British Raj tax revenue, and most significantly hurt the poorest Indians the most. Gandhi felt that this protest would dramatize Purna Swaraj in a way that was meaningful to the lowliest Indians. He also reasoned that it would build unity between Hindus and Muslims by fighting a wrong that touched them equally.

Satyagraha

Mahatma Gandhi, along with many members of the Congress Party, had a long-standing commitment to nonviolent civil disobedience, which he termed *satyagraha*, as the basis for achieving Indian independence. Referring to the relationship between *satyagraha* and *Purna Swaraj*, Gandhi saw "an inviolable connection between the means and the end as there is between the seed and the tree." He wrote, "If the means employed are impure, the change will not be in the direction of progress but very likely in the opposite. Only a change brought about in our political condition by pure means can lead to real progress."

Satyagraha is a synthesis of the Sanskrit words *Satya* (truth) and *Agraha* (holding firmly to). For Gandhi, satyagraha went far beyond mere "passive resistance" and became strength in practicing nonviolent methods. In his words:

Truth (satya) implies love, and firmness (agraha) engenders and therefore serves as a synonym for force. I thus began to call the Indian movement Satyagraha, that is to say, the Force which is born of Truth and Love or nonviolence, and gave up the use of the phrase "passive resistance", in connection with it, so much so that even in English writing we often avoided it and used instead the word "satyagraha"....

His first significant attempt in India at leading mass satyagraha was the Noncooperation movement from 1920-1922. Even though it succeeded in raising millions of Indians in protest against the British created Rowlatt Acts, violence broke out at Chauri Chaura, where a mob killed 22 unarmed policemen. Gandhi suspended the protest, against the opposition of other Congress members. He decided that Indians were not yet ready for successful nonviolent resistance.

The Bardoli Satyagraha in 1928 was much more successful. It succeeded in paralysing the British government and winning significant concessions. More importantly, due to extensive press coverage, it scored a propaganda victory out of all proportion to its size. Gandhi later claimed that success at Bardoli confirmed his belief in Satyagraha and Swaraj: "It is only gradually that we shall come to know the importance of the victory gained at Bardoli...Bardoli has shown the way and cleared it. Swaraj lies on that route, and that alone is the cure..." Gandhi recruited heavily from the Bardoli Satyagraha participants for the Dandi march, which passed through many of the same villages that took part in the Bardoli protests.

Preparing to March

On February 5, newspapers reported that Gandhi would begin civil disobedience by defying the salt laws. The salt satyagraha would begin on

March 12 and end in Dandi with Gandhi breaking the Salt Act on April 6. Gandhi chose April 6 to launch the mass breaking of the salt laws for a symbolic reason—it was the first day of "National Week", begun in 1919 when Gandhi conceived of the national hartal (strike) against the Rowlatt Act. Gandhi prepared the worldwide media for the march by issuing regular statements from Sabarmati, at his regular prayer meetings and through direct contact with the press. Expectations were heightened by his repeated statements anticipating arrest, and his increasingly dramatic language as the hour approached: "We are entering upon a life and death struggle, a holy war; we are performing an all-embracing sacrifice in which we wish to offer ourselves as oblation." Correspondents from dozens of Indian, European, and American newspapers, along with film companies, responded to the drama and began actively covering the event.

For the march itself, Gandhi wanted the strictest discipline and adherence to satyagraha and ahimsa. For that reason, he recruited the marchers not from Congress Party members, but from the residents of his own ashram, who were trained in Gandhi's strict standards of discipline. The 24 day march would pass through 4 districts and 48 villages. The route of the march, along with each evening's stopping place, was planned ahead of time based on recruitment potential, past contacts, and timing. Gandhi sent scouts to each village ahead of the march so he could plan his talks at each resting place, based on the needs of the local residents. Events at each village were scheduled and publicized in Indian and foreign press.

On March 2, 1930 Gandhi wrote to the Viceroy, Lord Irwin, offering to stop the march if Irwin met eleven demands, including reduction of land revenue assessments, cutting military spending, imposing a tariff on foreign cloth, and abolishing the salt tax. His strongest appeal to Irwin regarded the salt tax: If my letter makes no appeal to your heart, on the eleventh day of this month I shall proceed with such co-workers of the Ashram as I can take, to disregard the provisions of the Salt Laws. I regard this tax to be the most iniquitous of all from the poor man's standpoint. As the Independence movement is essentially for the poorest in the land, the beginning will be made with this evil.

Irwin did not take the threat of a salt protest seriously, writing to London, "At present the prospect of a salt campaign does not keep me awake at night." After the Viceroy ignored the letter and refused to meet with Gandhi, the march was set in motion. The eve of the march brought thousands of Indians to Sabarmati to hear Gandhi speak at the regular evening prayer. An American academic writing for The Nation reported that "60,000 persons gathered on the bank of the river to hear Gandhi's call to arms. This call to arms was perhaps the most remarkable call to war that has ever been made."

March to Dandi

On March 12, 1930, Gandhi and 78 male satyagrahis set out on foot for the coastal village of Dandi, Gujarat, over 390 kilometres (240 mi) from their starting point at Sabarmati Ashram. According to The Statesman, the official government newspaper which usually played down the size of crowds at Gandhi's functions, 100,000 people crowded the road that separated Sabarmati from Ahmedabad.

The first day's march of 21 kilometres (13 mi) ended in the village of Aslali, where Gandhi spoke to a crowd of about 4,000. At Aslali, and the other villages that the march passed through, volunteers collected donations, registered new satyagrahis, and received resignations from village officials who chose to end cooperation with British rule. As they entered each village, crowds greeted the marchers, beating drums and cymbals. Gandhi gave speeches attacking the salt tax as inhuman, and the salt satyagraha as a "poor man's battle." Each night they slept in the open, asking of the villagers nothing more than simple food and a place to rest and wash. Gandhi felt that this would bring the poor into the battle for independence, necessary for eventual victory.

Thousands of satyagrahis and leaders like Sarojini Naidu joined him. Every day, more and more people joined the march. At Surat, they were greeted by 30,000 people. When they reached the railhead at Dandi, more than 50,000 were gathered. Gandhi gave interviews and wrote articles along the way. Foreign journalists made him a household name in Europe and America. The New York Times wrote almost daily about the Salt March, including two front page articles on April 6 and April 7. Near the end of the march, Gandhi declared, "I want world sympathy in this battle of Right against Might."

Upon arriving at the seashore on April 5, Gandhi was interviewed by an Associated Press reporter. He stated: I cannot withhold my compliments from the government for the policy of complete non interference adopted by them throughout the march.... I wish I could believe this non-interference was due to any real change of heart or policy. The wanton disregard shown by them to popular feeling in the Legislative Assembly and their high-handed action leave no room for doubt that the policy of heartless exploitation of India is to be persisted in at any cost, and so the only interpretation I can put upon this non-interference is that the British Government, powerful though it is, is sensitive to world opinion which will not tolerate repression of extreme political agitation which civil disobedience undoubtedly is, so long as disobedience remains civil and therefore necessarily nonviolent.... It remains to be seen whether the Government will tolerate as they have tolerated the march, the actual breach of the salt laws by countless people from tomorrow.

The following morning, after a prayer, Gandhi raised a lump of salty mud and declared, "With this, I am shaking the foundations of the British Empire." He then boiled it in seawater, producing illegal salt. He implored his thousands of followers to likewise begin making salt along the seashore, "wherever it is convenient" and to instruct villagers in making illegal, but necessary, salt.

Mass Civil Disobedience

Mass civil disobedience spread throughout India as millions broke the salt laws by making salt or buying illegal salt. Salt was sold illegally all over the coast of India. A pinch of salt made by Gandhi himself sold for 1,600 rupees (equivalent to $750 dollars at the time). In reaction, the British government incarcerated over sixty thousand people by the end of the month. What had begun as a Salt Satyagraha quickly grew into a mass Satyagraha. British cloth and goods were boycotted. Unpopular forest laws were defied in the Maharashtra, Carnatic (now Karnataka), and Central Provinces. Gujarati peasants refused to pay tax, under threat of losing their crops and land. In Midnapore, Bengalis took part by refusing to pay the chowkidar tax. The British responded with more laws, including censorship of correspondence and declaring the Congress and its associate organizations illegal. None of those measures slowed the civil disobedience movement.

In Peshawar, satyagraha was led by a Muslim Pashto disciple of Gandhi, Ghaffar Khan, who had trained a 50,000 member army of nonviolent activists called Khudai Khidmatgar. On April 23, 1930, Ghaffar Khan was arrested. A crowd of Khudai Khidmatgar gathered in Peshawar's Kissa Khani (Storytellers) Bazaar. The British ordered troops to open fire with machine guns on the unarmed crowd, killing an estimated 200-250. The Pashtun satyagrahis acted in accord with their training in nonviolence, willingly facing bullets as the troops fired on them. One British Indian Army regiment, troops of the renowned Royal Garhwal Rifles, refused to fire at the crowds. The entire platoon was arrested and many received heavy penalties, including life imprisonment.

The civil disobedience in 1930 marked the first time women became mass participants in the struggle for freedom. Thousands of women, from large cities to small villages, became active participants in satyagraha. Gandhi had asked that only men take part in the salt march, but eventually women began manufacturing and selling salt throughout India. Usha Mehta, an early Gandhian activist, remarked that "Even our old aunts and great-aunts and grandmothers used to bring pitchers of salt water to their houses and manufacture illegal salt. And then they would shout at the top of their voices: 'We have broken the salt law!'" The growing number of women in the fight for independence was a "new and serious feature" according to Lord Irwin. A government report on the involvement of women stated "thousands of them emerged....from the seclusion of their homes...in order to join Congress demonstrations and assist in picketing: and their presence on these occasions made the work the police was required to perform particularly unpleasant."

There were outbreaks of violence in Calcutta (now Kolkata), Karachi, and Gujarat. Unlike his suspension of satyagraha after violence broke out during the Noncooperation movement, this time Gandhi was "unmoved". Appealing for violence to end, at the same time Gandhi honoured those killed in Chittagong and congratulated their parents "for the finished sacrifices of their sons.... A warrior's death is never a matter for sorrow." British documents show that the British government was shaken by satyagraha. Nonviolent protest left the British confused about whether or not to jail Gandhi. John Court Curry, a British police officer stationed in India, wrote in his memoirs that he felt nausea every time he dealt with Congress demonstrations in 1930. Curry and others in British government, including Wedgwood Benn, Secretary of State for India, preferred fighting violent rather than nonviolent opponents.

Aftermath

Gandhi himself avoided further active involvement after the march, though he stayed in close contact with the developments throughout India. He created a temporary ashram near Dandi. From there, he urged women followers in Bombay (now Mumbai) to picket liquor shops and foreign cloth. He said that "a bonfire should be made of foreign cloth. Schools and colleges should become empty."

For his next major action, Gandhi decided on a raid of the Dharasana Salt Works in Gujarat. He wrote to Lord Irwin, again telling him of his plans. Around midnight of May 4, as Gandhi was sleeping on a cot in a mango grove, the District Magistrate of Surat drove up with two Indian officers and thirty heavily-armed constables. He was arrested under an 1827 regulation calling for the jailing of people engaged in unlawful activities, and held without trial near Poona (now Pune).

The Dharasana Satyagraha went ahead as planned, with Abbas Tyabji, a seventy-six year old retired judge, leading the march with Gandhi's wife Kasturba at his side. Both were arrested before reaching Dharasana and sentenced to three months in prison. After their arrests, the march continued under the leadership of Sarojini Naidu, a woman poet and freedom fighter, who warned the satyagrahis, "You must not use any violence under any circumstances. You will be beaten, but you must not resist: you must not even raise a hand to ward off blows." Soldiers began clubbing the satyagrahis with steel tipped lathis in an incident that attracted international attention. United Press correspondent Webb Miller reported that: Not one of the marchers even raised an arm to fend off the blows. They went down like ten-pins. From where I stood I heard the sickening whacks of the clubs on unprotected skulls. The waiting crowd of watchers groaned and sucked in their breaths in sympathetic pain at every blow. Those struck down fell sprawling, unconscious or writhing in pain with fractured skulls or broken shoulders. In two or three minutes the ground was quilted with bodies. Great patches of blood widened on their white clothes. The survivors without breaking ranks silently and doggedly marched on until struck down.

Vithalbhai Patel, former Speaker of the Assembly, watched the beatings and remarked, "All hope of reconciling India with the British Empire is lost forever." Following attempts by the British to censor Miller's story, it eventually appeared in 1,350 newspapers throughout the world, and was read into the official record of the United States Senate. Salt Satyagraha succeeded in drawing the attention of the world. Millions saw the newsreels showing the march. Time magazine declared Gandhi its 1930 Man of the Year, comparing Gandhi's march to the sea "to defy Britain's salt tax as some New Englanders once defied a British tea tax." Civil disobedience continued until early 1931, when Gandhi was finally released from prison to hold talks with Irwin. It was the first time the two held talks on equal terms. The talks would lead to the Second Round Table Conference at the end of 1931.

Long Term Impact

Salt Satyagraha produced scant progress toward dominion status or independence for India, and did not win any major concessions from the British. It also failed to attract Muslim support—many Muslims actively boycotted the satyagraha. Congress leaders decided to end satyagraha as official policy in 1934. Nehru and other Congress members drifted further apart from Gandhi, who withdrew from Congress to concentrate on his Constructive Programme, which included his efforts to end untouchability. Even though British authorities were again in control by the mid 1930s, Indian, British, and world opinion increasingly began to recognize the legitimacy of claims by Gandhi and the Congress Party for independence. The Satyagraha campaign of the 1930s also forced the British to recognize that their control of India depended entirely on the consent of the Indians — Salt Satyagraha was a significant step in the British losing that consent.

Nehru considered Salt Satyagraha the high water mark of his association with Gandhi, and felt that its lasting importance was in changing the attitudes of Indians: Of course these movements exercised tremendous pressure on the British Government and shook the government machinery. But the real importance, to my mind, lay in the effect they had on our own people, and especially the village masses....Non-cooperation dragged them out of the mire and gave them self-respect and self-reliance....They acted courageously and did not submit so easily to unjust oppression; their outlook widened and they began to think a little in terms of India as a whole....It was a remarkable transformation and the Congress, under Gandhi's leadership, must have the credit for it.

More than thirty years later, Satyagraha and the March to Dandi exercised a strong influence on American civil rights activist Martin Luther King, Jr., and his fight for civil rights for blacks in the 1960s: Like most people, I had heard of Gandhi, but I had never studied him seriously. As I read I became deeply fascinated by his campaigns of nonviolent resistance. I was particularly moved by his Salt March to the Sea and his numerous fasts. The whole concept of *Satyagraha* (*Satya* is truth which equals love, and *agraha* is force; *Satyagraha*, therefore, means truth force or love force) was profoundly significant to me. As I delved deeper into the philosophy of Gandhi, my skepticism concerning the power of love gradually diminished, and I came to see for the first time its potency in the area of social reform.

Re-enactment in 2005

To commemorate the Great Salt March, the Mahatma Gandhi Foundation proposed a re-enactment on the 75th anniversary. The event was known as the "International Walk for Justice and Freedom". Mahatma Gandhi's great-grandson Tushar Gandhi and several hundred fellow marchers followed the same route to Dandi. The start of the march on March 12, 2005 in Ahmedabad was attended by Sonia Gandhi, Chairperson of the National Advisory Council, as well as several Indian Cabinet Ministers, many of whom walked for the first few kilometres. The participants halted at Dandi on the night of April 5, with the commemoration ending on April 7. A series of commemorative stamps were issued on the 75th anniversary of the Dandi March—denomination INR 5, Date of Issue: April 5, 2005.

5

Gandhian Principles and Thoughts

GANDHI'S PHILOSOPHY

What is Gandhian philosophy? It is the religious and social ideas adopted and developed by Gandhi, first during his period in South Africa from 1893 to 1914, and later of course in India. These ideas have been further developed by later "Gandhians", most notably, in India, Vinoba Bhave and Jayaprakash Narayan. Outside of India some of the work of, for example, Martin Luther King Jr. can also be viewed in this light. Understanding the universe to be an organic whole, the philosophy exists on several planes-the spiritual or religious, moral, political, economic, social, individual and collective. The spiritual or religious element, and God, is at its core. Human nature is regarded as fundamentally virtuous. All individuals are believed to be capable of high moral development, and of reform.

The twin cardinal principles of Gandhi's thought are truth and nonviolence. It should be remembered that the English word "truth" is an imperfect translation of the Sanskrit, "satya", and "nonviolence", an even more imperfect translation of "ahimsa". Derived from "sat"-"that which exists"-"satya"contains a dimension of meaning not usually associated by English speakers with the word "truth". There are other variations, too, which we need not go into here. For Gandhi, truth is the relative truth of truthfulness in word and deed, and the absolute truth-the Ultimate Reality. This ultimate truth is God (as God is also Truth) and morality-the moral laws and code-its basis. Ahimsa, far from meaning mere peacefulness or the absence of overt violence, is understood by Gandhi to denote active love-the pole opposite of violence, or "himsa", in every sense. The ultimate station Gandhi assigns nonviolence stems from two main points. First, if according to the Divine Reality all life is one, then all violence committed towards another is violence towards oneself, towards the collective, whole self, and thus "self"-destructive and counter to the universal law of life, which is love. Second, Gandhi believed that ahimsa is the most powerful force in existence. Had himsabeen superior to ahimsa, humankind would long ago have succeeded in destroying itself. The human race certainly could not have progressed as far as it has, even if universal justice remains far off the horizon. From both viewpoints, nonviolence or love is regarded as the highest law of humankind.

Although there are elements of unity in Gandhi's thought, they are not reduced to a system. It is not a rigid, inflexible doctrine, but a set of beliefs and principles which are applied differently according to the historical and social setting. Therefore there can be no dogmatism, and inconsistency is not a sin. Interpretation of the principles underwent much evolution during Gandhi's lifetime, and as a result many inconsistencies can be found in his writings, to which he readily admitted. The reader of Gandhi's works published by Navajivan Trust will notice that many are prefaced with the following quotation from an April 1933 edition of "Harijan", one of Gandhi's journals. He states straightforwardly: "I would like to say to the diligent reader of my writings and to others who are interested in them that I am not at all concerned with appearing to be consistent. In my search after Truth I have discarded many ideas and learnt many news things.... What I am concerned with is my readiness to obey the call of Truth, my God, from moment to moment, and therefore, when anybody finds any inconsistency between any two writings of mine, if he still has any faith in my sanity, he would do well to choose the later of the two on the same subject."

That there are inconsistencies in Gandhi's writings accords with the fact that the ideas are not a system. In coming to grips with Gandhi's way of thinking it is most important to understand that the perception of truth undergoes an ongoing process of refinement which is evolutionary in nature.

In Gandhi's thought the emphasis is on idealism, but on practical idealism. It is rooted in the highest religious idealism, but is thoroughly practical. One label (and almost the only one) Gandhi was happy to have pinned on him was that of "practical idealist". The important principle of compromise is relevant here, as is the acknowledgement that perfect truth and perfect nonviolence can never be attained while the spirit is embodied. As alluded to above, Gandhian philosophy is certainly considered by Gandhians as a universal and timeless philosophy, despite the fact that on the more superficial level it is set in the Indian social context. They hold that the ideals of truth and nonviolence, which underpin the whole philosophy, are relevant to all humankind. (Recently some have been suggesting that a distinction can be made between the core elements of Gandhi's thought and peripheral elements which, depending on the particular element under consideration, may or may not have timeless relevance.)

Also, it can be universal despite being fundamentally religious, as its religious position stresses not so much the Hindu interpretation of reality as the beliefs which are common to all major religions, and that commonality itself. It holds all religions to be worthy of equal respect and in one sense to be equal. As all are creations of mortal and imperfect human beings, no single religion can embody or reveal the whole or absolute truth. Gandhian philosophy is also compatible with the view that humankind is undergoing gradual moral evolution. While conflict is seen as inevitable, in fact not always undesirable, violence as the result of conflict is not regarded as inevitable. Simply put, human beings do have the capacity to resolve conflict nonviolently. This might be difficult, but it is not impossible. Liberation from a violent society is seen as requiring many decades or longer-but it is not an imposible ideal.

Importantly also, it is not an intellectual doctrine. Gandhi was not an intellectual. Rather, Gandhi's thought was conceived, to a great extent, out of action and as a guide to action, by a man of action. He hesitated to write about anything of which he did not have personal, first-hand experience. In the sense of it being a call to action, Gandhi's thought can also be seen as an ideology.

As a guide to action, Gandhian philosophy is a double-edged weapon. Its objective is to transform the individual and society simultaneously (rather than in sequence, as Marxism describes), in accordance with the principles of truth and nonviolence. The historic task before humankind is to progress towards the creation of a nonviolent political, economic and social order by nonviolent struggle. The social goal was described by Gandhi as Sarvodaya, a term he coined in paraphrasing John Ruskin's book Unto This Last, meaning the welfare of all without exception.

Its political aspect was expressed by the late eminent Gandhian Dr. R.R. Diwakar in the following words: "The good of each individual in society consists in his efforts to achieve the good of all." As the foundation of the Gandhian or nonviolent social order is religious or spiritual, economic and political questions are seen from the moral or humanistic perspective.

The welfare of human beings, not of systems or institutions, is the ultimate consideration. Materially, it centres on the following concepts and ideals:

- Political decentralisation, to prevent massive concentrations of political power in the hands of too few; rather, to distribute it in the hands of many. The Gandhian political order takes the form of a direct, participatory democracy, operating in a tier structure from the base village-level tier upward through the district and state levels to the national (and international) level.

- Economic decentralisation, to prevent massive concentrations of economic power in the hands of too few, and again, to distribute it in the hands of many. Therefore villages, which are anyway geographically decentralised, become the basic economic units. However, where unavoidable, certain industries may be organised on a more centralised basis, and their ownership and control come under the umbrella of the State.
- The minimisation of competition and exploitation in the economic sphere, and instead, the encouragement of cooperation.
- Production on the basis of need rather than greed, concentrating where India is concerned first on the eradication of poverty (and on the worst extreme of poverty).
- Recognition of the dignity of labour and the greater purity of rural life.
- The practice of extensive self-reliance by individuals, villages, regions and the nation.
- Absence of oppression on the basis of race, caste, class, language, gender or religion.
- A deep respect for mother nature, necessitating an economic system based upon the preservation rather than destruction of the natural environment.

Such concepts clearly represent pillars for a new social order.

A theory closely linked to the concept of Sarvodaya, also developed by Gandhi, is that of Trusteeship. Its fundamental objective is to create nonviolent and non-exploitative property relationships. Gandhi believed that the concepts of possession and private property were sources of violence, and in contradiction with the Divine reality that all wealth belongs to all people.

However, he recognised that the concept of ownership would not wither easily, nor would the wealthy be easily persuaded to share their wealth. Therefore a compromise was to encourage the wealthy to hold their wealth in trust, to use themselves only what was necessary and to allow the remainder to be utilised for the benefit of the whole society.

It is apparent that Gandhi's philosophy has much in common with several Western philosophies which uphold the ideal of a more just and equitable society. For example, the Gandhian social order has been described as "communism minus violence". (However, Marxists have traditionally rejected Gandhi because of what they regard as his "bourgeois" outlook. Gandhi rejected violent class conflict and the centralisation of political and economic power in the hands of the State as counterproductive to the development of a nonviolent society.) Nevertheless, Gandhian philosophy, particularly in the Sarvodaya ideal, does contain many socialist sentiments. In fact, such an entity as Gandhian Socialism emerged in theoretical literature during the 1970s and 1980s. Gandhi's thought has been likened also to Utopian Socialism and Philosophical Anarchism, and can be compared with strands of Maoist thought (though not a Western philosophy), and even Western liberal thought. However, Gandhi is incompatible with many aspects of Liberalism and is virtually entirely incompatible with the modern, intensely competitive, ecologically destructive and materialistic capitalism of the West.

As already observed, Gandhi's thought is equally a philosophy of self-transformation. The individual's task is to make a sincere attempt to live according to the principles of truth and nonviolence. Its fundamental tenets are therefore moral. They include-resisting injustice, developing a spirit of service, selflessness and sacrifice, emphasising one's responsibilities rather than rights, self-discipline, simplicity of lifestyle, and attempting to maintain truthful and nonviolent relations with others.

It should be understood that by simplicity is meant voluntary simplicity, not poverty, which has no element of voluntarism in it. If there is one thing Gandhi does not stand for, it is poverty. A Gandhian should also avoid political office. He or she should remain aloof from formal party politics and equi-distant from all political groupings. But this is not to say, and in my view Gandhi does not require, that the individual should remain aloof from all politics.

For often injustice cannot be resisted unless the political power holders and structures are engaged, nonviolently. What was the freedom struggle itself if not a political struggle, against the greatest concentration of political power the world had ever known, the British Empire? In my eyes, there is no particular virtue in attempting to avoid contact with politics. What must be avoided, however, is assumption of political power by a Gandhian (at least this is necessary in the short and medium terms in India), and cooperation with unvirtuous holders of political power on their terms. The ultimate responsibility of a Gandhian is to resist clear injustice, untruth, in conjunction with others or alone. Resistance should be nonviolent if at all possible. But Gandhi did condone use of violent means in certain circumstances, in preference to submission which he regarded as cowardice and equivalent to cooperation with evil. In relation to the use of violence he stated categorically: "Where there is only a choice between cowardice and violence I would advise violence..." As surprising as it no doubt sounds, Gandhi disliked most not violence, but cowardice and apathy. The eminent peace researcher Johan Galtung has correctly observed that Gandhi preferred first, nonviolent resistance, second, violence in a just cause, and third, meaning least of all, apathy. In general, however, it is held that immoral means, such as violence, cannot produce moral ends, as means are themselves ends or ends in the making.

For the individual self-transformation is attempted with deliberateness rather than with haste. One should not seek to become a Mahatma overnight, because such attempts will surely fail, but to reform oneself over the whole of one's life, as far as one is capable. (Nor should there be any question of superficial imitation of Gandhi.) Gandhi viewed his own life as a process of development undertaken "one step at a time". He saw the need to continually "experiment with truth" (from which he derived the title of his autobiography) in whatever field, in order to come to see the truthful path.

Though they were rooted in the highest idealism, the experiments were carried out on a very down-to-earth plane-India's moral, political and social needs as he saw them. Such an approach is available to all at all times. Gandhi believed his own moral and spiritual development to be far from complete at the time of his death. Despite the great heights he had attained, this was indeed true. He had not achieved perfection, as some of those who were close to him have testified.

The perception of what is the truthful path is largely a matter for the individual's reason and conscience, which therefore play key roles. The individual should subject each idea to the test of his or her own conscience and reason. Reason and rationality have enormous roles to play in the Gandhian way of thinking. This, I feel, is one of the major Western influences in Gandhi. If there is genuine, sincere disagreement, an idea can be discarded. However, once a principle is accepted a sincere attempt must be made to adhere to it. Ideally there should be harmony between thought, word and action. In this way the outer life becomes a true reflection of the inner, and a mental harmony is also achieved.

The remaining central concept in Gandhi's philosophy is Satyagraha. Defined most broadly (as Gandhi defined it), Satyagraha is itself a whole philosophy of nonviolence. Defined most narrowly, it is a technique or tool of nonviolent action. Because of the intention here to keep this discussion as simple as possible, Satyagraha will be described here in its latter guise. As a technique, Satyagraha was developed by Gandhi in South Africa to give the Indian population there a weapon with which to resist the injustices being perpetrated upon it by the colonial government. But Satyagraha can be practised in any cultural environment-provided the necessary ingredients are present, not least Satyagrahis (those capable of Satyagraha).

A Satyagraha campaign is undertaken only after all other peaceful means have proven ineffective. At its heart is nonviolence. An attempt is made to convert, persuade or win over the opponent. It involves applying the forces of both reason and conscience simultaneously. While holding aloft the indisputable truth of his or her position, the Satyagrahi also engages in acts of voluntary self-suffering. Any violence inflicted by the opponent is accepted without retaliation. But precisely because there is no retaliation (which can make the opponent feel his violence is justified), the opponent can only become morally bankrupt if violence continues to be inflicted indefinitely.

Several methods can be applied in a Satyagraha campaign, primarily noncooperation and fasting. The action is undertaken in the belief in the underlying goodness of the opponent, and in his or her ability to acknowledge the injustice of the action and to cease the injustice, or at least to compromise. Satyagrahain this sense is highly creative. It creates no enemies, hatred or lasting bitterness, but ultimately only mutual regard.

After a successful campaign there is not the least hint of gloating, nor is there any desire to embarrass the opponent. The former opponent becomes a friend. There are no losers, only winners. A truthful Satyagraha campaign, though it demands courage, self-discipline and humility on the part of the Satyagrahi, brings to bear tremendous moral pressure on the opponent and can bring about remarkable transformations.

Two factors are absolutely crucial to understand. There can be no Satyagraha in a cause which is not indisputably just and truthful. Nor can there be any element of violence or bitterness in a Satyagraha campaign-it must be conducted in a spirit of genuine nonviolence. Any campaign which is insincere in its spirit of nonviolence, or is not undertaken in a clearly just cause is not Satyagraha as Gandhi meant it. To sum up, Gandhian philosophy is not only simultaneously political, moral and religious, it is also traditional and modern, simple and complex.

It embodies numerous Western influences to which Gandhi was exposed, but being rooted in ancient Indian culture and harnessing eternal and universal moral and religious principles, there is much in it that is not at all new. This is why Gandhi could say: "I have nothing new to teach the world. Truth and nonviolence are as old as the hills." Gandhi is concerned even more with the spirit than with the form. If the spirit is consistent with truth and nonviolence, the truthful and nonviolent form will automatically re sult. Despite its anti-Westernism, many hold its outlook to be ultra-modern, in fact ahead of its time-even far ahead. Perhaps the philosophy is best seen as a harmonious blend of the traditional and modern. The multifaceted nature of Gandhi's thought also can easily lead to the view that it is extremely complex. Perhaps in one sense it is. One could easily write volumes in describing it! Yet Gandhi described much of his thought as mere commonsense. Dr. Diwakar sums up Gandhi's thought in a few words: "The four words, truth, nonviolence, Sarvodaya and Satyagraha and their significance constitute Gandhi and his teaching." These are indeed the four pillars of Gandhian thought.

TRUTH AND NON-VIOLENCE

Two basic principles, Truth and nonviolence, are the foundations of Gandhi's philosophy. At the highest level of experience they merge and become one with God. The ideal of reality is also the ideal of value-a distinctive mark of Hindu philosophy. God, therefore, has been referred to by Gandhi as Truth or Love (nonviolence in its perfection). His ideal of life, self-realisation, therefore, is couched in ideal terms, when the Unity of Man and God has also been achieved.

Gandhi, however, is fully aware that in actual fact, at the present level of human experience, there is a gulf between man and God; indeed, this gulf will never be completely bridged as long as we are in this body. "Being necessarily limited by the bonds of flesh we can achieve perfection only after the dissolution of the body." But while in this body, the gulf can certainly be narrowed. Thus recognising the imperfect nature of man, Gandhi's prescription would be to follow the relative truth persistently which he called "Satyagraha". This shows the dynamic character of his ideas.

In order to achieve this ideal, he prescribed an ethical discipline-the observance of vows which he defined as "doing at any cost something that one ought to do".

But taking of a vow does not mean that we are able to observe it completely from the very beginning, but it does mean "constant and honest effort in thought, word and deed, with a view to its fulfilment". It is no doubt true that in this way the practice of the ideal becomes very slippery indeed-anything could be justified as following the ideal.

But this is unavoidable as is the fate of all ethical ideals whose observance can hardly be a matter of strict objective scrutiny; it would ultimately depend on the spirit of the person who observes it and which no outsider can determine fully. At the same time, it does not condone the moral lapses of the individual; rather, this consciousness should make one strive to overcome the imperfections.

Gandhi's adoption of nonviolence as a method of pursuing truth is due to the fact that man, imperfect as he is, can only strive, he cannot command the result. Perfect nonviolence, being the attribute of God alone, cannot be practised by human beings.

Being a part of society, man cannot but participate in "himsa" that the very existence of society involves. Gandhi, therefore, would consider a person true to his faith if "there is an effort to avoid the violence that is inevitable in life".

That is how Gandhi's ideal of nonviolence is translated into actual practice. In essence, it consists "in allowing others the maximum of convenience at the maximum inconvenience to us, even at the risk of life. Everyone has to determine for himself the amount of inconvenience he is capable of putting up with. No third party can determine it for him." Gandhi believed that one should rather be conscious of one's imperfections than that one should lower one's ideal; this would spur the individual to perfect himself.

The application of nonviolence and Satyagraha to social and political fields has been a subject of great controversy. So complete was Gandhi's faith that he considered it a remedy against all social evils.

What makes it a unique method of bringing about change is the transformation of the whole atmosphere, satyagrahi and the opponent included. Its success or failure is not to be judged in terms of victory or defeat of one party but in terms of a change of heart of both. It is not merely a form of persuasion which is aimed in one direction only. If, in spite of the best efforts of the satyagrahi, some moral coercion is felt by the opponent, then such coercion is unavoidable because of the imperfect nature of the satyagrahi. However, he is obliged to try his best to reduce this unavoidable coercion to the minimum. That alone would make it different from passive resistance.

Ideally not even a group organisation is necessary. "A man or woman who is saturated with ahimsa has only to will a thing and it happens." This is because a perfect satyagrahi would be nearer to God; and what is beyond His power! Since such a perfect satyagrahi is not available, Gandhi realised the necessity of group action.

Also Satyagraha has its educative purpose, which is to bring about confidence in the community. Gandhi's method strongly emphasizes the need of ethical discipline, whose essential ingredient is courage-the courage of dying without killing. Having decided upon the rightness of a situation, Gandhi would not like one to be a passive spectator to evil.

That would be participation in the evil itself. If one does not have sufficient nonviolence to die without killing one should not shamefully flee from the danger in the name of nonviolence. Rather, Gandhi would advise killing and being killed. While for himself he did not believe in the use of arms at all, he would not hesitate to advise their use by those who had no faith in nonviolence. "If there was a national government, whilst I should not take any direct part in any war, I can conceive occasions when it would be my duty to vote for the military training of those who wish to take it.

For I know that all its members do not believe in nonviolence to the extent I do. It is not possible to make a person or a society nonviolent by compulsion."

Under certain circum stances, nonviolence may be only a matter of policy, as it was with the Indian National Congress. But this cannot be identified with the level of nonviolence which Gandhi personally was capable of.

There is not a uniform pattern of application of nonviolence for all individuals and societies. Gandhi is some times talking in terms of the ideal, sometimes from his personal level; and sometimes from the point of view of what he considered the Indian masses were capable of doing. It is this distinction, which is not always made explicit, that gives the impression of inconsistency.

Sometimes a confusion is made between the acts of the individual and those of the State, and it is expected that Gandhi's State is to be nonviolent. But how is the State to act nonviolently, when for Gandhi it "represents violence in a concentrated and organised form"?

Indeed a nonviolent State is a contradiction in terms. Ultimately, when nonviolence is the governing principle of society, we could not call it a State-it could only be called a nonviolent stateless society. And that is the ideal for Gandhi.

In such a society people would simply grow accustomed spontaneously to observe their social obligations without the operation of the state. The necessity of legal enforcement arises because of human imperfections.

The more the individuals have imbibed the spirit of nonviolence, the less the necessity of the state. This is the implication of Gandhi's concept of Swaraj. "The attempt to win Swaraj is Swaraj itself." It is a developing ideal and is "better than the best". Gandhi calls it "indefinable".

In the context of the Indian National Movement, he said that Swaraj did not mean merely political independence but "many other things". A Western style of parliamentary government lie would accept as Swaraj for the time being only. While in the ideal society there is no room for the military and the police, yet in the actual State there is provision for it according to the moral level of its citizens.

That is to say, a predominantly nonviolent State is the practical possibility and is the second best ideal of Gandhi. Failure to recognise the levels in Gandhi's thought results in such confused statements as this: "It is indeed clear that Gandhi held essential ideals in common with anarchists, that lie was willing, as they are not, to accept a degree of state organisation and control. He believed that government to be best which governs least, and yet he held that 'there are certain things which cannot be done without political power', even though there are 'numerous other things which do not at all depend upon political power'....

It would, of course, be incorrect to suppose that Gandhi thought of retaining the state as some intermediate step in a determined progress towards anarchical society."

Gandhi's actual State does concede the desirability of using the military and the police to deal with anti-social elements and defend the country. What, however, distinguishes his approach is the admission of weakness not of the doctrine of nonviolence or of Satyagraha, but of the individuals who practise it. Whatever political institutions Gandhi accepted, he did so only as a transitional device, to be transcended by better ones. No institutional device is final. They must evolve with the evolution of individuals. In actual practice, it would be a mixture: "A government cannot succeed in becoming entirely nonviolent because it represents all the people." He expected that the national policy would incline towards militarism of a modified character.

While fighting for the independence of India, Gandhi was conscious all the time of the necessity of moral uplift of the individuals who are to work the institutions after independence. In directing his energies towards political reform his method was equally directed "to educating the individuals to rise to a moral stature". He says : "Responsible government, which is a gift without the will and power of the people behind it, will be a mere paper responsibility hardly worth the paper on which it may be printed. If it is a fact that the atmosphere for immediate self government among the states is not propitious, and the people are not ready to pay the price, it follows that they should have the proper training."

When, therefore, Gandhi is criticised as a politician, such criticism is mainly based on his having one end in view, *viz.* the national independence of India; it ignores the other important principle of Gandhi, namely the moral training of the individual.

In the economic field, Gandhi holds to the ideal of Trusteeship. Ultimately he subscribes to "non-possession". But in actual life he admits that some possession is unavoidable for the maintenance of the body and its needs so that it may be used for performing its duties.

But property must always be held as a trust for the people and must satisfy this instrumental character. While absolute trusteeship is no doubt an abstraction and is unattainable, like Euclid's point, an effort in this direction will remove the hardships of inequality. In the actual world, Gandhi would not even mind State regulation, but with the minimum use of power-by which he means constitutional machinery.

He goes to the length of saying: "Every vested interest must be subjected to scrutiny and confiscation ordered where necessary-with or without compensation, as the case may be." This is what he said in 1932 at the Round Table Conference in London. As a part of a civil disobedience movement in 1942 he could expect "the peasants to stop taxes" and even "to seize the land". But this was not a matter of "advance", as Mr. Mukherji terms it; nor "a. signal change in Gandhi's ideology" as "dictated by politics"; it was indeed the application of his philosophy of property when trusteeship had failed.

Gandhi never failed to emphasise the need for his ideals which sometimes even seem to blur the distinction between the ideal and the actual.

He talked of independent India adopting,-with qualifications-the Satyagraha technique against aggression if India could acquire enough nonviolence. He knew very well that the people of India did not have nonviolence of his standard even to expel the British government: why then did he continue to talk of repelling armed aggression nonviolently?

For Gandhi, nonviolence was not merely a weapon to achieve self-government: for once independence was achieved, a constant effort was to be made to reach the ideal when it would, of course, be possible to defend the country non-violently. Such an ideal, it is true, was not to be realised immediately after the British government withdrew, but was to be striven for.

To conclude: Gandhi's philosophy lays down moral ideals for individuals and groups to strive for-their value consists in pointing out the direction, not in their realisation. They cannot be enforced from above but depend upon their voluntary acceptance. Unavoidable use of force he considers to be a necessary evil-but an evil all the same. The extent to which these ideals can be practised depends on the ethical capacity of individuals or groups. Accordingly, the actual practice of these ideals cannot be uniform. As a social and political reformer, Gandhi spoke from different levels at different times. But three levels mainly dominate his writings: first, that of the perfect ideal (unrealisable); second, that of his own personal point of view (admitting himself to be far from perfect, yet sufficiently advanced to practise his ideals); third, that of the point of view of the Indian masses. Yet what is implied throughout is this: that even though the ideal may be impossible of attainment, the very act of pursuing it generates the goodwill essential for the well-being of the corporate life.

THE POWER OF NONVIOLENCE

One of the first people to mention nonviolence in a broad social context was the Buddha (Siddhartha Gautama, circa 563-483 B.C.E.). He spoke at length about nonviolence, but only some centuries later did the idea percolate into Indian civilization. Nonviolence is the English word used by Gandhi and others for *Ahimsa*, the Sanskrit antonym of *himsa*, which means "hurt" or "harm." The idea of nonviolence is simple: not to hurt or harm. Nonviolence implicitly includes the "golden rule" which says that we should not treat others as we would not wish to be treated.

It is clear even from the word's etymology that a civilization that is not based on nonviolence will *ipso facto* generate violence — hence, pain, suffering, etc. This is why it is morally imperative that we collectively strive to reconstruct society along nonviolent principles. This chapter introduces the reader to the power and use of nonviolence, according to Gandhi and to the Bahá'ís.

MY MAHATMASHIP

No Mahatma

I do not feel like being one [a Mahatma]. But I do know that I am among the humblest of God's creatures. (YI, 27-10-1921, p.342) Often the title has deeply pained me; and there is not a moment I can recall when it may be said to have tickled me. (A, p. xiv)

My Mahatma ship is worthless. It is due to my outward activities, due to my politics which is the least part of me and is, therefore, evanescent. What is of abiding worth is my insistence on truth, non-violence and brahmacharya which is the real part of me. That part of me, however small, is not to be despised. It is my all. I prize even the failures and disillusionment's which are but steps towards success. (YI, 25-12-1926, pp78-79) The world knows so little of how much my so-called greatness depends upon the incessant toil and drudgery of silent, devoted, able and pure workers, men as well as women. (YI, 26-4-1928, p130)

Truth to me is infinitely dearer than the 'mahatmaship', which is purely a burden. It is my knowledge of my limitations and my nothingness which has so far saved me from the oppressiveness of the 'mahatmaship'. (YI, 1-11-1928, p361)

Sick of Adoration

I have become literally sick of the adoration of the unthinking multitude. I would feel certain of my ground if I was spat upon by them. Then there would be no need for confession of Himalayan and other miscalculations, no retracing, no re-arranging. (YI, 2-3-1922, p135)

In the majority of cases, addresses presented to me contain adjectives which I am ill able to carry. Their use can do good neither to the writers nor to me. They unnecessary humiliate me, for I have to confess that I do not deserve them. When they are deserved, their use is superfluous. It cannot add to the strength of the qualities possessed by me. They may, if I am not on my guard, easily turn my head. The good that a man does is more often than not better left unsaid. Imitation is the sincerest flattery. (YI, 21-5-1925, p176)

The Mahatma I must leave to his fate. Though a non-co-operator, I shall gladly subscribe to a Bill to make it criminal for anybody to call me Mahatma and to touch my feet. Where I can impose the law myself, *i.e.*, at the Ashram, the practice is criminal. (YI, 17-3-1927, p86)

True Honour

The highest honour that my friends can do me is to enforce in their own lives the programme that I stand for or to resist me to their utmost if they do not believe in it. (YI, 12-6-1924, p197)

It will be waste of good money to spend... on erecting a clay or metallic statue of the figure of a man who is himself made of clay and is more fragile than a bangle which can keep by preservation for a thousand years, whereas the human body disintegrates daily and undergoes final disintegration after the usual span of life. I have learnt from my Muslim friends, among whom I have passed the best part of my life, my dislike of statues and photographs of my figure....

Let these lines serve as a warning to those who want to honour me by erecting statues and having portraits of my figure, that I heartily dislike these exhibitions. I shall deem it ample honour if those who believe in me will be good enough to promote the activities I stand for. (H, 11-12-1939, p1)

No 'Avatar'

I hold it to be a blasphemy to represent me as Shri Krishna. I claim to be a humble worker and no more among many in a great cause, which can only be injured rather than advanced by glorification of its leaders. A cause has the best chance of success when it is examined and followed on its own merits. Measures must always, in a progressive society, be held superior to men, who are after all imperfect instruments, working for their fulfillment. (YI, 13-7-1921, p224)

The only virtue I want to claim is Truth and Non-violence. I lay no claim to superhuman powers. I want none. I wear the same corruptible flesh that the weakest of my fellow-beings wears, and am, therefore, as liable to err as any. My services have many limitations, but God has up to now blessed them in spite of the imperfections. (YI, 16-2-1922, p102)

I lay claim to nothing exclusively divine in me. I do not claim prophetship. I am but a humble seeker after Truth and bent upon finding It. I count no sacrifice too great for the sake of seeing God face to face. The whole of my activity, whether it may be called social, political, humanitarian or ethical, is directed to that end. And as I know that God is found more often in the lowliest of His creatures than in the high and mighty, I am struggling to reach the status of these. I cannot do so without their service. Hence my passion for the service of the suppressed classes. And as I cannot render this service without entering politics, I find myself in them. Thus I am no master. I am but a struggling, erring, humble servant of India and there through of humanity. (H, 11-9-1924, pp298)

It is curious how we delude ourselves. We fancy that one can make the perishable body impregnable and we think it impossible to evoke the hidden powers of the soul. Well, I am engaged in trying to show, if I have any of these powers, that I am as frail a mortal as any of us and that I never had anything extraordinary about me nor have any now. (YI, 6-5-1926, p164)

I do not consider myself worthy to be mentioned in the same breath with the race of prophets. I am a humble seeker after truth. I am impatient to realize myself, to attain moksha in this very existence. My national service is part of my training for freeing my soul from the bondage of flesh. Thus considered, my service may be regarded as purely selfish. I have no desire for the perishable kingdom of earth. I am striving for the Kingdom of Heaven, which is moksha. (YI, 3-4-1924, p114) I claim to be no more than an average man with less than average ability. Nor can I claim any special merit for such non-violence or continence as I have been able to reach with laborious research. I have not the shadow of a doubt that any man or woman can achieve what I have, if he or she would make the same effort and cultivate the same hope and faith. (H, 3-10-1936, p269) Some of my correspondents seem to think that I can work wonders. Let me say as a devotee of truth that I have no such gift... All the power I may have comes from God. But He does not work directly. He works through His numberless agencies. (H, 8-10-1938, p285)

AWARENESS OF LIMITATIONS

I consider myself to be a sagacious worker and my sagacity means no more and no less than a fine perception of my limitations. I hope I never travel beyond my limits. Certainly, I have never done so consciously. (YI, 23-6-1920, p3). I am conscious of my own limitations. That consciousness is my only strength. Whatever I might have been able to do in my life has proceeded more than anything else out of the realization of my own limitations. (YI, 13-11-1924, p378)

If I was what I want to be, the fast would not have been necessary. I would not then need to argue with anyone. My word would go straight home. Indeed, I would not even need to utter the word. The mere will on my part would suffice to produce the required effect. But I am painfully aware of my limitations. (H, 15-4-1939, p86)

I shall continue to confess blunders each time the people commit them. The only tyrant I accept in this world is the 'still small voice' within. And even though I have to face the prospect of a minority of one, I humbly believe I have the courage to be in such a hopeless minority. (YI, 2-3-1922, p135)

I claim to be a fairly accurate student of human nature and vivisector of my own failings. I have discovered that man is superior to the system he propounds. (MGI, p241) I hope there is no pride in me. I feel I recognize fully my weakness. But my faith in God and His strength and love is unshakable. I am like clay in the Potter's hand. (YI, 26-1-1922, p49)

I have no desire for prestige anywhere. It is furniture required in courts of Kings. I am a servant of Mussalmans, Christians, Parsis and Jews as I am of Hindus. And a servant is in need of love, not prestige. That is assured to me so long as I remain a faithful servant. (YI, 26-3-1925, p112)

READINESS FOR MARTYRDOM

There are certain things which you cannot escape all at once, even whilst you are avoiding them. This earthly case in which I am locked up is the bane of my life, but I am obliged to put up with it and even indulge it. (YI, 27-10-1921, p342)

I implicitly believe in the truth of the saying that not a blade of grass moves but by His will. He will save it [my life] if He needs it for further service in this body. None can save it against His will. (EF, p114)

Do not seek to protect me. The Most High is always there to protect us all. You may be sure that when my time is up, no one, not even the most renowned in the world, can stand between Him and me. (YI, 2-4-1931, p64-55)

I must be true to my Maker, and the moment I feel that life is insupportable for me, I hope not to be found wanting. What better reparation can I do than willing surrender of the body that has ceased to evoke response and may be a hindrance to the discovery of the true way? (ibid, p60)

I am not aching for martyrdom, but if it comes in my way in the prosecution of what I consider to be the supreme duty in defense of the faith I hold... I shall have earned it. (H, 29-6-1934, p156)

Whilst I prize the unbounded affection of the people, let them realize that my life is not worth keeping if anxiety to save it deflects the attention of the nation from the main purpose. (H, 11-3-1939, p44)

Assaults have been made on my life in the past, but God has spared me till now, and the assailants have repented for their action. But if someone were to shoot me in the belief that he was getting rid of a rascal, he would kill not the real Gandhi, but the one that appeared to him a rascal. (BC, 9-8-1942)

God alone is my protector. How can puny man, who is not sure even of his own tomorrow, presume to protect another? I am content to be under God's care. He may protect or destroy. I know He sometimes even destroys to protect. (H, 9-6-1946, p170)

I do not want to die... of a creeping paralysis of my faculties-a defeated man. An assassin's bullet may put an end to my life. I would welcome it. But

I would love, above all, to fade out doing my duty with my last breath. (MGMLP, I, p562)

I am not afraid to die in my mission, if that is to be my fate. (H, 27-4-1947, p127)

Avoidance of Anger

I have learnt through bitter experience the one supreme lesson to conserve my anger, and as heat conserved is transmuted into energy, even so our anger controlled can be transmuted into a power which can move the world. (YI, 15-9-1920, p6) I spare neither friend nor foe when it is a question of departing from the code of honour. (YI, 2-3-1922, p140)

It is not that I do not get angry. I do not give vent to anger. I cultivate the quality of patience as angerlessness, and, generally speaking, I succeed. But I only control my anger when it comes. How I find it possible to control it would be a useless question, for it is a habit that everyone must cultivate and must succeed in forming by constant practice. (H, 11-5-1935, p98)

If I had no sense of humour, I should long ago have committed suicide. (YI, 18-8-1921, p238)

I am an irrepressible optimist, because I believe in myself. That sounds very arrogant, doesn't it? But I say it from the depths of my humility. I believe in the supreme power of God. I believe in Truth and, therefore, I have no doubt in the future of this country or the future of humanity.

I am an optimist because I expect many things from myself. I have not got them, I know, as I am not yet a perfect being. If I was one, I should not even need to reason with you. When I am a perfect being, I have simply to say the word and the nation will listen. I want to attain that perfection by service. (YI, 13-8-1925, pp.279-80)

My philosophy, if I can be said to have any, excludes the possibility of harm to one's cause by outside agencies. The harm comes deservedly and only when the cause itself is bad or, being good, its champions are untrue, faint-hearted or unclean. (H, 25-7-1936, p185)

I Know the Path

I know the path. It is straight and narrow. It is like the edge of a sword. I rejoice to walk on it. I weep when I slip. God's word is: 'He who strives never perishes.' I have implicit faith in that promise. Though, therefore, from my weakness I fail a thousand times, I will not lose faith, but hope that I shall see the Light when the flesh has been brought under perfect subjection, as some day it must. (YI, 17-6-1926, p215)

My soul refuses to be satisfied so long as it is a helpless witness of a single wrong or a single misery. But it is not possible for me, a weak, frail, miserable being, to mend every wrong or to hold myself free of blame for all the wrong I see.

The spirit in me pulls one way, the flesh in me pulls in the opposite direction. There is freedom from the action of these two forces, but that freedom is attainable only by slow and painful stages.

I cannot attain freedom by a mechanical refusal to act, but only by intelligent action in a detached manner. This struggle resolves itself into an incessant crucifixion of the flesh so that the spirit may become entirely free. (YI, 17-11-1921, p368)

SEARCH FOR TRUTH

I am but a seeker after Truth. I claim to have found a way to it. I claim to be making a ceaseless effort to find it. But I admit that I have not yet found it. To find Truth completely is to realize oneself and one's destiny, *i.e.*, to become perfect. I am painfully conscious of my imperfections, and therein lies all the strength I posses, because it is a rare thing for a man to know his own limitations. If I was a perfect man, I own I should not feel the miseries of neighbours as I do. As a perfect man I should take note of them, prescribe a remedy, and compel adoption by the force of unchallengeable Truth in me. But as yet I only see as through a glass darkly and, therefore, have to carry conviction by slow and laborious processes, and then, too, not always with success. That being so, I would be less than human if, with all my knowledge of avoidable misery pervading the land and of the sight of mere skeletons under the very shadow of the Lord of the Universe, I did not feel with and for all the suffering but dumb millions of India. (ibid, p377)

Trust in God

I am in the world feeling my way to light 'amid the encircling gloom'. I often err and miscalculate... My trust is solely in God. And I trust men only because I trust God. If I had no God to rely upon, I should be like Timon, a hater of my species. (YI, 4-12-1924, p398) I will not be a traitor to God to please the whole world. (H, 18-2-1933, p4)

Whatever striking things I have done in life, I have not done prompted by reason but prompted by instinct, I would say, God. (H, 14-5-1938, p110)

I am a man of faith. My reliance is solely on God. One step is enough for me. The next step He will make clear to me when the time for it comes. (H, 20-10-1940, p330)

No Secrecy

I have no secret methods. I know no diplomacy save that of truth. I have no weapon but non-violence. I may be unconsciously led astray for a while, but not for all time. (YI, 11-12-1924, p406) My life has been an open book. I have no secrets and I encourage no secrets. (YI, 19-3-1931, p43)

I am but a poor struggling soul yearning to be wholly good-wholly truthful and wholly non-violent in thought, word and deed, but ever failing to reach the ideal which I know to be true. I admit it is a painful climb, but the pain of it is a positive pleasure for me. Each step upward makes me feel stronger and fit for the next. (YI, 9-4-1924, p126) When I think of my littleness and my limitations on the one hand and of the expectations raised about me on the other, I become dazed for the moment, but I come to myself as soon as I realize that these expectations are a tribute not to me, a curious mixture of Jekyll and Hyde, but to the incarnation, however imperfect but comparatively great in me, of the two priceless qualities of truth and non-violence. I must, therefore, not shirk the responsibility of giving what aid I can to fellow-seekers after truth from the West. (YI, 3-10-1925, p344)

Guidance

I claim to have no infallible guidance or inspiration. So far as my experience goes, the claim to infallibility on the part of a human being would be untenable, seeing that inspiration too can come only to one who is free from the action of opposites, and it will be difficult to judge on a given occasion whether the claim to freedom from pairs of opposites is justified.

The claim to infallibility would thus always be a most dangerous claim to make. This, however, does not leave us without any guidance whatsoever. The sum-total of the experience of the sages of the world is available to us and would be for all time to come.

Moreover, there are not many fundamental truths, but there is only one fundamental truth which is Truth itself, otherwise known as Non-violence. Finite human being shall never know in its fullness Truth and love which is in itself infinite. But we do know enough for our guidance. We shall err, and sometimes grievously, in our application. But man is a self-governing being, and self-government necessarily includes the power as much to commit errors as to set them right as often as they are made. (YI, 21-4-1927, p128)

I deny being a visionary. I do not accept the claim of saintliness. I am of the earth, earthly... I am prone to as many weakness as you are. But I have seen the world. I have lived in the world with my eyes open. I have gone through the most fiery ordeals that have fallen to the lot of man. I have gone through this discipline. (SW, p531)

Self-sacrifice

I am asking my countrymen in India to follow no other gospel than the gospel of self-sacrifice which precedes every battle. Whether you belong to the school of violence or non-violence, you will still have to go through the fire of sacrifice and of discipline. (ibid, p532)

I want to declare to the world, although I have forfeited the regard of many friends in the West-and I must bow my head low; but even for their friendship or love, I must not suppress the voice of conscience,-the promptings of my inner basic nature today. There is something within me impelling me to cry out my agony. I have known humanity. I have studied something of psychology. Such a man knows exactly what it is. I do not mind how you describe it. That voice within tells me, "You have to stand against the whole world although you may have to stand alone. You have to stare in the face the whole world although the world may look at you with blood-shot eyes. Do not fear. Trust the little voice residing within your heart." It says: "Forsake friends, wife and all; but testify to that for which you have lived and for which you have to die." (MN, pp201-2)

No Defeatism

Defeat cannot dishearten me. It can only chasten me..... I know that God will guide me. Truth is superior to man's wisdom. (YI, 3-7-1924, p218)

I have never lost my optimism. In seemingly darkest hours hope has burnt bright within me. I cannot kill the hope myself. I must say I cannot give an ocular demonstration to justify the hope. But there is no defeat in me. (H, 25-1-1935, p399)

I do not want to foresee the future. I am concerned with taking care of the present. God has given me no control over the moment following...

Trust

It is true that I have often been let down. Many have deceived me and many have been found wanting. But I do not repent of my association with them. For I know how to non-co-operate, as I know how to co-operate. The most practical, the most dignified way of going on in the world is to take people at their word, when you have no positive reason to the contrary. (YI, 26-12-1924, p430)

I believe in trusting. Trust begets trust. Suspicion is fetid and only stinks. He who trusts has never yet lost in the world. (YI, 4-6-1925, p193)

A breach of promise shakes me to my root, especially when I am in any way connected with the author of the breach. And if it cost my life which, after all, at the age of seventy has no insurance value, I should most willingly give it in order to secure due performance of a sacred and solemn promise. (H, 11-3-1939, p46)

To my knowledge, throughout my public and private career, I have never broken a promise. (H, 22-4-1939, p100)

MY LEADERSHIP

They say I claim to understand human nature as no one else does. I believe I am certainly right, but if I do not believe in my rightness and my methods, I would be unfit to be at the helm of affairs. (YI, 1-1-1925, p8)

As for my leadership, if I have it, it has not come for any seeking, it is a fruit of faithful service. A man can as little discard such leadership as he can the colour of his skin. And since I have become an integral part of the nation, it has to keep me with all my faults and shortcomings, of some of which I am painfully conscious and of many others of which candid critics, thanks be to them, never fail to remind me. (YI, 13-2-1930, p52)

It is a bad carpenter who quarrels with his tools. It is a bad general who blames his men for faulty workmanship. I know I am not a bad general. I have wisdom enough to know my limitations. God will give me strength enough to declare my bankruptcy if such is to be my lot. He will perhaps take me away when I am no longer wanted for the work which I have been permitted to do for nearly half a century. But I do entertain the hope that there is yet work for me to do, that the darkness that seems to have enveloped me will disappear, and that, whether with another battle more brilliant than the Dandi March or without, India will come to her own demonstrably through non-violent means. I am praying for the light that will dispel the darkness. Let those who have a living faith in non-violence join me in the prayer. (H, 23-7-1938, p193)

My Work

I am content with the doing of the task in front of me. I do not worry about the why and wherefore of things... Reason helps us to see that we should not dabble in things we cannot fathom. (H, 7-9-1935, p234)

My work will be finished if I succeed in carrying conviction to the human family, that every man or woman, however weak in body, is the guardian of his or her self-respect and liberty. This defense avails, though the whole world may be against the individual resister. (Hst, 6-8-1944)

It will be time enough to pronounce a verdict upon my work after my eyes are closed and this tabernacle is consigned to the flames. (YI, 4-4-1929, p107)

My Mission

I am not a visionary. I claim to be a practical idealist. The religion of non-violence is not meant merely for the rishis and saints. It is meant for the common people as well. Non-violence is the law of our species as violence is the law of the brute. The spirit lies dormant in the brute and he knows no law but that of physical might. The dignity of man requires obedience to a higher law-to the strength of the spirit. (YI, 11-8-1920, p3)

There are more instances than one in my public life when, with the ability to retaliate, I have refrained from doing so and advised friends to do likewise. My life is dedicated to the spread of that doctrine. I read it in the teachings of all the greatest teachers of the world-Zoroaster, Mahavir, Daniel, Jesus, Muhammad, Nanak and a host of others. (YI, 9-2-1922, p85)

Non-violence is the first article of my faith. It is also the last article of my creed. (YI, 23-3-1922, p166)

I am but an humble explorer of the science of non-violence. Its hidden depths sometimes stagger me just as much as they stagger fellow-workers. (YI, 20-11-1924, p382)

GANDHI'S THOUGHT TO RELIGIOUS STUDIES TODAY

In modern universities, the discipline of religious studies seeks to understand religion and religions in all of their richness. Much as geographers analyse elements of physical and cultural landscapes, or historians investigate the relationships among past events, students of religion analyse phenomena that we call "religious," phenomena that Robert Bellah defines as "a set of symbolic forms and actions that relate man to the ultimate conditions of his existence" or to an ultimate reality.

In our study ofreligion, we ask questions that can help us appreciate the structures, histories, origins, goals and logic of religion in general and of the numerous world religions. And to answer such questions, we employ methods drawn from across the intellectual spectrum, including psychological, literary-critical, sociological and linguistic methods. Ultimately, religious studies in the university aims to appreciate the complexity of religion as a human activity, to foster critical thinking skills, and to build a stronger appreciation and toleration of the world's religions and ultimately of other people. It is worth noting, too, that the fundamental approach to religious studies is academic or critical: religious studies has no desire to accept (or to deny) truth claims of religions, but rather to describe and assess them as human endeavours, without appeal to faith or religious authority.

To a point, this critical approach to the study of religion is satisfying. But only to a point. As I reflect on my stance as both a student of religion and a participant in religion, in particular as an admirer of the religious principles of Gandhi, I wonder whether there is more room in religious studies to accommodate and acknowledge the value of religion to our lives. In the university, I wear an "observer's hat" and teach about religion without investment in my own or others' religious well being. As a human who thinks about how we can align ourselves to ultimate reality, though, I wear a "participant's hat": I strongly believe, as many of us do, in principles espoused by Gandhi, including a commitment to nonviolence and to the fundamental unity of life. While I hope that I would remain objective and never teach students that one religious stance is normative or "better" than another, I also believe that many of Gandhi's principles are noble, are practically universal, and are worth sharing. And there are precedents for this stance: certain of my own professors have taught me, explicitly and through their personal example, that we can do more to embrace and respect others, and to raise consciousness of Gandhian principles. Are there, then, ways in which Gandhi's thought can find a place within the academic teaching of religion?

I submit that Gandhi's thought can inform today's teaching about religion. My insight is not novel: work by Glyn Richards among others has demonstrated the timeliness of Gandhian thought to religious studies.

I believe that we can further apply Gandhian thought in ways that will enrich our study of religion yet also maintain its academic objectivity. In what follows, I shall outline some Gandhian principles and then suggest that certain of these principles are consonant with and so can enhance, the teaching of religion in universities.

Gandhi on Post-Secondary Education

Perhaps the most direct means to discover Gandhi's value for teaching religion is to examine his thinking on education. From at least the 1920s, Gandhi wrote and lectured on the kind of education that India required to function well as a sovereign state. For Gandhi, the basic purposes of all education are social and religious.

On the one hand, education has a social purpose: to equip people to "serve their country." Put more precisely, the purpose of education is to inculcate in students the virtues of swaraj and sarvodaya.

The term swaraj or "self-rule" denotes intellectual and manual skills that foster autonomy and build in their turn a just and equitable society for all. Critically for Gandhi, education must impart such swaraj.

Education must train individuals and families in skills to help them support themselves and their families (for instance, trade skills that produce good income, as well as skills in maintaining one's own clothing, healthy accommodation and food). Similarly, education must train citizens about their nation's history and culture, using national languages, so that citizens will appreciate and in turn keep the interests and well being of the nation, the people of the nation, front and centre.

Sarvodaya is a second virtue that Gandhi believed needed the support of education. Often translated as the "uplift of all," sarvodaya denotes the amelioration of the lives of as many people as possible. Significantly, Gandhi held that education had to equip citizens for sarvodaya; education needed both to teach moral values of service and compassion, and to emphasize practical skills that can express such compassion, whether in natural science, medicine, engineering, or philosophy.

For Gandhi, the centre of gravity in post-secondary education is to foster social well-being; it places no premium on individual achievement in the form of income or professional status.

Underlying and infusing these social purposes, on the other hand, Gandhian education has at its core a religious purpose: to teach students to value truth, the essence of which is ultimate reality (or God) as well as one's real self (or Atman).

Manifestations of truth in our world include the moral principles of nonviolence and of love that recognizes others as fundamentally linked to oneself; indeed, truth manifests itself in the social values of swaraj and sarvodaya. Education should inculcate precisely these values.

Thus far, we have described Gandhi's views on the purposes of education. What role did teaching specifically about religion play in achieving these purposes? Gandhi believed that in schools and universities, students ought to become aware of the world's religions and study them in a manner that was, as Richards puts it, empathetic. By learning about other religions, and also by taking one's learning back to nurture a better appreciation of one's own religious tradition, the student could gain a better and fuller grasp of truth.

Gandhi's Relevance to Religious Studies

I believe that Gandhian philosophy can "fit" within and indeed support the contemporary teaching about religion in publicly funded, secular universities. Already Richards has observed that Gandhi anticipates modern teaching about religion, for instance in his concern for examining world religions and for a tolerant and equitable method of study. Richards is entirely correct; I would add only that Gandhi can further inform the study of religion in ways that do not compromise the discipline—indeed, in ways that are consonant with the aims of a university as a whole.

To their credit, certain university departments of religious studies already teach in ways that reflect, consciously or unconsciously, the influence of Gandhi. Be that as it may, I propose that four tenets of Gandhian thought can fit comfortably into any religious studies program: sarvodaya, nonviolence, inter-religious dialogue and the importance of seeking after truth.

First, the teaching of religion can comfortably afford to encourage sarvodaya. For instance, in a department's required religious studies course, such as a course in method and theory, students could write about ways in which their study might help them pursue meaningful social service after graduation. Reflection on the social value of one's discipline certainly does not compromise its academic integrity; it simply extends our studies beyond academic training into contributions to others' welfare. And no university would deny (I hope!) that we apply our academic training to the welfare of society; indeed, universities aim to promote such welfare through disciplines as diverse as medicine, music and physics.

Some universities offer courses that concern religion and violence, but there does not exist to my knowledge a course specifically about religion and nonviolence.

Such a course would be highly valuable in raising awareness of Gandhi and others' teachings on the benefits of nonviolence. This kind of course needs not compel students to take a stance on the appropriateness of violence and nonviolence (even though it would seem hard to argue against nonviolence as a universal value). Teaching about nonviolence in world religions would encourage students to reflect on the values of nonviolence for themselves.

A third application of Gandhi's thought to the teaching of religion is in inter-religious dialogue. Gandhi believed in what scholars call a dialogical method of study, whereby students could reflect on similarities between one's own traditions and other traditions, and so come to better appreciate truth.

University courses in inter-religious dialogue could serve this very aim. In Canada, some universities already offer courses in dialogue among religions. Established though these courses may be, we can afford to offer more such courses.

Finally, the teaching of religion can and should accommodate Gandhi's cardinal principle that it is our obligation to pursue understanding of truth — to "experiment" and adapt our lives accordingly with truth. Gandhi described truth in terms that could appeal to adherents of any religion.

I believe that it is important in teaching about religion to encourage students to use their knowledge in their own quest for truth. Often, the practice of religious studies — and here I include my own practice — deconstructs religious phenomena in ways that are necessary but which forget to remind us that, outside the classroom, religion and its quest for truth is highly noble and necessary. And once again, this quest for truth need not be phrased in a "religious" manner; after all, universities have for centuries prided themselves on the effort to discover truth, however one might conceive it; the motto of the university that I attended as an undergraduate is that "truth conquers all."

CORPORATE SANITATION

Civil Conscience

Corporate cleanliness can only be ensured if there is a corporate conscience and a corporate insistence on cleanliness in public places. Untouchability has a great deal to answer for the insanitation of our streets and our latrines, whether private or public.

In its inception, untouchability was a rule of sanitation, and still is in all parts of the world outside India. That is to say, an unclean person or thing is untouchable, but immediately his or its uncleanliness is shed, he or it is no linger untouchable.

Therefore, a person who is to attend to scavenging, whether it is a paid BHANGI or an unpaid mother, they are unclean until they have washed themselves clean of their unclean work. (H, 11-2-1933, p.8)

Municipalities

No municipality can cope with insanitation and congestion by the simple process of taxation and paid services. This vital reform is possible only by wholesale and voluntary cooperation of the people, both rich and poor. (YI, 26-11-1925, p. 416) If I were a taxpayer within the jurisdiction of a local board or a municipality, I would refuse to pay a single pie by way of additional taxation and advise others to do likewise unless the money we pay is returned fourfold.

Those who enter local boards and municipalities as representatives go there not to seek honour or to indulge in mutual rivalries, but to render a service of love and that does not depend upon money.

Ours is a pauper country. If our municipal councilors are imbued with a real spirit of service, they will convert themselves into unpaid sweepers, BHANGIS and road makers, and take pride in doing so. They will invite their fellow-councilors, who may not have come on the Congress ticket, to join them and if they have faith in themselves and their mission, their example will not fail to evoke response.

This means that a municipal councilor has to be whole-timer. He should have no axe of his own to grind.

The next step would be to map out the entire adult population within the jurisdiction of the municipality or the local board. All should be asked to make their contribution to municipal activities. A regular register should be maintained. Those who are too poor to make any money contribution but are able-bodied and physically fit can be asked to give their free labour. (H, 18-2-1939, p. 22)

Offences against Nature

Anyone who fouls the air by spitting about carelessly, throwing refuse and rubbish, or otherwise dirtying the ground, sins against man and nature. Man's body is the temple of God. Anyone who fouls the air that is to enter that temple desecrates it. He takes the name of RAMA in vain. (H, 7-4-1946, p. 69)

A sense of national or social sanitation is not a virtue among us. We may take a kind of a bath, but we do not mind dirtying the well or the tank or the river by whose side or in which we perform ablution. I regard this defect as a great vice which is responsible for the disgraceful state of our villages and the sacred banks of the sacred rivers and for the diseases that spring that spring from insanitation. (CP, p. 15)

Communal Harmony

If not during my life-time, if know that after my death both Hindus and Mussalmans will bear witness that I had never ceased to yearn after communal peace. (YI, 11-5-1921, p. 148)

My longing is to be able to cement the two [Hindus and Muslims] with my blood, if necessary. (YI, 25-9-1924, p. 314)

I have the same love for the Mussalman as for the Hindu. My heart feels for the Mussalman as much as for the Hindu. If I could tear it open, you would discover there are no compartments in it, one reserved for the Hindu, another for the Mussalman and so on. (YI, 13-8-1921, p. 215)

Meaning of Unity

Hindu-Muslim unity has been my passion from early youth. I count some of the noblest of Muslims as my friends. I have a devout daughter of Islam as more than daughter to me. She lives for that unity and would cheerfully die for it. I had the son of the late Muezzin of the Jama Masjid of Bombay as a staunch inmate of the Ashram. (H, 30-4-1938, p. 99)

Hindu-Muslim unity consists in our having a common purpose, a common goal and common sorrows. It is best promoted by co-operating to reach the common goal by sharing of one another's sorrows and by mutual toleration. (YI, 25-2-1920, p. 3)

Hindu-Muslim unity means not unity only between Hindus and Mussalmans, but between all those who believe India to be their home, no matter to what faith they belong. (YI, 11-5-1921, p. 148)

Love is the basis of our friendship as it is of religion. I seek to gain Mussalman friendship by right of love. And if love persists even on the part of one community, unity will become a settled fact in our national life. (YI, 20-10-1921, p. 333)

One Family: The golden way is to be friends with the world and to regard the whole human family like members of one family. He who distinguishes between one's family and another's mis-educates the members of his own and opens the way for discord and irreligion. (H, 17-11-1946, p. 402)

Communal Riots

The lawlessness [of communalism] is a monster with many faces. It hurts all in the end, including those who are primarily responsible for it. (H, 15-9-1940, p.284)

If one side ceases to retaliate, the riots will not go on. (H, 14-7-1946, p. 219)

To retaliate against the relatives of the co-religionists of the wrongdoer is a cowardly act. (H, 17-11-1946, p.408)

There must arise in Islam as well as Hinduism men who, being comparatively pure in character, would work among such men (GOONDAS). (YI, 29-8-1924, p. 181)

We would convert and control the hooligan elements. (H, 7-4-1946, p. 74) There is no room for GOONDAISM in any religion worth the name, be it Islam, Hinduism or any other. (H, 5-1-1947, p. 478)

Respect for Religions

Each must respect the other's religion must refrain from even secretly thinking ill of the other. (YI, 7-5-1919)

No propaganda can be allowed which reviles other religions. (YI, 29-5-1924, p.180)

To revile one another's religion, to make reckless statements, to utter untruth, to break the heads of innocent men, to desecrate temples or mosques is a denial of God. (YI, 25-9-1924, p. 313)

The key to the solution of the [communal] tangle lies in every one following the best in this own religion and entertaining equal regard for the other religions and their followers. (H, 4-1-1948, p. 497)

In trying to explore the hidden treasures of ancient culture, I have come upon this inestimable boon that all that is permanent in ancient Hindu culture is also to be found in the teaching of Jesus, the Buddha, Mohamed and Zoroaster. (WGC, p. 131)

Hinduism has absorbed the best of all the faiths of the world and in that sense is not an exclusive religion. Hence it can have no quarrel with Islam or its followers. (H, 28-9-1947, p. 349)

The sword is no emblem of Islam. But Islam was born in an environment where the sword was, and still remains, the supreme law... The sword is yet too much in evidence among the Mussalmans. It must be sheathed if Islam is to be what it means-peace. (YI, 30-12-1926, p. 458)

Islam distinctive contribution..... is its unadulterated belief in the oneness of God and a practical application of the truth of the brotherhood of man for those who are nominally within its fold. (YI, 21-3-1929, p. 95)

Islam means peace. The peace cannot be confined to the Muslims. It must mean peace for the whole world. (H, 22-8-1940, p. 294)

Proselytization: The days of forcible conversion are gone. (YI, 30-12-1926, p. 148)

It is the transference of allegiance from one fold to another and the mutual denying of rival faiths which gives rise to mutual hatred. (YI, 6-1-1927, p. 1)

There is nothing in the Quran to warrant the use of force for conversion. (YI, 29-9-1921, p. 307). Just as we do not break one another's heads in respect of civil matters, so may we not do even in respect of religious matters. (YI, 29-5-1924, p. 176)

I am convinced that the masses do not want to fight, if the leaders do not. If therefore the leaders agree that mutual rows should be, as in all advanced countries, erased out of our public life as being barbarous and irreligious, I have no doubt that the masses will quietly follow them. (ibid, p.182)

Arbitration: It [arbitration] is an age-long method and a civilized method. (H, 24-5-1942, p. 166)

Mutual toleration is a necessity for all time and for all races. (YI, 25-2-1920, p. 3)

Honest public opinion should make it impossible for grieved parties to take the law into their own hands and every case [of dispute] must be referred to private arbitration or to law courts.... (YI, 5-6-1924, p. 188)

Music before Mosques: Where the Hindus have long been deliberately observing the custom to stop music before mosques, they must not break it. But where they have been playing music without interference, the practice should continue. Where trouble is apprehended and facts are disputed both communities ought to refer the matter to arbitration. (YI, 18-9-1924, p. 312)

The Cow: The Hindu's religion consists in saving the cow, but it can never be his religion to save the cow by a resort to force towards a non-Hindu. (ibid, p. 311)

It would be unwise... and improper for a Hindu majority to coerce by legislation a Mussalman minority into submission to statutory prohibition of cow slaughter. (YI, 29-1-1925, p. 38)

Scripts: My advice about the adoption of the scripts (Hindi and Urdu) by Hindus and Muslims is based on the unitary method. (H, 1-2-1942, p. 27)

The Services: It will be fatal to good government if we introduce there [in Government departments] the communal spirit. (YI, 29-5-1924, p. 182)

Minorities are entitled to the fullest justice. Efficiency and merit alone should count... (H, 27-7-1947, p. 50)

Toleration: The unity we desire will last only if we cultivate an yielding and charitable disposition towards one another. (YI, 11-5-1921, p. 148)

Toleration is the only thing that will enable persons belonging to different religions to live as good neighbours and friends. (H, 3-11-1946, p. 383)

Secularism: Nationalism is greater than sectarianism. And in that sense, we are Indians first and Hindus, Mussalmans, Parsis and Christians after. (YI, 26-1-1922, p.62)

The state is bound to be wholly secular... All subjects will thus be equal in the eye of the law. But every single individual will be free to pursue a religion without let or hindrance so long as it does not transgress the common law. (H, 31-8-1947, p. 297)

Equal Citizenship: The minorities must be made to realize that they are as much valued citizens of the State they live in as the majority to look to for justice. (H, 7-9-1947, p. 310)

If the Hindu majority treasure their religion and duty, they will be just at all cost. They will overlook the limitations or mistakes of the minority who have no one but the majority to look to for justice. (H, 31-8-1947, p. 298)

You should treat the Muslims as equal citizens. Equality of treatment demands respect for the Urdu script. (H, 26-10-1947, p.383)

No oppression should be felt by the minorities, however small they may be. There is need for the gentlest handling of all such questions [as language, script] (ibid, p. 387)

My one aim with respect to the Hindu-Muslim question is that the solution will be complete only when the minority, whether in the Indian Union or Pakistan, feels perfectly safe, even if they are in the minority of one. (H, 14-9-1947, p. 323)

Hindu and Sikh women should go to the Muslim sisters and establish friendship with them. They should invite them on ceremonial occasions and be invited. Muslim girls and boy should be attracted to common schools, not communal. They should mix in sports. (H, 25-1-1940, p. 536)

SUPERIOR TO VIOLENCE

According to Darwinian theories of evolution, it usually makes more sense to kill than to be killed, because it is not possible for a dead individual to procreate and to have offspring. This is certainly true of our animal aspect, but humans are more than animals. We are thinking, intelligent beings, capable of creating not only biological offspring but also poetry, music, ideas, theories, social movements, etc. The act of creation, after all, is not limited to the act of procreation! Hence, it is sometimes possible that a person can create more through physical death than through staying alive. Human history celebrates the lives of those who sacrificed their lives for a greater cause. Gandhi and Martin Luther King Jr. are recent examples of people who, though dead, continue to exert an influence as though still alive. Their lives attest to the truth that it can sometimes be better to be killed than to kill. More generally, it can be better to suffer harm than to hurt others. This truth captures the essential idea underlying the principle of nonviolence.

Gandhi is famous for his emphasis on nonviolence. He even felt that violent methods are unbecoming of intelligent human beings:

Non-violence is the law of our species as violence is the law of the brute.

There is nothing very wonderful in killing and being killed in the process. But the man who offers his neck to the enemy for execution, but refuses to bend to his will, shows courage of a far higher type.

The concept of nonviolence is also emphasized in the Bahá'í Faith and can be traced to its earliest days. Some years after the 1850 public execution of the Báb by firing-squad,** Bahá'u'lláh emerged as the leader of the new Faith and began to teach the surviving believers that "if ye be slain, it is better for you than to slay." By 1863, when the Bahá'í Faith was founded by Bahá'u'lláh, the Bábí believers — now called Bahá'ís — had become distinctly nonviolent in their ethics as well as in their methods. Shoghi Effendi concisely sums up this change in direction in the following sentence taken from *God Passes By*, his masterpiece history of the first Bahá'í century:

The dissociation of the Bábí Faith from every form of political activity and from all secret associations and factions; *the emphasis placed on the principle of non-violence;*** the necessity of strict obedience to established authority; the ban imposed on all forms of sedition, on back-biting, retaliation, and dispute; the stress laid on godliness, kindliness, humility and piety, on honesty and truthfulness, chastity and fidelity, on justice, toleration, sociability, amity and concord, on the acquisition of arts and sciences, on self-sacrifice and detachment, on patience, steadfastness and resignation to the will of God — all these constitute the salient features of a code of ethical conduct to which the books, treatises and epistles, revealed during those years, by the indefatigable pen of Bahá'u'lláh, unmistakably bear witness.

Violence, oppression, tyranny are all categorically and repeatedly condemned in the Bahá'í writings. 'Abdu'l-Bahá explains that while violent methods might have been tolerable in earlier stages of human evolution, now we are more mature and have no excuse to resort to violence:

O ye lovers of God! In this, the cycle of Almighty God, violence and force, constraint and oppression, are one and all condemned.

There are many other instances where nonviolence is emphasized in the Bahá'í Faith. For example, in the opening page of the 1976 edition of Esslemont's book, *Bahá'u'lláh and the New Era,* we read that the Bahá'í Faith takes "firm worldly positions in vital areas affecting modern man," including "Nonviolent Means."

A COHESIVE FORCE

It may be difficult for many people to accept that nonviolence is really superior to violence, for old ways of thinking die hard. One of the reasons why the power of nonviolence and compassion has been historically underestimated is that they are creative, cohesive forces — difficult to notice. In contrast, violence and hatred are destructive and repulsive forces, hence trivial to understand — every murderer can be considered an expert. It is quite instructive, if not amazing, to compare the views of 'Abdu'l-Bahá and of Gandhi on this subject. Gandhi writes:

Scientists tell us that, without the presence of the cohesive force amongst the atoms that comprise this globe of ours, it would crumble to pieces and we would cease to exist; and even as there is cohesive force in blind matter, so must there be in all things animate, and the name for that cohesive force among animate beings is Love. We notice it between father and son, between brother and sister, friend and friend. But we have to learn to use that force among all that lives, and in the use of it consists our knowledge of God. Where there is love there is life; hatred leads to destruction.

The fact that mankind persists shows that the cohesive force is greater than the disruptive force...

The force of love is the same as the force of the soul or truth. We have evidence of its working at every step. The universe would disappear without the existence of that force...

Though there is repulsion in Nature, she *lives* by attraction. Mutual love enables nature to persist. Man does not live by destruction. Self-love compels regard for others. Nations cohere because there is mutual regard among individuals composing them. Some day, we must extend the national law to the universe, even as we have extended the family law to form nations — a larger family.

'Abdu'l-Bahá writes on the same subject: Love is the most great law that ruleth this mighty and heavenly cycle, the unique power that bindeth together the divers elements of this material world, the supreme magnetic force that directeth the movements of the spheres in the celestial realms. Love revealeth with unfailing and limitless power the mysteries latent in the universe. Love is the spirit of life unto the adorned body of mankind, the establisher of true civilization in this mortal world, and the shedder of imperishable glory upon every high-aiming race and nation.

Therefore attraction and composition between the various elements is the means of life, and discord, decomposition and division produce death. Thus the cohesive and attractive forces in all things lead to the appearance of fruitful results and effects, while estrangement and alienation of things lead to disturbance and annihilation.

Through affinity and attraction all living things like plants, animals and men come into existence, while division and discord bring about decomposition and destruction. Consequently, that which is conducive to association and attraction and unity among the sons of men is the means of the life of the world of humanity, and whatever causeth division, repulsion and remoteness leadeth to the death of humankind.

A CREATIVE POWER

Since nonviolence is a creative rather than destructive power, therefore it allows individuals and communities who draw upon it to prosper spiritually relative to those that are ignorant of it. Until now, the power of nonviolence has not been fully appreciated by the majority of humankind. Hence people consider it extraordinary — almost miraculous — that the Bahá'í Faith nonviolently withstood the concerted and violent efforts of the Persian and Ottoman Empires to destroy it, or that Gandhi obtained independence for his native land without armies. It is perhaps a sign of the times that people consider it surprising that nonviolent, creative, energies can overcome the destructive furies of violence.

Gandhi believed that nonviolent methods are inherently more powerful than violence: The fact is that non-violence does not work in the same way as violence. It works in the opposite way. An armed man naturally relies upon his arms. A man who is intentionally unarmed relies upon the Unseen Force called God by poets, but called the Unknown by scientists. But that which is unknown is not necessarily non-existent. God is the Force among all forces known and unknown. Non-violence without reliance upon that Force is poor stuff to be thrown in the dust. Non-violence is an active force of the highest order. It is soul force or the power of Godhead within us. Imperfect man cannot grasp the whole of that Essence — he would not be able to bear its full blaze, but even an infinitesimal fraction of it, when it becomes active within us, can work wonders. The sun in the heavens fills the whole universe with its life-giving warmth. But if one went too near it, it would consume him to ashes. Even so it is with Godhead. We become Godlike to the extent we realize non-violence; but we can never become wholly God.

This idea that what Gandhi calls "soul force" can produce apparently incredible results is a constant theme in the Bahá'í writings. Bahá'u'lláh writes concerning the nonviolent response of the Bahá'ís towards their oppressors: Gracious God! This people need no weapons of destruction, inasmuch as they have girded themselves to reconstruct the world. Their hosts are the hosts of goodly deeds, and their arms the arms of upright conduct, and their commander the fear of God.

Blessed that one that judgeth with fairness. By the righteousness of God! Such hath been the patience, the calm, the resignation of contentment of this people that they have become the exponents of justice, and so great hath been their forbearance, that they have suffered themselves to be killed rather than kill, and this notwithstanding that these whom the world hath wronged have endured tribulations the like of which the history of the world hath never recorded, nor the eyes of any nation witnessed.

What is it that could have induced them to reconcile themselves to these grievous trials, and to refuse to put forth a hand to repel them? What could have caused such resignation and serenity? The true cause is to be found in the ban which the Pen of Glory hath, day and night, chosen to impose, and in Our assumption of the reins of authority, through the power and might of Him Who is the Lord of all mankind.

'Abdu'l-Bahá implies that the use of nonviolent methods is not as difficult as it may appear to be: Be self-sacrificing in the path of God, and wing thy flight unto the heavens of the love of the Abhá Beauty, for any movement animated by love moveth from the periphery to the centre, from space to the Day-Star of the universe.

Perchance thou deemest this to be difficult, but I tell thee that such cannot be the case, for when the motivating and guiding power is the divine force of magnetism it is possible, by its aid, to traverse time and space easily and swiftly.

Esslemont further explains the apparently paradoxical power of nonviolence: The soundness of Bahá'u'lláh's nonresistance policy has already been proved by results. For every believer martyred in Persia, the Bahá'í faith has received a hundred new believers into its fold, and the glad and dauntless way in which these martyrs cast the crowns of their lives at the feet of their Lord has furnished to the world the clearest proof that they had found a new life for which death has no terrors, a life of ineffable fullness and joy, compared with which the pleasures of earth are but as dust in the balance, and the most fiendish physical tortures but trifles light as air.

Nonviolent Power Structures

Nonviolence can be artfully employed in the life of the individual, but its greatest effect is to be seen on our collective community lives. Since excessive centralization of political and economic power necessarily involves some degree of violence towards those in the periphery of society, therefore a nonviolent civilization must be based upon decentralized power structures. Gandhi explains:

All society is held together by non-violence, even as the earth is held in her position by gravitation. But when the law of gravitation was discovered, the discovery yielded results of which our ancestors had no knowledge. Even so, when society is deliberately constructed in accordance with the law of non-violence, its structure will be different in material particulars from what it is today.

Centralization as a system is inconsistent with non-violent structure of society.

What I would personally prefer would be not a centralization of power in the hands of the State, but an extention of the sense of trusteeship, as, in my opinion, the violence of private ownership is less injurious than the violence of the State. However, if that is unavoidable, I would support a minimum of state ownership.

Similar ideas occur in the writings of 'Abdu'l-Bahá: It is very evident that in the future there shall be no centralization in the countries of the world, be they constitutional in government, republican or democratic in form. The United States may be held up as the example of future government— that is to say, each province will be independent in itself, but there will be federal union protecting the interests of the various independent states. It may not be a republican or a democratic form. To cast aside centralization which promotes despotism is the exigency of the time. This will be productive of international peace.

Nonviolent Administration

In our contemporary civilization, social order is maintained because disobedience of the law leads to punishment: fines, prison terms, even capital punishment for serious crimes. This arrangement is not without its drawbacks, however. So long as people think they will not "get caught" or punished, they may convince themselves that there is nothing to be lost in breaking the law. Have not even many heads of state and of government in various countries attempted to break the law with impunity? Has today's civilization been able to proclaim victory over drug abuse, forced prostitution, smuggling, or environmental crimes? No sooner are new laws enacted than the "criminals" find new loopholes. Indeed, so long as we do not get caught or punished, it pays to commit crimes in our civilization.

Is there not a better method of ensuring social order that is based on the application of nonviolent spiritual principles? Both Gandhi and the Bahá'ís believe that a nonviolent, approach to social order is indeed possible. Gandhi explains: The principles on which a non-violent organization is based are different from and the reverse of what obtains in a violent organization. For instance, in the orthodox army, there is a clear distinction made between an officer and a private.

The latter is subordinate and inferior to the former. In a non-violent army, the general is just the chief servant — first among equals. He claims no privilege over or superiority to the rank and file...

The second difference between a military organization and a peace organization is that in the former the rank and file have no part in the choice of their general and their officers. These are imposed upon them and enjoy unrestricted power over them. In a non-violent army, the general and the officers are elected or are as if elected when their authority is moral and rests solely on the willing obedience of the rank and file.

It may interest the reader to note that both these principles can be found put into practice in the Bahá'í community. All administrative authority is vested in elected consultative institutions at the local, national, and international levels. Individual members of such bodies have no authority and do not enjoy extra powers, but rather typically consider themselves fortunate to have been chosen to serve.

Regarding nonviolent law enforcement, Gandhi writes further:... I have concluded that even in a non-violent State a police force may be necessary... The police of my conception will, however, be of a wholly different pattern from the present-day force. Its ranks will be composed of believers in non-violence. They will be servants, not masters, of the people. The people will instinctively render them every help, and through mutual co-operation they will easily deal with the ever-decreasing disturbances. The police force will have some kind of arms, but they will be rarely used, if at all. In fact the policemen will be reformers. Their police work will be confined primarily to robbers and dacoits. Quarrels between labour and capital and strikes will be few and far between in a non-violent state, because the influence of the non-violent majority will be so great as to command the respect of the principal elements in society. Similarly there will be no room for communal disturbances.

'Abdu'l-Bahá also addressed the subject of law enforcement:... communities must punish the oppressor, the murderer, the malefactor, so as to warn and restrain others from committing like crimes. But the most essential thing is that the people must be educated in such a way that no crimes will be committed; for it is possible to educate the masses so effectively that they will avoid and shrink from perpetrating crimes, so that the crime itself will appear to them as the greatest chastisement, the utmost condemnation and torment.

Therefore, no crimes which require punishment will be committed...... communities are day and night occupied in making penal laws, and in preparing and organizing instruments and means of punishment. They build prisons, make chains and fetters, arrange places of exile and banishment, and different kinds of hardships and tortures, and think by these means to discipline criminals, whereas, in reality, they are causing destruction of morals and perversion of characters.

The community, on the contrary, ought day and night to strive and endeavour with the utmost zeal and effort to accomplish the education of men, to cause them day by day to progress and to increase in science and knowledge, to acquire virtues, to gain good morals and to avoid vices, so that crimes may not occur.

At the present time the contrary prevails; the community is always thinking of enforcing the penal laws, and of preparing means of punishment, instruments of death and chastisement, places for imprisonment and banishment; and they expect crimes to be committed. This has a demoralizing effect.

But if the community would endeavour to educate the masses, day by day knowledge and sciences would increase, the understanding would be broadened, the sensibilities developed, customs would become good, and morals normal; in one word, in all these classes of perfections there would be progress, and there would be fewer crimes. It has been ascertained that among civilized peoples crime is less frequent than among uncivilized — that is to say, among those who have acquired the true civilization, which is divine civilization — the civilization of those who unite all the spiritual and material perfections.

As ignorance is the cause of crimes, the more knowledge and science increases, the more crimes will diminish.

See then how wide is the difference between material civilization and divine. With force and punishments, material civilization seeketh to restrain the people from mischief, from inflicting harm on society and committing crimes. But in a divine civilization, the individual is so conditioned that with no fear of punishment, he shunneth the perpetration of crimes, seeth the crime itself as the severest of torments, and with alacrity and joy, setteth himself to acquiring the virtues of humankind, to furthering human progress, and to spreading light across the world.

NONVIOLENCE

The concept of nonviolence (ahinsa) and nonresistance has a long history in Indian religious thought and has had many revivals in Hindu, Buddhist, Jain, Jewish and Christian contexts.

Gandhi explains his philosophy and way of life in his autobiography The Story of My Experiments with Truth. He was quoted as saying:

"When I despair, I remember that all through history the way of truth and love has always won. There have been tyrants and murderers and for a time they seem invincible, but in the end, they always fall-think of it, always."

"What difference does it make to the dead, the orphans, and the homeless, whether the mad destruction is wrought under the name of totalitarianism or the holy name of liberty and democracy?"

"An eye for an eye makes the whole world blind."

"There are many causes that I am prepared to die for but no causes that I am prepared to kill for."

In applying these principles, Gandhi did not balk from taking them to their most logical extremes. In 1940, when invasion of the British Isles by Nazi Germany looked imminent, Gandhi offered the following advice to the British people (Non-Violence in Peace and War):

"I would like you to lay down the arms you have as being useless for saving you or humanity. You will invite Herr Hitler and Signor Mussolini to take what they want of the countries you call your possessions.... If these gentlemen choose to occupy your homes, you will vacate them. If they do not give you free passage out, you will allow yourselves, man, woman, and child, to be slaughtered, but you will refuse to owe allegiance to them."

However, Gandhi was aware that this level of nonviolence required incredible faith and courage, which he realized not everyone possessed. He therefore advised that everyone need not keep to nonviolence, especially if it was used as a cover for cowardice:

"Gandhi guarded against attracting to his satyagraha movement those who feared to take up arms or felt themselves incapable of resistance. 'I do believe,' he wrote, 'that where there is only a choice between cowardice and violence, I would advise violence.'"

"At every meeting I repeated the warning that unless they felt that in non-violence they had come into possession of a force infinitely superior to the one they had and in the use of which they were adept, they should have nothing to do with non-violence and resume the arms they possessed before. It must never be said of the Khudai Khidmatgars that once so brave, they had become or been made cowards under Badshah Khan's influence. Their

bravery consisted not in being good marksmen but in defying death and being ever ready to bare their breasts to the bullets."

VEGETARIANISM

As a young child, Gandhi experimented in meat-eating. This was due partially to his inherent curiosity as well as his rather persuasive peer and friend Sheikh Mehtab. The idea of vegetarianism is deeply engrained in Hindu and Jain traditions in India, and, in his native land of Gujarat, many Hindus were vegetarian. The Gandhi family was no exception. Before leaving for his studies in London, Gandhi made a promise to his mother, Putlibai and his uncle, Becharji Swami that he would abstain from eating meat, taking alcohol, and engaging in promiscuity. He held fast to his promise and gained more than a diet, he gained a basis for his life-long philosophies. As Gandhi grew into adulthood, he became a strict vegetarian, though he was not against the consumption of eggs.

He wrote articles on the subject, some of which were published in the London Vegetarian Society's publication: "The Vegetarian." Gandhi inspired many people around the world to become vegetarian. Gandhi, himself, became inspired by many great minds during this period and befriended a chairman of the London Vegetarian Society, Dr. Josiah Oldfield.

Having also read and admired the work of Henry Stephens Salt, the young Mohandas met and often corresponded with the vegetarian campaigner. Gandhi spent much time advocating vegetarianism during and after his time in London. To Gandhi, a vegetarian diet would not only satisfy the requirements of the body, it would also serve an economic purpose as meat was, and still is, generally more expensive than grains, vegetables, and fruits. Also, many Indians of the time struggled with low income, thus vegetarianism was seen not only as a spiritual practice but also a practical one. He abstained from eating for long periods, using fasting as a form of political protest. He refused to eat until his death or his demands were met. It was noted in his autobiography that vegetarianism was the beginning of his deep commitment to Brahmacharya; without total control of the palate his success in Bramacharya would have been likely to falter.

Brahmacharya

This decision was deeply influenced by the philosophy of Brahmacharya-spiritual and practical purity-largely associated with celibacy and asceticism. Gandhi saw brahmacharya as a means of going close to God and as a primary foundation for self realization. In his autobiography he tells of his battle against lustful urges and fits of jealousy with his childhood bride, Kasturba.

He felt it his personal obligation to remain celibate so that he could learn to love, rather than lust. For Gandhi brahmacharya meant control of the senses in thought, word and deed.

Simplicity

Gandhi earnestly believed that a person involved in social service should lead a simple life which he thought could lead to Brahmacharya. His simplicity began by renouncing the western lifestyle he was leading in South Africa. He called it "reducing himself to zero", which entailed giving up unnecessary expenditure, embracing a simple lifestyle and washing his own clothes. On one occasion he returned the gifts bestowed to him from the natals for his diligent service to the community.

Gandhi spent one day of each week in silence. He believed that abstaining from speaking brought him inner peace. This influence was drawn from the Hindu principles of mouna (silence) and shanti (peace). On such days he communicated with others by writing on paper. For three and a half years, from the age of 37, Gandhi refused to read newspapers, claiming that the tumultuous state of world affairs caused him more confusion than his own inner unrest. Returning to India from South Africa, where he had enjoyed a successful legal practice, he gave up wearing Western-style clothing, which he associated with wealth and success. He dressed to be accepted by the poorest person in India, advocating the use of homespun cloth (khadi). Gandhi and his followers adopted the practice of weaving their own clothes from thread they themselves spun, and encouraged others to do so. While Indian workers were often idle due to unemployment, they had often bought their clothing from industrial manufacturers owned by British interests. It was Gandhi's view that if Indians made their own clothes, it would deal an economic blow to the British establishment in India. Consequently, the spinning wheel was later incorporated into the flag of the Indian National Congress. He would wear a dhoti all his life to show simplicity.

FAITH

Gandhi was born a Hindu and practised Hinduism all his life, deriving most of his principles from Hinduism. As a common Hindu, he believed all religions to be equal, and rejected all efforts to convert him to a different faith. He was an avid theologian and read extensively about all major religions. He had the following to say about Hinduism:

"Hinduism as I know it entirely satisfies my soul, fills my whole being... When doubts haunt me, when disappointments stare me in the face, and when I see not one ray of light on the horizon, I turn to the Bhagavad Gita, and find a verse to comfort me; and I immediately begin to smile in the midst of overwhelming sorrow. My life has been full of tragedies and if they have not left any visible and indelible effect on me, I owe it to the teachings of the Bhagavad Gita." Gandhi believed that at the core of every religion was Truth and Love (compassion, nonviolence and the Golden Rule). He also questioned hypocrisy, malpractices and dogma in all religions and was a tireless social reformer. Some of his comments on various religions are:

> *"Thus if I could not accept Christianity either as a perfect, or the greatest religion, neither was I then convinced of Hinduism being such. Hindu defects were pressingly visible to me. If untouchability could be a part of Hinduism, it could but be a rotten part or an excrescence. I could not understand the raison d'etre of a multitude of sects and castes. What was the meaning of saying that the Vedas were the inspired Word of God? If they were inspired, why not also the Bible and the Quran? As Christian friends were endeavouring to convert me, so were Muslim friends. Abdullah Sheth had kept on inducing me to study Islam, and of course he had always something to say regarding its beauty." (source: his autobiography)*

> *"As soon as we lose the moral basis, we cease to be religious. There is no such thing as religion over-riding morality. Man, for instance, cannot be untruthful, cruel or incontinent and claim to have God on his side."*

> *"The sayings of Muhammad are a treasure of wisdom, not only for Muslims but for all of mankind."*

Later in his life when he was asked whether he was a Hindu, he replied:

"Yes I am. I am also a Christian, a Muslim, a Buddhist and a Jew."

In spite of their deep reverence to each other, Gandhi and Rabindranath Tagore got involved in protracted debates more than once. These debates exemplify the philosophical differences between the two most famous Indians at the time. On January 15, 1934, an earthquake hit Bihar and caused extensive damage and loss of life. Gandhi maintained this was because of the sin committed by upper caste Hindus by not letting untouchables in their temples (Gandhi was committed to the cause of improving the fate of untouchables, referring to them as Harijans, people of Krishna). Tagore vehemently opposed Gandhi's stance, maintaining that an earthquake can only be caused by natural forces, not moral reasons, however repugnant the practice of untouchability may be.

LEGACY

Gandhi's birthday, 2 October is a national holiday, Gandhi Jayanti.

The word Mahatma, while often mistaken for Gandhi's given name in the West, is taken from the Sanskrit words maha meaning Great and atma meaning Soul. Most sources, such as Dutta and Robinson's Rabindranath Tagore: An Anthology, state that Rabindranath Tagore first accorded the title of Mahatma to Gandhi. Other sources state that Nautamlal Bhagavanji Mehta accorded him this title on January 21, 1915. In his autobiography, Gandhi nevertheless explains that he never felt worthy of the honour. According to the manpatra, the name Mahatma was given in response to Gandhi's admirable sacrifice in manifesting justice and truth.

Time Magazine named Gandhi the Man of the Year in 1930, the runner-up to Albert Einstein as "Person of the Century" at the end of 1999, and named The Dalai Lama, Lech Walesa, Dr. Martin Luther King, Jr., Cesar Chavez, Aung San Suu Kyi, Benigno Aquino Jr., Desmond Tutu, and Nelson Mandela as Children of Gandhi and his spiritual heirs to non-violence. The Government of India awards the annual Mahatma Gandhi Peace Prize to distinguished social workers, world leaders and citizens. Nelson Mandela, the leader of South Africa's struggle to eradicate racial discrimination and segregation, is a prominent non-Indian recipient. In 1996, the Government of India introduced the Mahatma Gandhi series of currency notes in rupees 5, 10, 20, 50, 100, 500 and 1000 denomination. Today, all the currency notes in circulation in India contain a portrait of Mahatma Gandhi. In 1969, the United Kingdom issued a series of stamps commemorating the centenary of Mahatma Gandhi. In the United Kingdom, there are several prominent statues of Gandhi, most notably in Tavistock Square, London (near University College London), where he studied law. January 30 is commemorated in the United Kingdom as the "National Gandhi Remembrance Day." In the United States, there are statues of Gandhi outside the Union Square Park in New York City and the Martin Luther King, Jr. National Historic Site in Atlanta, and in Waikiki, Hawaii. The city of Pietermaritzburg, South Africa, where Gandhi was ejected in 1893 from a first-class train, now hosts a commemorative statue. There are wax statues of Gandhi at the Madame Tussaud's wax museums in New York and London, and other cities around the world.

Gandhi never received the Nobel Peace Prize, though he was nominated five times between 1937 and 1948. Decades later, the Nobel Committee publicly declared its regret for the omission, and admitted to deeply divided nationalistic opinion denying the award. Mahatma Gandhi was to receive the Prize in 1948, but his assassination prevented the award from coming to him. The war breaking out between the newly created states of India and Pakistan could have been a complicating factor for Mahatma Gandhi not being presented with the Prize in 1948. The Prize was not awarded in 1948, the year of Gandhi's death, on the grounds that "there was no suitable living candidate" that year, and when the Dalai Lama was awarded the Prize in 1989, the chairman of the committee said that this was "in part a tribute to the memory of Mahatma Gandhi". The Committee felt so terrible it had not conferred the prize on Mahatma Gandhi that it kept looking at "other Indians" over the years. Those considered over the years were Jawaharlal Nehru and Vinoba Bhave.

Neither Saint, Nor Sinner

I think that the word 'saint' should be ruled out of present life. It is too sacred a word to be lightly applied to anybody, much less to one like myself who claims only to be a humble searcher after Truth, knows his limitations, makes mistakes, never hesitates to admit them when he makes them, and frankly confesses that he, like a scientist, is making experiments about some 'of the eternal verities' of life, but cannot even claim to be a scientist because he can show no tangible proof of scientific accuracy in his methods or such tangible results of his experiments as modern science demands. (YI, 12-5-1920, p2)

To clothe me with sainthood is too early even if it is possible. I myself do not feel a saint in any shape or form. But I do feel I am a votary of Truth in spite of all my errors of unconscious omission and commission.

POLICY OF TRUTH

I am not a 'statesman in the garb of a saint'. But since Truth is the highest wisdom, sometimes my acts appear to be consistent with the highest statesmanship. But, I hope I have no policy in me save the policy of Truth and ahimsa. I will not sacrifice Truth and ahimsa even for the deliverance of my country or religion. That is as much as to say that neither can be so delivered. (YI, 20-1-1927, p21)

I see neither contradiction nor insanity in my life. It is true that, as a man cannot see his back, so can he not see his errors or insanity. But the sages have often likened a man of religion to a lunatic. I therefore hug the belief that I may not be insane and may be truly religious. Which of the two I am in truth can only be decided after my death. (YI, 14-8-1924, p267)

It seems to me that I understand the ideal of truth better than that of ahimsa, and my experience tells me that if I let go my hold of truth, I shall never be able to solve the riddle of ahimsa..... In other words, perhaps, I have not the courage to follow the straight course. Both at bottom mean one and the same thing, for doubt is invariably the result of want or weakness of faith. 'Lord, give me faith' is, therefore, my prayer day and night. (A, p336)

I claim to be a votary of truth from my childhood. It was the most natural thing to me. My prayerful search gave me the revealing maxim 'Truth is God', instead of the usual one 'God is Truth'. That maxim enables me to see God face to face as it were. I feel Him pervade every fibre of my being.

Faith in Right

I remain an optimist, not that there is any evidence that I can give that right is going to prosper, but because of my unflinching faith that right must prosper in the end..... Our inspiration can come only from our faith that right must ultimately prevail. (H, 10-12-1938, p372)

Somehow I am able to draw the noblest in mankind, and that is what enables me to maintain my faith in God and human nature. (H, 15-4-1939, p86)

No Ascetic

I have never described myself as a sannyasi. Sannyas is made of sterner stuff. I regard myself as a house-holder, leading a humble life of service and, in common with my fellow-workers, living upon the charity of friends..... The life I am living is entirely very easy and very comfortable, if ease and comfort are a mental state. I have all I need without the slightest care of having to keep any personal treasures. (YI, 1-10-1925, p338)

My loin cloth is an organic evolution in my life. It came naturally, without effort, without premeditation. (YI, 9-7-931, p175)

I hate privilege and monopoly. Whatever cannot be shared with the masses is taboo to me. (H, 2-11-1934, p303)

It is wrong to call me an ascetic. The ideals that regulate my life are presented for acceptance by mankind in general. I have arrived at them by gradual evolution. Every step was thought out, well considered, and taken with greatest deliberation. Both my continence and non-violence were derived from personal experience and became necessary in response to the calls of public duty. The isolated life I had to lead in South Africa, whether as a householder, legal practitioner, social reformer or politician, required for the due fulfillment of these duties the strictest regulation of sexual life and a rigid practice of non-violence and truth in human relations, whether with my own countrymen or with Europeans. (H, 3-10-1936, p268)

Mine is a life full of joy in the midst of incessant work. In not wanting to think of what tomorrow will bring for me, I feel as free as a bird..... The thought that I am ceaselessly and honestly struggling against the requirements of the flesh sustains me. (YI, 1-10-1925, p338)

Work without faith is like an attempt to reach the bottom of a bottomless pit. (H, 3-10-1936, pp268-9)

Shedding the Ego

I know that I have still before me a difficult path to traverse. I must reduce myself to zero. So long as man does not of his own free will put himself last among his fellow-creatures, there is no salvation for him. Ahimsa is the farthest limit of humility. (A, p371)

If we could erase the 'It's' and the 'Mine's' from religion, politics, economics, etc., we shall soon be free and bring heaven upon earth. (YI, 3-9-1926, p336)

A drop in the ocean partakes of the greatness of its parent, although it is unconscious of it. But it is dried up as soon as it enters upon an existence independent of the ocean. We do not exaggerate when we say that life is a mere bubble.

A seeker after truth cannot afford to be an egotist. One who would sacrifice his life for others has hardly time to reserve for himself a place in the sun. (YI, 16-10-1930, p2)

There are limits to the capacity of an individual, and the moment he flatters himself that he can undertake all tasks, God is there to humble his pride. For myself, I am gifted with enough humility to look even to babes and suckling for help. (YI, 12-3-1931, p32) Fates decide my undertakings for me. I never go to see them. They come to me almost in spite of me. That has been my lot all my life long, in South Africa as well as ever since my return to India. (YI, 7-5-1925, p163)

LITTLE BOOK KNOWLEDGE

I admit my limitations. I have no university education worth the name. My high school career was never above the average. I was thankful if I could pass my examinations. Distinction in the school was beyond my aspiration. (H, 9-7-1938, p176)

During the days of my education I had read practically nothing outside textbooks, and after I launched into active life, I had very little time left me for reading. I cannot, therefore, claim much book knowledge. However, I believe I have not lost much because of this enforced restraint. On the contrary, the limited reading may be said to have enabled me thoroughly to digest what I did read. Of these books, the one that brought about an instantaneous and practical transformation in my life was Unto This Last. I translated it later into Gujarati, entitling it Sarvodaya (the welfare of all). I believe that I discovered some of my deepest convictions reflected in this great book of Ruskin, and that is why it so captivated me and made me transform my life. (A, p220)

I was living in South Africa then. It was the reading of Unto This Last on a railway journey to Durban, in 1904, when I was thirty-five, that made me decide to change my whole outward life. There is no other word for it, Ruskin's words captivated me. I read the book in one go and lay awake all the following night, and I there and then decided to change my whole plan of life. Tolstoy I had read much earlier. He affected the inner being. (ICS, p245)

Service of the Poor

The heart's earnest and pure desire is always fulfilled. In my own experience, I have often seen this rule being verified. Service of the poor has been my heart's desire and it has always thrown me amongst the poor and enabled me to identify myself with them. (A, p110)

I have always had a love for the poor all my life and in abundance. I could cite illustrations after illustrations from my past life that it was something innate in me. I have never felt that there was any difference between the poor and me. I have always felt towards them as my own kith and kin. (H, 11-5-1935, p99)

I have no desire for the perishable kingdom of earth. I am striving for the Kingdom of Heaven which is moksha. To attain my end it is not necessary for me to seek the shelter of a cave. I carry one about me, if I would but know it.

A cave-dweller can build castles in the air whereas a dweller in a palace, like Janak, has no castles to build. The cave-dweller who hovers round the world on the wings of thought has no peace. A Janak, though living in the midst of 'pomp and circumstance', may have peace that passeth understanding. For me the road to salvation lies through incessant toil in the service of my country and therethrough of humanity. I want to identify myself with everything that lives. (YI, 3-4-1924, p114)

My life is an indivisible whole, and all my activities run into one another; and they all have their rise in my insatiable love of mankind. (H, 2-3-1934, p24)

I am used to misrepresentation all my life. It is the lot of every public worker. He has to have a tough hide. Life would be burdensome if every misrepresentation had to be answered and cleared. It is a rule of life with me never to explain misrepresentations except when the cause requires correction. This rule has saved much time and worry. (YI, 27-5-1926, p193)

I have been known as a crank, faddist, mad man. Evidently the reputation is well deserved. For wherever I go, I draw to myself cranks, faddists and mad man. (YI, 13-6-1929, p193)

Practical Dreamer

I believe in absolute oneness of God and, therefore, also of humanity. What though we have many bodies? We have but one soul. The rays of the sun are many through refraction. But they have the same source. I cannot, therefore, detach myself from the wickedest soul (nor may I be denied identity with the most virtuous). Whether, therefore, I will or not, I must involve in my experiment the whole of my kind. Nor can I do without experiment. Life is but an endless series of experiments. (YI, 25-9-1924, p313)

I must be taken with all my faults. I am a searcher after truth. My experiments I hold to be infinitely more important than the best-equipped Himalayan expeditions.(YI, 3-12-1925, p422)

It has been my misfortune or good fortune to take the world by surprise. New experiments, or old experiments in new style, must sometimes engender misunderstanding. (EF, p132)

I am indeed a practical dreamer. My dreams are not airy nothings. I want to convert my dreams into realities as far as possible. (H, 17-11-1933, p6)

If any action of mine claimed to be spiritual is proved to be unpractical, it must be pronounced to be a failure. I do believe that the most spiritual act is the most practical in the true sense of the term. (H, 1-7-1939, p181)

My Fallibility

I claim to be a simple individual liable to err like any other fellow-mortal. I own, however, that I have humility enough in me to confess my errors and to retrace my steps. I own that I have an immovable faith in God and His goodness, and unconsumable passion for truth and love. But, is that not what every person has latent in him? (YI, 6-5-1926, p164)

Those who have at all followed my humble career even superficially cannot have failed to observe that not a single act of my life has been done to the injury of any individual or nation..... I claim no infallibility. I am conscious of having made Himalayan blunders, but I am not conscious of having made them intentionally or having even harboured enmity towards any person or nation, or any life, human or sub-human. (EF, p133)

I have made the frankest admission of my many sins. But I do not carry their burden on my shoulders. If I am journeying Godward, as I feel I am, it is safe with me. For I feel the warmth of the sunshine of His presence. My austerities, fastings and prayers are, I know, of no value if I rely upon them for reforming me. But they have an inestimable value, if they represent, as I hope they do, the yearnings of a soul striving to lay his weary head in the lap of his Maker. (H, 18-4-1936, p77)

Kinship with All

Whenever I see an erring man, I say to myself I have also erred; when I see a lustful man, I say to myself so was I once; and in this way, I feel kinship with every one in the world and feel that I cannot be happy without the humblest of us being happy. (YI, 10-2-1927, p44)

I shall have to answer my God and my Maker if I give any one less than his due, but I am sure that He will bless me if He knows that I gave someone more than his due. (YI, 10-3-1927, p80)

I am too conscious of the imperfections of the species to which I belong to be irritated against any single member thereof. My remedy is to deal with the wrong wherever I see it, not to hurt the wrong-doer, even as I would not like to be hurt for the wrongs I continually do. (YI, 12-3-1930, pp89-90)

I can truthfully say that I am slow to see the blemishes of fellow-beings, being myself full of them and, therefore, being in need of their charity, I have learnt not to judge any one harshly and to make allowances for defects that I may detect. (H, 11-3-1939, p47)

Regard for Opponents

Differences of opinion should never mean hostility. If they did, my wife and I should be sworn enemies of one another. I do not know two persons in the world who had no difference of opinion, and as I am a follower of the Gita, I have always attempted to regard those who differ from me with the same affection as I have for my nearest and dearest. (YI, 17-3-1927, p82)

It is to me a matter of perennial satisfaction that I retain generally the affection and trust of those whose principles and policies I oppose. The South Africans gave me personally their confidence and extended their friendship.

In spite of my denunciation of British policy and system, I enjoy the affection of thousands of Englishmen and women, and in spite of unqualified condemnation of modern materialistic civilization, the circle of European and American friends is ever widening. It is again a triumph of non-violence. (ibid, p86)

I cannot intentionally hurt anything that lives, much less fellow-human beings, even though they may do the greatest wrong to me and mine. (YI, 12-3-1930, p93) It would be impossible for any person to point to a single act of mine during the past 50 years which could be proved to have been antagonistic to any person or community. I have never believed anyone to be my enemy. My faith demands that I should consider no one as such. I may not wish ill to anything that lives. (H, 17-11-1933, p4)

6

Democracy Though of Gandhi

Gandhi's democratic thought in order to examine the nature and extent of the influence British political thought and practice thereon. The first section will trace the origins of Gandhi's democratic thought up to his return to India in 1914 and the following section will examine its development through to his death in 1948.

THE ORIGINS OF GANDHI'S SOCIALIST THOUGHT UP TO 1914

This period contains several seminal events in Gandhi's life that contributed to the development of his socialist thought in particular. Gandhi's activities within London vegetarian circles during the period 1888-1891 merit closer attention. Stephen Hay considered that these activities were of much importance in the development of Gandhi's political thought. For example, he stated: "During his student years in London, Gandhi's membership in the London Vegetarian Society (L. V. S.) brought with it the most powerful set of influences on his whole outlook on life and how he should live it."

According to Gandhi's secretary Pyarelal, these activities "brought him into contact with some of the finest types of Englishmen, and this in turn bred in him a deep admiration for some traits in British character." Similarly for Tendulkar:

Through the cult of vegetarianism Gandhi came into contact with many interesting persons who had to do with *[sic]* new movements in England - socialism, anarchism, atheism, theosophy and birth control.

Vegetarianism was part of the wider social reform movement which was composed of many, often connected, groups active at this time including the emerging socialist organizations. It is evident that through the vegetarian movement Gandhi became aware of many social reformers including, Henry Salt (1851-1939) and Edward Carpenter who were humanitarian socialists as well as vegetarians. According to Hay, after reading Salt's *A Plea for Vegetarianism* (1886) Gandhi become a vegetarian by choice rather than in deference to his mother. Since Gandhi contributed articles to the L. V. S. periodical, *The Vegetarian,* it is reasonable to assume that he read other articles in that publication. In particular, Hay observed the similarities between editorials that appeared in *The Vegetarian* and aspects of Gandhi's thought. The most significant of these were those concerning "the failure of modern civilization and the urban blight it created" which appeared in *The Vegetarian* in November 1890 and February 1891. Gandhi's discovery of vegetarianism in Britain also provided a British endorsement of a cherished aspect of Gandhi's traditional Indian culture. The importance of vegetarianism to Gandhi ensured a link between Indian and British influences connected to those circles.

An aspect of Gandhi's stay in London related to his vegetarian activities was his exposure to theosophy. Gandhi was introduced to Annie Besant, who was also a vegetarian, and Madame Blavatsky (1831-1891) in 1891 and thereafter read Besant's *Why I Became A Theosophist* (1891) and Blavatsky's *Key to Theosophy* (1889). Gandhi also became an Associate member of the Blavatsky Lodge of the Theosophical Society in March 1891. Hay believed that the enthusiastically pro-Hindu aspect of theosophy provided evidence of western validation for Gandhi's traditional culture which helped to reinforce his belief in the qualities of Indian civilization. The reasonableness of this assumption is reinforced by Gandhi's explanation of his motives for coming to study in Britain, which he gave in an interview in *The Vegetarian.* Gandhi said that in addition to becoming a barrister he would be able to see, "England, the land of philosophers and poets, the very centre of civilization." Thus for Gandhi it was significant that it was not merely a western endorsement of Hindu culture but a *British* endorsement. Gandhi was evidently much enamoured with Britain at this time which lends credence to the notion of him being susceptible to those aspects of British culture which endorsed or coincided with Indian practices. The fact that vegetarianism was often connected through its adherents to some of the most progressive, reformist and radical elements of British society provided Gandhi with an exposure to them he might not have had otherwise. In particular vegetarianism provided a link between Gandhi's traditional heritage and the social reformist and anti-industrial strain of British socialist thought.

Gandhi also developed the religious and spiritual background to his socialist thought whilst in London. This included Christianity, theosophy and Hindu influences and was also connected to vegetarianism. In his autobiography Gandhi recalled that he met a "good Christian from Manchester" in a vegetarian boarding house who gave him a

If Gandhi did read it he would have done so probably in London and in English further reinforcing the strength of his British connection. Further,

Hay emphasised the similarity between the lectures that Annie Besant gave in London whilst Gandhi was a student and his ideaion of truth. Gandhi explained that although he struggled through the old testament, the new testament and "especially the Sermon on the Mount went straight to" his "heart." As a student at the Inner Temple, Gandhi often attended sermons at the Temple Church. There is also some evidence that during his first trip to London, by visiting Cardinal Manning to congratulate him on assisting the striking dockers, Gandhi was concerned with the less advantaged groups in society. Further evidence which supports this appears in a letter that Gandhi wrote to his friend Charles Freer Andrews in 1927. Gandhi told Andrews that he recalled "the controversy that was carried out in the Public Press in 1889 or 1890 in London in connection with the expensive upkeep of the Bishop of London with his Palace." Gandhi also became a member of Edward Maitland (1824-1897) and Anna Kingsford's (1846-1888) Esoteric Christian Union. Later, Gandhi commented on the influence of Christianity and admit that his "regard for the life of Jesus" was "very great indeed," especially "his ethical teaching, his ordinary sense" and "his sacrifice." Gandhi's theosophist friends also introduced him to Sir Edwin Arnold (1832-1904) and his translation of the Indian classic the Gita, *The Song Celestial* (1885), and his life of the Buddha, *The Light of Asia* (1879). This reading encouraged Gandhi to discover other works on religious teachers, including Carlyle's *Heroes and Hero-Worship* (1841) and in particular the part concerning the life of the prophet. Thus not only was Gandhi influenced by Christianity through British sources but he was introduced to the great Hindu works in English translation. These wider religious influences permeated Gandhi's socialist thought throughout his life and reinforced his faith in the merits of Indian civilization.

After returning from London, Gandhi left India to pursue his legal career in South Africa. In 1904, whilst in South Africa, Gandhi read Ruskin's *Unto This Last,* which became a very important British power on his thought. The book was given to Gandhi by Henry Polak, a British friend he had met in a vegetarian restaurant. He recalled in his *Autobiography* how the book "gripped him" and "brought about an instantaneous and practical transformation" of his life. In fact Gandhi claimed that he had "discovered" some of his "deepest convictions reflected in this great book of Ruskin." Gandhi summarised the teachings that he understood from *Unto This Last:*

1. That the good of the individual is contained in the good of all.
2. That a lawyer's work has the same value as the barber's, inasmuch as all have the same right of earning their livelihood from their work.
3. That a life of labour, i.e. the life of the tiller of the soil and the handicraftsman is the life worth living.

The first of these I knew. The second I had dimly realized. The third had never occurred to me. In South Africa, Gandhi proceeded to put these ideas into practice and established a farm community called the Phoenix settlement. Gandhi's 1908 paraphrase translation into Gujarati of Ruskin's *Unto This Last,* which he called *Sarvodaya* or the welfare of all, constituted an important contribution to his socialist thought. In the preface Gandhi observed that in the west "happiness" was equated with "material happiness" or 'economic prosperity." However, Gandhi noted that Ruskin, "an Englishman of great learning," held, contrary to the prevailing view in the west, that the pursuit of "happiness in violation of moral principles" was "contrary to divine law." Therefore, Gandhi believed that although it was "necessary to imitate the west in certain respects" it was evident that "many western ideas are wrong." Crucially, according to Gandhi the British had "survived so long... not because they had lived up to the maxims of economics, but because they have had heroes who have questioned them and followed instead" the "principles of moral conduct." However, the result of the materialism, that had gripped Britain latterly, was that:

In England and elsewhere factories have multiplied because of the spread of these ideas. Large numbers of men leave their farms and concentrate in cities.... As a result, the nation grows weaker, and avarice and immorality increase.

The arrangements dictated by modern economics were "at the root of the starvation prevalent in England. In the conclusion Gandhi stated that Ruskin's work, while intended for a British audience, was "a thousand times more applicable to Indians."

This suggests that Gandhi was often seeking to identify those British influences which either endorsed or were applicable to Indian practices and conditions. Parel noted that Gandhi adapted Ruskin to suit his own reason so that where, "Ruskin saw the value of handicrafts even in an industrial society; Gandhi saw the value of the spinning-wheel and handicrafts for the whole of India." In sum, Ruskin was an important influence from the anti-industrial strain of British socialist thought.

Gandhi's years in South Africa also included further British influences. Gandhi maintained his interest in Christianity attending Christian prayer meetings, reading on the subject and mixing with Christians. His reading included Maitland's *The Perfect Way* (1882), which Gandhi claimed to have "liked" because it "seemed to support Hinduism." According to Pyarelal: "Edward Maitland's writings left a deep impression on Gandhiji's mind." This religious interpretation proceeded to include Tolstoy's *The Kingdom of God is Within You* (1893) which "left an abiding impression" on Gandhi. The Christian influence was reinforced by the work of Ruskin which possessed a strong quasi-religious element. It was also in South Africa in 1914 that Gandhi met the Cambridge educated, Anglican missionary, Charles Andrews who would become a life long friend and influence on him. British Christian influences can be usefully considered as an important part of wider religious and moral influences on Gandhi that also included Indian influences and Christian influences from non-British sources.

Gandhi's 1906 visit to Britain was a short political mission and reveals little of Gandhi's developing socialist thought, however his 1909 visit is of greater significance, not least because it was on the return journey to South Africa that Gandhi wrote *Hind Swaraj.* Gandhi arrived in London in July and stayed until November 1909 at the same luxury hotel as in 1906, The Cecil in the Strand. However, despite this indulgence, Gandhi had read Edward Carpenter's *Civilization, Its Cause and Cure* in September, and its critique of modern civilization had a significant impact on his socialist, thought. Reflecting on this visit years later, Gandhi recalled a meeting with Lord Ampthill (1869-1935), a pro-Indian peer, in which he "discussed the main points of his book," referring to *Hind Swaraj.* Gandhi recommended to Ampthill that England should discard "modern civilization," which he claimed was "ensouled" with a "spirit of selfishness and materialism," as well as being "vain and reasonless" and as such a "negation of the spirit of Christianity." Gandhi also condemned "railways, machinery and corresponding increase of indulgent habits" as "badges of slavery of the Indian people" as well for Europeans. It is obvious that Gandhi first aired his views on civilisation to a Briton and whilst in Britain.

During this period Gandhi's most important contribution to his socialist thought was *Hind Swaraj.* It contains Gandhi's critique of modern civilization and three of the twenty chapters can be considered in the context of his socialist thought. The first of these includes Gandhi's discussion of modem civilization. At the beginning of this chapter Gandhi quoted the "great English writer," author of *"Civilization: Its Cause and Cure"* who likened civilization to a "disease." This was Edward Carpenter the humanitarian socialist and vegetarian. Gandhi believed that the disease of modem civilization had afflicted the English and drew them to India to trade and having been brought to India by the British, the disease soon established itself there as well. Modern civilization ignored morality and religion and made "bodily welfare the object of life" and meant that workmen are required to work in 'factories or mines" under conditions "worse than that of beasts." These appalling working conditions not only applied to men but women as well and this "awful fact," according to Gandhi, "was one of the causes of the daily growing suffragette movement." Since the culprit was modern rather than British civilization *per se*, the English people, rather than being blamed, deserved sympathy. These manifestations of modern civilization had many harmful effects, including the spread of disease, increased quarrels, immorality and sin in India. Gandhi pursued his analysis of modern civilization as a disease, which he had obtained from Carpenter, in a chapter devoted to the medical profession in India. Gandhi began the chapter by stating: One writer has likened the whole modern system to the Upas tree. Its branches are represented by parasitical professions, including those of the law and medicine, and over the trunk has been raised the axe of true religion. Immorality is at the root of the tree.

He then explained how the medical profession, as a manifestation of modern civilization, was used by the English to maintain their position in India by inducing Indians to rely on its services and participate in the profession. Gandhi summarised the crux of the problem with that profession as follows: "I have indulged in vice, I contract a disease, a doctor cures me, the odds are that I shall repeat the vice." He proceeded to link the deficiencies of the medical profession with India's predicament: "The fact remains that the doctors induce us to indulge, and the result is that we have become effeminate. In these circumstances, we are unfit to serve the country." In this way Gandhi was able to apply Carpenter's analogy to the Indian situation in support of his call for independence and his ideaion of manliness. At the same time Gandhi utilised Carpenter to support his own critique of modern civilization which was so crucial to his socialist thought.

Edward Carpenter was clearly an important power on Gandhi's socialist thought. Carpenter describes modern civilization as a disease in the very first paragraph of *Civilisation: Its Cause and Cure.* Carpenter explained that he used the term disease because he believed societies everywhere had found that: "Whenever Civilisation touches them, they die like flies from the small-pox, drink, and worse evils it brings along with it, and often its mere contact is sufficient to destroy whole races." As evidence Carpenter had cited the existence of "23,000 medical men" in Britain who, organised as a profession, made a "fetish of disease" rather than attempting to "contradict" the disease itself. The maladies of "civilised man" and the attendant physicians, Carpenter cited as evidence of a "national sickness" which had been caused by the *"break up* of the unity" of man's nature which in turn was a result of a civilisation founded on private property. From this passage it is clear that Gandhi had obtained his analysis of the medical profession from Carpenter. As an alternative to modern civilization based on private property, Carpenter described a "Communism" in which: "Gladly will each man, and more gladly still each woman, take his or her treasures, except what are immediately or necessarily in use, to the ordinary centre, where there value will be increased a hundred and a thousand fold by the greater number of those who can enjoy them, and where far more perfectly and with far less toil they can be tended than if scattered abroad in private hands." This seems to be a similar to the kind of trusteeship that Gandhi would advocate later and as such Carpenter represents an important and enduring influence on *Hind Swaraj* and Gandhi's later socialist thought.

In the chapter on machinery, Gandhi claimed it was "machinery" that had "impoverished India" and had also "begun to desolate Europe." It is apparent that Gandhi associated machinery with Britain, when he observed: "It is difficult to measure the harm that Manchester has done to us." He made numerous references to Manchester and its association with the textile trade with India, which had led to the situation where, "Indian handicraft has all but disappeared." Further, it was not only India that was suffering from the advent of machinery, because Gandhi believed:

Ruination is now knocking at the English gates." Machinery and the destruction of the Indian textile industry by competition from Manchester had also had an equally damaging impact on the Indian "moral being." However, Gandhi appreciated that it was "not easy to do away with a thing that is established" because machinery had spread its tentacles widely and facilitated the development of "large cities... tram-cars and railways [and]... electric light." Significantly, Gandhi observed that: "English villages do not boast of these things." Gandhi concluded his analysis: "I cannot recall a single good point with machinery." This chapter reveals an interesting mix of British influences, from Gandhi's knowledge of the textile trade to his example of a pre-industrial English village. The former had been harmful to both Britain and India whilst the latter demonstrated that civilisation and equipment may have spread from England to India it had not engulfed England entirely. Thus Gandhi championed the English village and the Indian village against the evils of urbanization.

The crux of Gandhi's critique of modem civilization was set out in his translation of *Unto This Last* and in *Hind Swaraj*. The fundamental assumption on which Gandhi's critique rested was his opposition to the materialism of western civilization. Gandhi was always careful to differentiate between modem civilization and western or British civilization. However, clearly, and almost exclusively, Gandhi's direct experience of modern civilization was gained either in British India, Great Britain or South Africa. Similarly, his knowledge of modern civilization from written works included predominantly those by British authors and even those works by other Indian authors discussed British civilization. In fact in *Hind Swaraj* Gandhi admitted that Britain had been affected by the disease of modern civilization. Therefore, it is reasonable to assume that Gandhi's ideaion of modern civilization was overwhelmingly the product of British influences. Yet, significandy, Gandhi felt that the British were just as much victims of modern civilization as Indians. Moreover, in distinguishing modem civilization from both British and western civilisation, Gandhi was able on occasion to condemn the former whilst recognising strengths in the latter.

Gandhi's critique reveals considerable power from both British writers and friends and his experiences in Britain and British India. This is demonstrated, for example, by the fact that many of the ideas in *Hind Swaraj* were evident in Carpenter's work, Gandhi's translation of Ruskin and his discussion with Lord Ampthill. Basham emphasises the significance of British influence and noted that "Gandhi's objection to mechanized twentieth-century life" had "no counterpart in the attitudes of ancient India, which was never averse to innovations of a practical kind." This suggests that Gandhi's critique was significantly influenced by writers like Ruskin and Carpenter. However, Rudrangshu Mukherjee cautions against overemphasising the influence of Carpenter and Ruskin because Gandhi was "thoroughly eclectic and his borrowings were not impaired by any considerations of scientific and theoretical rigour." Nevertheless, it is reasonable to assume that Gandhi found in Ruskin and Carpenter a source of criticism which coincided with his own interpretations of his traditional Hindu culture and which he could apply to the Indian situation. By virtue of Gandhi's early British influences he was orientated towards sources from Britain which he could incorporate into his developing thought. It is also important to note that Gandhi's knowledge of traditional Indian influences came to him first through British sources. These British sources were introduced to him via vegetarian contacts in London and the English language. So while Gandhi may have been selective in his borrowings from the British sources of Ruskin and Carpenter his selectivity was informed by his own ideaion of his traditional Indian culture which had in part been gained indirectly via British influences. Gandhi's critique also possesses a spiritual dimension which seems to have been, at least partially, influenced by British Christian sources.

Some of the explanations of Gandhi's critique of modern civilization and his rejection of modernization centre on his over reliance on his reading of Ruskin and Carlyle and his experience of the effects of the industrial revolution in England. For example, Aiyar summarised this position as follows:

His study of the writings of Carlyle and Ruskin and his acquaintance with the evils of the industrial revolution - a passing phase of England's social transformation -left a permanent impression on his mind and he did little to correct that impression in the light of social and economic changes which were taking place in England in the last quarter of the nineteenth century.

The over reliance on Gandhi's British connection implied in this explanation contrasts with Aiyar's subsequent, and rather contradictory, analysis of *Hind Swaraj* and the "socialist ideas" therein for which "there was little or no evidence for this philosophy from a foreign source." This analysis aside there is evidence to support Aiyar's former explanation that Gandhi had adopted the social reformist conscience of the late Victorian era and did not discard it. For example, Hay, concluding his study of Gandhi's first trip to England, describes him as possessing "all the social and cultural skills of a late-Victorian gentleman." Similarly, Hunt concluded his study of Gandhi's visits to Britain: "He was most often in the midst of the urban middle classes, and showed a strong affinity for earnest Nonconformist Christians and evangelical reformers such as the vegetarians and Theosophists." Gandhi found in the circles in which he moved in London a critique of modern, British civilization which happened to coincide with his own predilections. Gandhi was exposed to many of these important British influences at the most formative period of his life when he was still in awe of Britain and seeking to follow a legal career.

THE ORIGINS OF GANDHI'S DEMOCRATIC THOUGHT, UP TO 1914

As well as being a significant power in its own right, Gandhi's experience in South Africa, adds an important dimension to British influence on his democratic thought. Gandhi regarded South Africa as an application of British political practice and himself as a British subject. Consequently, Gandhi's democratic thought at this time was conceived wholly within a British framework and, significantly, he was a democrat before becoming a nationalist. Gandhi's democratic thought during the mid-1890s found expression in his demands for equality of treatment for the Indians in South Africa. Gandhi's appeal to the imperial authorities took the form of a number of petitions to British officials in London, South Africa and India. In 1895, Gandhi made an appeal to Britons in South Africa on behalf of the Indian community, entitled *The Indian Franchise.* Gandhi dismissed a number of the arguments against the Indian franchise which were circulating in South Africa. The first of these claimed Indians were unprepared for, and unschooled in, democracy. Gandhi countered that Indians possessed the franchise in India, albeit a limited one, and moreover, India had possessed a form of representative democracy since ancient times. Specifically, the Indian form of representation that Gandhi identified as existing from "the earliest ages" was the "*Panchayat.* " Interestingly there is a British influence on this aspect of Gandhi's democratic thought.

Henry Sumner Maine had discussed the existence and significance of Indian *panchayat-based* democracy in *Village Communities in the East and the West.* Gandhi cited this work in *Hind Swaraj* in 1909 and the influence of Maine. It is unclear whether Gandhi had read Maine's work prior to that time but his argument here suggests he might have done.

Secondly, Gandhi denied the argument that India was a conquered country and as such Indians were not entitled to the same rights as other subjects of the Empire.

In support of this view, Gandhi claimed, "many British writers think that India is under England with her consent," including Professor Seeley, whom Gandhi quoted. The gist of the pamphlet revealed Gandhi's contention that the curtailment of the Indian franchise represented an affront to the "fundamental principles" of the British constitution.

It is obvious that Gandhi used the work of Seeley to support his contention that Indians in South Africa should enjoy the same democratic rights as other British subjects. In particular, Gandhi used Seeley's argument that India was not a conquered country and, by extension, Britain governed India with the consent of the Indian people for their mutual benefit. The implication of this for Gandhi's democratic thought was two-fold. Firstly, since India was governed by mutual consent, Indians were entitled to certain rights, in return for which their consent had been obtained. Seeley admitted that India's relation to Britain was different to that of the colonies like Australia and New Zealand, but nevertheless India was "not a conquered country" because: "England has not seized lands in India, and after displacing the native proprietors assigned them to Englishmen."

Further, and in summary, Seeley concluded: "The truth is that, though the present relation between India and England was historically created by war, yet England does not, at least openly, claim any rights over India in virtue of this fact." Secondly, there was a tacit agreement, that Gandhi shared with Seeley, that the methods and objectives of British rule, including particularly democracy, were both desirable and beneficial. In this respect Seeley constitutes a significant British influence on Gandhi's democratic thought. The Boer war provides a demonstration of the practical implications of British influences on Gandhi's democratic thought in a number of ways. Firstly, in his *Autobiography,* Gandhi explained his reason for assisting the British:

> Suffice it to say that my loyalty to the British rule drove me to participation with the British in that war. I felt that, if I demanded rights as a British citizen, it was also my duty, as such, to participate in the defence of the British Empire. I held then that India could achieve her complete emancipation only within and through the British Empire.

Similarly, in his account of the South African years, Gandhi justified his participation in the war as a demand for rights which must be accompanied by the performance of duty:

I advanced these arguments in 1899, and even today I do not see any reason for modifying them. That is to say, if I had today the faith in the British Empire which I then entertained, and if I now cherished the hope, which I did at that time, of achieving our freedom under its aegis, I would advance the same arguments, for word for word, in South Africa, and, in similar circumstances even in India.

Secondly, Gandhi recalled the relations that he had had with British soldiers during the war: "They were friendly with us and thankful for our being there to serve them." This sentiment reveals Gandhi's affection for the British people, dating from his time in London as a student, and can be contrasted with his experience in South Africa which was typified by harassment and discriminatory legislation. For example, Gandhi recognised in the oppressive nature of the Asiatic Bill, nothing "except the hatred of Indians."

Finally, Gandhi observed that the war had brought many soldiers and officers from India to South Africa. Gandhi believed that this produced a noticeable and significant effect. With the coming of the officers from Asia, came also its autocracy, and the habits that the autocrats had imbibed there. In South Africa there was a kind of responsible government or democracy, whereas the commodity imported from Asia was autocracy pure and simple.

This emphasises Gandhi's growing realization that there was a contrast between the theory and practice of British constitutional principles in Britain, South Africa and India. Gandhi's contributions to his periodical *Indian Opinion* also provide evidence of both his faith in the British constitution and his determination for Indians to enjoy equality in the application of its principles in South Africa. The editorial of the first issue claimed that the Indians in South Africa were "loyal subjects" but were labouring "under a number of legal disabilities" which were "undeserved and unjust." Gandhi discussed the rights he believed that Indians possessed in an article in *Indian Opinion* on Queen Victoria's proclamation of 1858.

Gandhi remarked that the "memorable proclamation" had been "rightly termed 'the Magna Charta of British Indians,'" and as such was especially applicable to the situation in South Africa. The proclamation, Gandhi argued, gave "the people of India full privileges and rights of British subjects" and therefore Indians had invoked it "whenever any attempt" had been "made to curtail their liberties or their rights as British subjects." Significantly, Gandhi also noted "that in it there is absolutely no qualification whatsoever with reference to the place where the people to whom it was given are to enjoy the fulfilment of the promises given therein." In another article that month Gandhi discussed the argument he had encountered in South Africa that because India had been conquered Indians were "not entitled to the same rights as real Britishers." Gandhi dismissed this chapter for two reasons, the first he had used previously and was taken from Seeley's *Expansion of Great Britain*. Seeley, Gandhi argued, did not consider India a conquered country "in the real sense of the term" but rather it was "British because the vast majority of its people have, perhaps for selfish reasons, accepted British rule." Secondly, Gandhi recalled: "British statesmen have times without number disavowed any connection whatsoever with the idea of inequality necessarily existing between the conquerors and the conquered... and they have done this more especially with regard to the British Indians." Finally, Gandhi contended that it was "these very principles which have made Great Britain what she is" and they "guide her policy, maybe with temporary aberration, from day to day." This sentiment reveals the extent to which Gandhi had subscribed to the ideals and rhetoric of the Empire, either for reasons of expedience, self-interest or more substantively.

It is apparent that Gandhi used Seeley to support the contention that India was not a conquered country. Additionally, Gandhi's argument that there was no inequality between the 'conquerors' and the 'conquered' is also traceable to Seeley. In particular, Seeley identified the importance of the 1858 proclamation in this respect:

> In the Queen's proclamation of November 1st, 1858, by which the open assumption of the government by the Queen was announced, occur the express words 'We hold ourselves bound to the natives of our Indian territories by the same obligations of duty which bind us to all our other subjects.' That is, conquest confers no peculiar rights, or India is not for practical reasons a conquered country.

Since Gandhi had deployed other aspects of Seeley's argument, it seems certain that Seeley alerted Gandhi to the significance of the 1858 proclamation. It was then left to Gandhi to compare this proclamation with the Magna Carta, which provided a link between his observations of political practice in Britain and India and the situation in South Africa.

Gandhi led a delegation to London in the autumn of 1906 on behalf of the Indians in South Africa. Its objective was to present the case of the Indian community, who had been the subject of discriminatory legislation, to the British authorities. As such, and in terms of his democratic thought, the deputation can be regarded as further evidence of Gandhi's attempt to obtain the same democratic rights for the Indians in South Africa as those enjoyed by other subjects of the Empire, according to the principles of the British constitution. In an interview on the day of his arrival in London, Gandhi explained that the deputation sought to protest against a law that, "intended to make every Indian settled in the Transvaal carry a pass, just as the kaffirs are required to do." Gandhi also observed that "the disabilities of British Indians in the Transvaal were one of the causes of the late war." The deputation provided a number of important British influences which Gandhi incorporated into his democratic thought.

Gandhi made several contributions to *Indian Opinion* from London which reveal various British influences on his democratic thought at that time. In a number of articles Gandhi recorded the development of the women's suffrage movement which he had evidently been observing keenly. These observations are significant since Gandhi admired the women's methods and courage and sympathised with their objective which was similar to his own: the attainment of the franchise. In this respect Gandhi believed that the Indians in South Africa could learn much from the movement. Not only did it have a similar goal, but also that goal was being withheld by the same authority. In October, Gandhi remarked of the willingness of the women not to confine themselves to 'words' but to include action in support of their cause: 'They are bound to succeed and gain the franchise, for the simple reason that deeds are better than words." In November, Gandhi mentioned the movement again and repeated his advice: "Every Indian in the Transvaal should take to heart the example of these brave women.'* Finally, towards the end of the deputation's time in London, Gandhi observed that the Indians in South Africa would have to contemplate going to jail to obtain their rights, just as the suffragettes had done. This was because Gandhi anticipated the failure of the deputation, which appeared unable to prevent the attainment of Royal Assent of the offending legislation. It is evident that despite the frustrations encountered by the deputation, Gandhi did not abandon his hope that he could obtain equality for the Indians in South Africa.

Gandhi led a subsequent deputation to London on behalf of the Indians in South Africa in 1909. Gandhi mentioned the women's suffrage movement in at least twelve articles which appeared in *Indian Opinion* at the time. In these articles, Gandhi praised: the women's capacity and willingness to suffer; their organizational skills; their endurance; their willingness to fast; their courage and their fund raising abilities. Consequently, Gandhi commented: "We can learn quite a few things and draw much inspiration from it." Gandhi also attended at least two women's suffrage meetings. At one of them he met Mrs Pankhurst and he mentioned the meeting in a letter to his friend Henry Polak, to whom he also enclosed a copy of their weekly publication "Votes for

Women." Tendulkar also noted the importance of Gandhi's observations of the movement, and concluded: "He took a keen interest in all their work, and learnt much of the value and methods of passive resistance from the British women." In defining his policy of *Satyagraha* several years later, in his account of the South African struggle, Gandhi referred to the women's suffrage movement, and also British political practice 163 more generally. Gandhi explained that passive resistance, the English equivalent of *Satyagraha,* had been used successfully in Britain:

But among the English people, whenever a small minority did not approve of some obnoxious piece of legislation, instead of rising in rebellion they took the passive or milder step of not submitting to the law and inviting the penalties of such non-submission upon their heads. When the British Parliament passed the Education Act some years ago, the Non-conformists offered passive resistance under the leadership of Dr. Clifford. The great movement of the English women for the vote was also known as passive resistance.

In sum Gandhi was influenced by the women's suffrage movement and incorporated lessons he learnt from it into his democratic thought. There is one additional lesson from the suffrage movement that Gandhi observed and which he felt the Indians in South African would be well advised to heed. Gandhi noticed that as it wore on and the women became impatient with the lack of progress they abandoned non-violent methods. The articles in *Indian Opinion* in August and September are almost entirely positive and full of praise for the movement whereas in later articles the praise is qualified by Gandhi's criticism of the violent turn the movement was beginning to take. For example, in October 1909, Gandhi reported that the women had broken Asquith's windows:

If the British women mean to fight in the spirit of Satyagraha, they cannot adopt tactics. There is no room for impatience in Satyagraha. Those who want the franchise are in a minority, whereas the majority of women oppose the demand; so the minority has no option but to suffer for a long time.

Thus Gandhi warned his readers: "We ought never to forsake the sword of Satyagraha and grow impatient." There was also a subtler lesson to be learnt from the women's adoption of violence. It indicated to Gandhi that the British may well be very reluctant to concede rights to the disenfranchised Indians and therefore the struggle was likely to prove long and arduous: "We may observe that the British will not concede any rights even to women in their country without putting them to the test." Just as Gandhi rejected the violent extremism of the suffrage movement he rejected that of the Indian nationalists which he encountered in London at this time. While Gandhi was in London, Sir William Curzon-Wylie, the *aide-de-camp* to the Secretary of State for India, was assassinated by an Indian extremist. Gandhi commented on this assassination in *Indian Opinion:* "I must say that those who believe and argue that such murders may do good to India are ignorant men indeed." There is a striking parallel between Gandhi's condemnation of the violence of both the suffragettes and the Indian extremists. *Hind Swaraj* represents a very significant source of Gandhi's democratic thought and reveals a number of significant British influences. Four of the twenty chapters can be considered contributions to Gandhi's democratic thought. In the first two of these chapters, Gandhi questioned the existing goal of Indian nationalism and provided a devastating critique of the English model on which it was based. Consequently, he rejected this goal which sought the kind of self-government that had been granted to Canada and South Africa. Gandhi criticized those who wished to merely remove the British whilst maintaining their system of government in India:

You want the tiger's nature, but not the tiger; that is to say, you would make India English. And when it becomes English, it will be called not Hindustan but *Englistan.* That is not the Swaraj that I want

In support of his criticism Gandhi discussed the British Parliament in terms similar to the assessment made during the deputations. For Gandhi, the so called "Mother of Parliaments" was rather more "like a sterile woman and a prostitute." It was like a "sterile woman" because it had "not yet of its own accord done a single good thing" and it was "like a prostitute because it is under the control of ministers who change from time to time." Gandhi also attacked the composition of the British Parliament. Its members were "hypocritical and selfish" and they had "been seen to stretch themselves and to doze" during important debates or, conversely, they talk "away until the listeners are disgusted." In support of this view, Gandhi quoted Carlyle, who he said had called Parliament "the talking shop of the world." In dismissing Parliament as a "costly toy," Gandhi claimed that: "If the money and the time wasted by Parliament were entrusted to a few good men, the English nation would be occupying today a much higher platform." He added that "these views" were not "peculiar" to him and "some great English thinkers have expressed them." In support of his assessment, Gandhi cited another British source of criticism: "One of the members of that Parliament recently said that a true Christian could not become a member of it." Finally, Parliament was not entirely honest or beyond corruption. Gandhi cautioned:

If they are to be considered honest because they do not take what are generally known as bribes, let them be so considered, but they are open to subtler influences. In order to gain their ends, they certainly bribe people with honours.

Gandhi explained the variability and changeability of the British Parliament as a reflection of the British people whom it claimed to represent. However, the people were victims of the "dishonest" newspapers, from whom they "take their cue," and consequently they "change their views frequently." Gandhi claimed that the root cause of the problem was not the 'English people" themselves but "modern civilization." Thus Gandhi believed that: "If India copies England... she will be ruined." Gandhi's analysis of British political practice condemned Parliament as a manifestation of modem civilization. In the third chapter concerning democracy, Gandhi surveyed nineteenth century British political history in support of his assessment of the problems of British political practice and the lessons Indians should learn from them. This chapter examined the paucity of rights secured by violence that Gandhi considered characteristic of the British experience. The first example Gandhi gave was the "Proclamation of 1857 *[sic]*" which he explained was made "at the end of a revolt... [but] when the peace was secured... its full effect was toned down." The second example was from Britain. "The English in 1833," Gandhi claimed, had "obtained greater voting power by violence." It seems likely that Gandhi was referring to the Great Reform Act of 1832, the single year error in the date matches his error in the date of Queen Victoria's proclamation. Although there was some violence in 1831 associated with its passage it was largely an evolutionary rather than revolutionary development Nevertheless, according to Gandhi, the use of violence meant that the English had not obtained real rights, since: "[R]eal rights are a result of the performance of duty." Gandhi believed that in England there was a problem of "everybody wanting and insisting on his rights, [and] nobody thinking of his duty." Consequently, if Indians wanted their rights they should be obtained through duty rather than violence. It is evident that Gandhi considered "soul-force" or "passive resistance" to be an important part of this duty and he explained that it should back claims for rights:

A petition of an equal is a sign of courtesy; a petition from a slave is a symbol of his slavery. A petition backed by force is a petition from an equal and, when he transmits his demand in the form of a petition, it testifies to his nobility.

Thus Gandhi used two British examples to support his critique of political violence. His analysis of Queen Victoria's proclamation is particularly poignant given his earlier praise of that 'Indian Magna Carta' and reveals the extent of his disaffection with the gulf between British political theory and practice as it was applied in the empire.

Having condemned the use of force Gandhi's elaborate his idea of *Satyagraha* or passive resistance. Gandhi explained that there was a "proverb among Englishman" that all history is the history of war and therefore a nation with "no history... is a happy nation." However, Gandhi disagreed and contended that: "The fact that there are so many men still alive in the world shows that it is based not on the force of arms but on the force of truth or love." In summary, "passive resistance is a method of securing rights by personal suffering." Gandhi explained that "Man-made laws are not necessarily binding" and, in fact, "it is unmanly to obey laws that are unjust." Therefore, for Gandhi: "Real Home Rule is possible only where passive resistance is the guiding force of the people." Far from being "a weapon of the weak," passive resistance was superior to physical force because: 'Those alone can follow the path of passive resistance who are free from fear, whether as to their possessions, false honour, their relatives, the government, bodily injuries or death." Gandhi concluded that the 'duty' of passive resistance was the most effective and only acceptable method of supporting a claim for 'rights' in society.

Gandhi cited Henry Sumner Maine's *Village Communities,* as an authority he recommended, in the Appendix to *Hind Swaraj.* Maine discussed traditional Indian village society and in particular identified the existence of vestiges of democratic institutions. For example, Maine observed:

But I have good authority for saying that, in those parts of India in which the village community is most perfect and in which there are the clearest signs of an original proprietary equality between all the families composing the group, the authority exercised elsewhere by the Headman is lodged with the Village Council. It is always viewed as a representative body, and not as a body possessing inherent authority, and, whatever be its real number, it always bears a name which recalls its ancient constitution of Five persons. These village councils, Maine explained, exercised "quasi-judicial, [and] quasi-legislative power." Gandhi had called for a return to village-based democracy in *Hind Swaraj* and Maine seems to have endorsed Gandhi's faith in such a system. In summary, it is apparent that Maine's work identified and provided at least an endorsement of the democratic credentials of traditional Indian society of which Gandhi was aware and utilised in his developing democratic thought. It is instructive to compare Maine's position with Seeley to illustrate how far Gandhi had moved from his early thinking. Seeley, in *The Expansion of England,* had claimed: "Of liberty, of popular institutions, there exists scarcely a trace in the whole extent of Indian history or tradition." This sentiment in Seeley would suggest that Gandhi had either not read Maine until several years after he read Seeley or had not integrated Maine's analysis with the frustrations he had experienced in his struggle in South Africa. Thus Gandhi used British sources both initially, when he used a liberal like Seeley, and latterly when he used a conservative like Maine, to support his changing democratic thought.

Edward Carpenter was another authority that Gandhi cited in *Hind Swaraj*. Carpenter considered that government in society, prior to the growth of civilization based on the ownership of property, was "essentially democratic," although it only existed in "rudimentary form." However, the development of civilization had heralded the age of aristocracy which had been followed by the commercial age. In the commercial age: "Parliaments and Constitutions and general Palaver are the order of the day." This is followed, according to Carpenter, by the breakdown into "the era of anarchy - the democracy of Carlyle; the rule of the rabble, and mob-law." This, for Carpenter, was "no true democracy," or the "rule of the Demos in every man." Rather, Carpenter believed that eventually the false democracy parts aside for the disclosure of true Democracy which has been formed beneath it - which is not an external government at all, but an inward rule - the rule of the mass - Man in each unit - man.

In conclusion, Carpenter predicted: "As to External Government and Law, they will disappear; for they are only the travesties and transitory substitutes of Inward Government and Order." Carpenter's criticism of modern civilization and the type of democracy which was based on it and his vision of true democracy bear a remarkable similarity with Gandhi's democratic thought as it began to develop from this time onwards.

In an article in 1910 Gandhi discussed the struggle of the Indian community in South Africa in terms of the definition of liberty given by Lord Hugh Cecil. Gandhi began by quoting Cecil's definition of liberty as the ability "to obey our own conscience rather than the will and conscience of others." Gandhi remarked that the struggle in South Africa had often been regard as a struggle for liberty and this interpretation was supported when judged according to Cecil's definition and therefore it should "command universal sympathy." According to Gandhi, who used Cecil's terms, the Indians were "exercising the power to obey their will and conscience rather than the will of the State." Gandhi developed this analysis of the struggle, quoting Cecil again, who held that the "true ground for maintaining liberty is that, without it, there cannot be any true sense of virtue or righteousness." Moreover, Gandhi's quotation of Cecil continued: "Virtue does not consist in doing right, but in choosing to do right." Finally, Gandhi linked Cecil's definition of liberty to the problem of its attainment, a subject which he felt Cecil had overlooked. Therefore, Gandhi postulated: "If liberty be ability to act according to the dictates of our conscience, we certainly cannot achieve it by force of arms." Thus Gandhi was able to combine Cecil's definition of liberty with his own preferred method of non-violence: "It is attainable only by suffering in our own persons until our opponents see the error of their ways and cease to harass us by trying to impose their will on us." Therefore, Cecil constitutes another important British influence on Gandhi's democratic thought that has been overlooked.

Lord Hugh Cecil represents another British influence that Gandhi used to support his demand for equality of treatment for Indians in South Africa. Cecil's address to the Associated Societies of the University of Edinburgh was published as *Liberty and Authority,* and therefore constitutes the most likely source. Cecil began by defining liberty almost exactly as Gandhi had quoted: *"Liberty consists in being able to obey your own will and conscience rather than the will and conscience of others.* Cecil claimed that Mill's definition of liberty was wrong, because he was "obliged to say his principle does not apply to children or to savage nations, but only to those Western peoples who have become civilised." Hidden within this proviso, Cecil believed, was "that vulgar notion that civilisation consists of the British Isles and a few contiguous places, and that all the more distant parts of the earth are savage." Whilst Cecil accepted that the "natives of Africa are savage" he doubted the same could be said "of those in India, with their ancient civilisation." This analysis, acknowledging the ancient Indian civilization and the universality of the principle of liberty would have appealed to Gandhi. Therefore, for Cecil, liberty was "not a right" and "the sound *ground for maintaining liberty* is that liberty is the essential condition of human progress, and that without it there cannot be in any *true sense virtue or righteousness.* Cecil continued to link his ideaion of liberty with virtue: "Virtue is attained in proportion as liberty is attained: for *virtue does not consist in doing right, but in choosing to do right.* It is this definition that Gandhi quoted in his article in support of his struggle for the liberty of the Indians in South Africa.

Cecil proceeded to converse the relationship between liberty and equality. Gandhi did not mention this part of Cecil's address but it is pertinent to the development of Gandhi's democratic thought. Whilst Cecil regarded liberty as "the very essential of human progress," he believed that equality, at least absolute equality, was an "unreal delusion." Cecil believed that Britain had not attempted to achieve such equality, either domestically or within the empire, but rather it had sought only to attain political equality or justice. In particular, British policy in respect of equality, accepting natural inequalities, had manifested itself in British success in its dealings with "inferior races." In summary, Cecil stated:

I believe that the success of the British Empire in dealing with its vast dependencies results more from this quality than any other - that we, unlike other parts of the Anglo-Saxon race, unlike the French or the Belgians have always denied the equality of men, and always proceeded on the principle that men are unequal but are alike entitled to be treated with justice. To put the matter in one sentence, it is because we believe in liberty and do not believe in equality that we have not unworthily fulfilled our great imperial vocation.

Cecil's claim that the British had based their empire on justice seems to resemble Gandhi's understanding of the basis of the relationship and the framework upon which he demanded the rights of the Indians in South Africa. Finally, Cecil concluded his address by revealing the ethical foundation of his thought: For it is in the growth of liberty, in the growth of the free choice of good and free rejection of evil that we move towards the ideal of a divine society which religion and natural reflection alike set before us as the goal of our hope.

Certainly, there is much in this passage that Gandhi would have endorsed. Gandhi's emphasis on the importance of self-rule and the control of one's passions, reflected in the importance he placed on vows and abstinence as important facets of his democratic thought, could be included within Cecil's framework.

Finally, Gandhi's visit to London in 1914, on his way back to India from South Africa, provided an opportunity for him to assess the struggle and in doing so revealed more of his democratic thought at that time. In a farewell letter, immediately before

Gandhi left South Africa, he discussed the 'Settlement' between the Indian community and the South African authorities which his campaign had achieved. The 'Settlement' to which Gandhi referred was The Indians' Relief Act 1914 which claimed: 'To make provision for the redress of certain grievances and the removal of certain disabilities of His Majesty's Indian subjects in the Union and other matters incidental thereto."

Significantly, Gandhi described the 'Settlement' as "the Magna Charta of our liberty in this land." Gandhi explained that he described the 'Settlement' as such for a number of reasons, including the fact that it established the rights of the Indian community and especially because it confirmed "the theory of the British Constitution that there should be no legal racial inequality between different subjects of the Crown, no matter how much practice may vary according to local circumstance."

Finally, Gandhi considered that the 'Settlement' had "vindicated passive resistance," which had proved itself "an infinitely superior force to that of the vote, which history shows has often been turned against the voters themselves." In a farewell speech in Cape Town, Gandhi claimed:

I have always believed there is something subtle, something fine in the ideals of the British Constitution. Tear away those ideals and you tear away my loyalty to that Constitution; keep those ideals and I am ever a bondman.

Gandhi repeated his comparison between the 'Settlement' and the Magna Carta when he arrived in London. In a speech at a reception he claimed that is was "the Magna Charta of British Indians" both in its "substance" and its "spirit" which heralded a "change of attitude" by the South African authorities. At this time, despite the emergence of some doubts, Gandhi still had faith in the British model.

THE DEVELOPMENT OF GANDHI'S DEMOCRATIC THOUGHT. 1915-1948

In this period the framework within which Gandhi's democratic thought was founded changed from the British empire to an independent India. In 1920, Gandhi stated that *swaraj* meant Indians "feeling and being the equals of Englishmen." It was also the life of "perfect freedom even though it may be full of defects." In this respect, and quoting the British statesman Henry Campbell-Bannerman, Gandhi observed: "Good government is no substitute for self-Government." Iyer noted that: "Gandhi would not regard good government as better than self-government because he believed there was a connection between individual and national self-rule." The apparent contradiction between Iyer's claim and Gandhi's use of Campbell-Bannerman's dictum illustrates the two different senses in which Gandhi used his ideaion of *swaraj* or self-rule or government. Gandhi differentiated between *swaraj* for India and *swaraj* for Indians. Gandhi came to believe that the former was preferable to 'good government' whilst he never accepted the same for the latter. Whilst this would seem to explain, at least partially, the motivation behind Gandhi's use of Campbell-Bannerman's phrase it is evident that Gandhi altered his position from that in his early years in South Africa when he sought 'good government' within the framework of the empire. However, it was apparent that Gandhi came to realize that good government was not achievable under that framework. Faced with this situation Gandhi was then able to explain why that was the case and link this to his democratic thought.

In the early 1920s, Gandhi's shift in favour of democracy conceive in an Indian, rather than a British, framework is represented by his use of Campbell-Bannerman's dictum concerning good and self-government. It is perhaps curious that Gandhi did not utilise Campbell-Bannerman in support of his struggle until 1920. Gandhi was familiar with Campbell-Bannerman during the early years of the century and met him in London during the 1906 Indian deputation. Gandhi wrote an article on Campbell-Bannerman, on the occasion of his death, which appeared in *Indian Opinion* in 1908. Gandhi described him as follows: "Sir Henry was a man of kind nature and noble mind. His sympathies were not confined to his own people." Gandhi also described how Campbell-Bannerman had been supportive of the 1906 Indian deputation:

When the [Transvaal] Indian deputation visited England in connection with the campaign against the law, he was very sympathetic [to the Indian case]. It is said he played some part in bringing pressure on Lord Elgin [to veto the Asiatic Law Amendment Ordinance].

Finally, Gandhi claimed that much could be learnt from Campbell-Bannerman's example as a worker for the "public good." Gandhi chided those Indians who had retired at "forty" from active life but still complained that India had not been "granted self-government." In contrast to these Indians, Campbell-Bannerman, Gandhi observed, had continued working until his seventies. Given his knowledge and admiration of Campbell-Bannerman it is likely that prior to 1920 Gandhi did not subscribe to his dictum and still had faith in democracy within a British framework.

Whilst in Britain during the Round Table Conference, in a 1931 speech at Chatham House, Gandhi revealed a number British influences as well as admitting to some problems in traditional Indian society. He also referred to *The Village Communities of India [sic]* and explained that Maine had described the Indian villages as "self-contained 'little republics.'" Gandhi quoted a British source in support of his demand for independence and home rule: "Sir Henry Campbell-Bannerman had said that good government was no substitute for self-government." Gandhi returned to Campbell-Bannerman's remark in a speech at the London School of Economics the following month. Having repeated the quotation Gandhi implied that British rule was not even good government: Those who are concerned do not feel that British rule has done good." It is interesting to note Desai's account of Gandhi's excursions to Oxford and Cambridge where he met a variety of scholars including Lindsay, Coupland, Gilbert Murray, Lowes Dickinson and Barker. Desai concluded: "With all deference to their studies, and their breadth of outlook, and above all to their earnest desire to understand and help, I am afraid, no one, whether in Oxford or Cambridge, seems to appreciate the truth of Henry Campbell-Bannerman's great maxim: 'Good government is no substitute for self-government.'" On this subject, Hunt concluded that: "Gandhi agreed with the dons on the positive values of British political theory; [but] he thought they overestimated the degree of effectiveness with which that theory operated in India." This assessment strikes at the core of the development of Gandhi's democratic thought. Gandhi had consistently supported the ideals of British political theory but had suffered and became disillusioned with its practice first in South Africa and then in India.

Louis Fischer's report of his conversations with Gandhi during June 1942 also reveals something of Gandhi's democratic thought at that time. In particular the conversation involved a discussion of the nature of Gandhi's village-based democracy and his criticism of the practice of democracy in Britain. In reply to a question concerning the welfare of the Indian peasants Gandhi explained that ideally he would improve their lot by ensuring that: "The village would become a self-governing unit living its own life." When Fischer enquired whether these village units would require a national government, Gandhi replied:

"I realize," Gandhi said, shaking his head, "that despite my views there will be a central government administration. However, I do not believe in the accepted Western form of democracy with its universal voting for parliamentary representatives."

As a replacement for directly elected parliaments, Gandhi envisaged a hierarchical system of representative institutions, elected by the villagers. Despite the impracticality of Gandhi's ideal Fischer pushed him to expand on its nature and Gandhi replied:

"There are seven hundred thousand villages in India. Each would be organized according to the will of its citizens, all of them voting. Then there would be seven hundred thousand votes and not four hundred million. Each village, in other words, would have one vote. The villages would elect their district administrations, and the district administrations would elect the provincial administrations and these in turn would elect a president who would be the national chief executive."

Fischer then remarked that the Congress had been criticised for being rather authoritarian. In its defence Gandhi retorted: "Do you think all questions are decided in the House of Commons or are decisions taken in party caucuses and in the clubs of London? Congress officers are elected by the members of Congress, and ministers who are members of Congress abide by the principles of Congress. Sir Samuel Hoare has told me a few things about the workings of democracy in Britain."

This passage reflects Gandhi's criticism of British political practice that he had first made in his observation of the House of Commons as early as 1909. Gandhi also urbanized the idea of decentralized, village-based *swaraj* in his contributions to *Harijan* in the 1940s. In an article in 1942 Gandhi explained: "My idea of Village Swaraj is that it is a complete republic, independent of its neighbours for its vital wants, and yet interdependent for many others in which dependence is a necessity."

Turning to the government of these villages Gandhi explained that it "will be conducted by the Panchayat of five persons, annually elected by the adult villagers, male and female, possessing minimum prescribed qualifications." Gandhi returned to the nature of these village republics in 1946. He explained that "every village will be a republic or panchayat having full powers" and as such "capable of managing its affairs." Within the villages "ultimately, it is the individual who is the unit." However, the villages would not be completely independent or isolated and Gandhi's plan would "not exclude dependence on and willing help from neighbours or from the world." Gandhi also described how the system of villages would interact:

In this structure composed of innumerable villages there will be ever widening, never ascending circles. Life will not be a pyramid with the apex sustained by the bottom. But it will be an oceanic circle whose centre will be the individual always ready to perish for the village, the latter ready to perish for the circle of villages, till at last the whole becomes one life composed of individuals, never aggressive in their arrogance but ever humble, sharing the majesty of the oceanic circle of which they are integral units.

Gandhi admitted that this was a "Utopian" ideal: "Let India live for this true picture, though never realizable in its completeness." In a speech in 1946, Gandhi referred to his *Harijan* article when he discussed his idea of village based democracy. Gandhi stated that he hoped that the village units would be "economically and politically as autonomous as possible." Correspondingly, political power would as far as possible "rest in the unit itself and not at the top, "on Mt. Everest," as it was under the British. This situation would constitute a return to the ancient Indian village system which Gandhi noted had been identified by Maine who had said that "India was a congeries of village republics." Since it was well over thirty years since Gandhi had first cited Maine, and possibly much longer since he had first read him, it is evident that Maine was an important British influence. This is reinforced by the increasing importance that village-based democracy attained in Gandhi's later democratic thought. Conclusion,

This chapter has identified a number of British influences on Gandhi's democratic thought. Positively, Gandhi incorporated a number of British sources directly into his democratic thought including Seeley, Maine, Carpenter, Cecil and Campbell-Bannerman.

Gandhi used the ideas of these authors to varying extents either on their own terms, as purely British ideas, or as British sources which endorsed traditional Indian ideas. Negatively, Gandhi used aspects of the works of these authors to support his criticism of British political practice. Conversely, and more positively, Gandhi also incorporated a number of aspects of British political practice. Initially, Gandhi sought to apply the ideals and principles of the British constitution, as he understood them, to the situation in South Africa. Ultimately, however, Gandhi rejected the British model, as he came to believe it was fundamentally flawed, being founded on modern civilization. In this sense, the influence of British political practice was at first positive and became negative but it continually constituted the wider framework within which Gandhi developed his democratic thought.

Socialism Thought of Gandhi

Gandhi's later socialist thought up to 1914 and the following section will examine the period up to his death in 1948. Finally, a conclusion will summarise the findings of the chapter.

THE DEVELOPMENT OF GANDHI'S SOCIALIST THOUGHT. 1915-1948

In a speech in 1916 Gandhi developed his assertion that by adopting the "modem materialistic craze" India had gone "down hill in the path of progress." He stated that "economic progress' of the materialistic kind was "antagonistic to real progress." In a speech to the Muir College Economic Society, Gandhi related that when he was asked to make the speech he had to admit that he "knew very little of economics" and he "had not even read books on economics by such well-known authorities as Mill, Marshall, [and] Adam Smith." This remark is interesting in that it not only reveals that Gandhi had read few traditional writers on economics up until that time but also the few authorities he cited were all British and classical.

Later in life, Gandhi read Adam Smith's *Wealth of Nations* and whilst discussing this work in 1934, described how his "economics of khadi" equated to one of Smith's "disturbing factors" which "prevented economic laws from having free play." Conversely, Gandhi read Marx's work but not until even later in his life, and was unconvinced of its merit. Pradhan concluded his study: "Although Gandhi's socialist thought was enriched by the heritage both of the East and the West... his indebtedness by no stretch of the imagination can be traced to the Scientific Socialism of Marx and Engels." Pandiri's survey of Gandhi's reading suggests only a few other possible sources of his socialist thought. These include: *Equality* (1897) by Edward Bellamy (1850-1898); *Economic History of India Under Early British Rule* (1901) by Romesh Chunder Dutt (1848-1909); and *Poverty and Un-British Rule in India* (1901) by Dadabhai Naoroji. None of these can really be classified as pure Marxist influences. This supports the explanation of British humanitarian, religious, and traditional Indian sources as being the strongest influences on Gandhi's socialist thought. For example, according to Adi Doctor: "Gandhi derived many of his economic views from Ruskin."

In contrast to the paucity of other possible sources for Gandhi s socialist thought the influence of British sources like Ruskin and Carpenter assumes a high degree of significance.

In an editorial in *Young India* in 1931 Gandhi criticised the Indian communists who, did "not seem to live the life of Communism," whilst claiming that he tried "to live up to the ideal of Communism in the best sense of the term." Gandhi made it clear that his socialism was not the socialism of the Congress Socialist Party. For example, commenting on the Congress Socialist Party's programme in 1934, Gandhi said he disliked it because it ignored "Indian conditions" and assumed "antagonism between the classes." Similarly, later that year Gandhi advised a member of the party to present "the country with practical socialism in keeping with Indian conditions instead of scientific socialism." Gandhi also rejected entirely the idea of class war on similar grounds. In 1934 he stated: "Class war is foreign to the essential genius of India which is capable of evolving a form of communism broad-based on the fundamental rights of all and equal justice to all." Elsewhere that year, Gandhi claimed that class war would be an "impossibility" if the "non-violent method" was adopted. For Gandhi socialism should be an action orientated philosophy, beginning with the individual, rather than an overtly theoretical one. Thus Gandhi stressed the importance of his own example in rejecting materialism and embracing asceticism. Additionally, Gandhi rejected the atheism of Marxism and stressed the importance of the spiritual and moral dimension of his socialist thought. Finally, Marxism was also an entirely alien ideology developed within, and for, the industrial west. Gandhi considered that:

Socialism and communism of the West are based on certain ideaions which are fundamentally different from ours. One such ideaion is their belief in the essential selfishness of human nature. I do not subscribe to it.

Therefore, Gandhi cautioned against being "obsessed with catchwords and seductive slogans imported from the West." Consequently, for Gandhi socialism and communism of the Marxist variety were not appropriate for India. Gandhi developed on his idea of trusteeship in the 1930s. He believed that "owners" should "act as trustees," or "owners" on behalf of, "those whom they have exploited." In 1937 Gandhi admitted that his ideaion of "trusteeship" had "yet to prove its worth." In practical terms Gandhi's "trusteeship" sought "to secure the best use of property for the people by competent hands." Trusteeship meant that the owners of wealth should hold it as trustees for the rest of society. For Gandhi trusteeship had a religious aspect since the owner of property should regard their wealth "as a bequest" put in their "possession by God." Therefore, Gandhi held that: 'The man who takes for himself only enough to satisfy the needs customary in his society and spends the rest for social service becomes a trustee." The feasibility of trusteeship followed from Gandhi's idealism and his anathema of class conflict and any violent redistribution of wealth. Gandhi claimed that trusteeship was based on traditional Indian practices.

However, the idea of trusteeship is one that Gandhi would have been familiar with from his legal studies. The British influence on Gandhi's idea of trusteeship has been acknowledged by Adi Doctor who observed that "it was to some extent inspired by

Gandhi s study of English jurisprudence and particularly Snell's *Equity.* "^ Gandhi read this book as a law student in London and mentions in his autobiography that he found it "full of interest, but a bit hard to understand." According to Pradhan, Snell's work describes Gandhi's idea of trusteeship very closely: "[Tjhe legal owner of property may himself hold the property" not for his own benefit "but for the benefit of another person, the real beneficiary of the property." In addition to the influence of Gandhi's legal studies, trusteeship therefore reveals further British influences. The elitism and paternalism implied by trusteeship also finds resonance with aspects of British socialism, although not those that Gandhi was particularly influenced by, Fabianism, for example. Additionally, it resembles some of Carpenter's ideas expressed in *Civilization, its Cause and Cure,* a work with which Gandhi was familiar. In 1941 Gandhi's *Constructive Programme* provided a brief outline of his framework for an independent India. Acknowledging the difficulties of implementing the ideas outlined in *Hind Swaraj,* Gandhi began by accepting that "practice will always fall short of the theory." However, Gandhi was adamant that to whatever extent practice might fall short of the ideal, that ideal could not be achieved through violence because in this way "perfect equality, economic or otherwise, is-inconceivable." For Gandhi *khadi,* the "symbol of Indian humanity, of its economic freedom and equality," was important because it would contribute to the Indian villages becoming "largely self-contained" and as such free them from "exploitation" and "ruin" by the cities of India and Britain. In particular the "khadi mentality" stood for "decentralization of the production and distribution of the necessaries of life." Gandhi accepted that there would be heavy industries but emphasised that they should be "centralized and nationalized" and occupy responsible for exploiting rural India. The least part of the vast national activity which will mainly be in the villages." Finally, Gandhi restated his belief in economic equality and his faith in the doctrine of trusteeship.

In defining the nature of his socialist thought towards the end of his life, Gandhi stressed the importance of economic equality. In an article in 1940 Gandhi developed his vision of equality and integrated it with his idea of trusteeship. For Gandhi, "equal distribution" meant that "each man shall have the wherewithal to supply all his natural needs and no more." Gandhi explained that the "root" of his "doctrine of equal distribution" was "the trusteeship of the wealthy for the superfluous wealth possessed by them" because "the rich cannot accumulate wealth without the co-operation of the poor in society." In discussing the differences between "Gandhism" and socialism or communism in 1946, Gandhi stressed that he would "bring about economic equality through non-violence" which meant "converting the people" and "by harnessing the forces of love as against hatred." Gandhi had been aware of the importance of equality ever since reading *Unto This Last.* In 1946 when asked about his economic programme Gandhi replied: "[That] if mankind was to progress and to realize the ideal of equality and brotherhood, it must adopt and act on the principle of *Unto This Last.*" In an interview in 1946, Gandhi again acknowledged his debt to Ruskin when expanding on his idea of equality. For Gandhi *Unto This Last* "marked the turning point" in his life, from whence he realized that "all should have equal opportunity" because "every human being has the same opportunity for spiritual growth." Equality would be improved for Gandhi if emphasis was instead placed on the 'moral being,' rather than the material, as had been done traditionally in India. This emphasis coincided with Gandhi's interpretation of Ruskin, including the lesson from *Unto This Last* that all work was equally valuable to the individual and to society. Conclusion

This chapter has outlined the nature, origins and development of Gandhi's socialist thought. It was a complex blend of humanitarianism, social reformism, and socialism defined by his critique of modern civilization. Gandhi's socialist thought was based on a genuine concern for the welfare of the masses and a broad based equality. Gandhi's programme for economic development was designed to ensure that the spiritual and moral element of Indian civilization was never overwhelmed by the materialism so evident in modern civilization. His socialist thought reveals several important British influences including critics of industrialism and modern civilization, like Carpenter and Ruskin. It also possessed a strong spiritual dimension that was in part a result of Christian influences, including that from British friends and acquaintances, his reading and his observations of Britain. Gandhi's legal training was also an important influence on his doctrine of trusteeship, which became such a central component of his socialist thought.

7

Gandhi and Satyagraha

Satyagraha is basically a way of life in which truth and nonviolence, the realization of truth through nonviolence and loving action, is the ideal. Everything else, thought or acted, has to be subservient to that ideal.

Love and nonviolence in the broadest sense have been the most cohesive and cementing forces of human society and of human relations since the beginning of man's life on earth. The progress of human society from the tribal to the international level would not otherwise have been a possibility. From violence to nonviolence, from fear to fearlessness, from hatred to love; from the gross to the subtle has been the progress of civilization and culture.

While, thus, the trend of evolution is towards truth and nonviolence, towards construction and achievement, while the inner aspiration of man is towards the good and the true, the beautiful and the everlasting, untruth, evil, violence, hatred and destruction are still acting as anti-evolutionary forces. The progressive realization of the true nature and power as well as the increasing and effective use of goodness and truth, of love and nonviolence, is and can be the highest and the only goal of self-conscious humanity. The measure of success man attains in this venture is the measure of real progress in his evolution towards an ideal humanity, living in peace and joy and fulfilment.

Seen in this perspective, Gandhi may be said to have placed himself in the hands of the human evolutionary urge itself. He is the spearhead and symbol of future humanity. For him, the evolutionary urge meant predominantly the quest of the truth of life in terms of the needs of human progress, and its realization through the means of love and through action prompted by nonviolence.

It is true that insistence on clinging to truth firmly, and defence as well as establishment of truth through nonviolent behaviour and through love and self-suffering, are not entirely new. They are as old as humanity and as ancient as the first emergence of saints. But Gandhi developed the technique not merely as a weapon to be used by individuals and almost entirely in the religious field but as a method which can be used by organized' groups universally and in all fields and conflicts. It is this that has opened new vistas and inspired in mankind a fresh hope that this may be helpful not only as an equivalent of war but also for eliminating war ultimately.

True, Gandhi acted in a certain environment and led his people to success under given circumstances. He was faced directly with specific problems, the liberation of his own country being one of the most important of them. He solved many problems and that of liberation during his own lifetime. He organized and disciplined vast masses on nonviolent lines, though there were some occasional lapses on the part of his followers.

But it should be remembered that invasion of one country by another, international war, the replacement of war as an instrument for solving international conflicts, the solution o£ such conflicts by peaceful methods only, these were not the problems that he had to face directly as a satyagrahi. He has no doubt written a lot about all these situations, but they are in the nature of obiter dicta. The remedies which he has suggested indicate only the direction. Though he had no occasion to act and demonstrate his principles in the circumstances indicated above, he firmly believed that a nonviolent way was bound to be available for the solution of every problem in human relationship and that it was also bound to be successful, That he held this belief firmly and from the beginning is evident from his statements on many occasions.

The fact of the matter is that Satyagraha is not a mechanical formula or a mathematical theory. It is a living, dynamic principle and philosophy of life which is yet to unfold itself and evolve fully. It may be said to be "the law of being" of coming humanity. It has yet to replace fully and effectively the operation of physical force and coercion in social evolution and social dynamics. Love, nonviolence, is the law of our species, no doubt, but it has yet to establish itself firmly and fully. Nevertheless it is progressively advancing. It is struggling, with reason as its helpmate, to control the irrational urges for possession and power of present-day humanity.

It is, of course, doubtful if organized political States as such will ever entertain a plan of action based on the principles of Satyagraha because every State is founded on physical force as its basic and final sanction. That has been the theory of State since the beginning of all politics. In its dealings with its own subjects or with its neighbours a State may occasionally use methods which are in their externals somewhat similar to those of a satyagrahi, such as persuasion, negotiation, compromise and so on. But there the similarity ends. nonviolent methods are used by States as being expedient or less costly but never as a principle of action or as the final sanction. Self-suffering, for instance, has no place at all in a State's policy. A State guides its steps mainly along the line of immediate as well as ultimate self interest. So to expect at present even the smallest State to think in terms of the principles of Satyagraha is to live in an imaginary world. It is equally futile to expect even the most powerful State, which keeps swearing by peace, to cease to add to its striking power. "Keeping the powder dry" is the only policy that all States follow. A State which would train and discipline its citizens in the science and art of Satyagraha is yet to be horn. Even India, which won its freedom by predominantly nonviolent means, has not been able, as a State, to do anything either in the way of unilateral disarmament or in the way of organizing a "nonviolent army".

But we need not despair at the fact that States, constituted as they are today, can never think in terms of Satyagraha. Certainly such States as are not out for war, such as are peace-minded and in dead earnest to see that the ways of peace and friendliness are ultimately substituted for those of war and violence, can help create circumstances which would promote the methods of Satyagraha by the people. They can certainly add to the common efforts of mankind to bring about an atmosphere of peace. They can do this both in the political and in the diplomatic field.

The first and most important step that a State could take to lessen the prevailing tension and the chances of war-I mean a major war-is to refrain from joining the power-groups, or powerblocs as they are called. This is a kind of "noncooperation with evil". Of course, the question could be asked whether these nations which stand outside the blocs have themselves abjured violence and war as a means of solving international conflicts, and whether they have disbanded their armies and established the rule of nonviolence in their own areas. The obvious answer is that they have clone nothing of the kind. And yet it cannot be gainsaid that they have helped by non-alignment in creating an atmosphere for peace, be it in ever so humble a way.

Following this first step could come complete noncooperation, boycott and education of public opinion within the borders of, the war-mongering States by a sufficiently well-organized group of non-bloc countries. They may use their collective influence to insist that there should be complete disarmament, that there should be no war henceforward and that means and methods other than violence and war should be brought into use, both for preventing international conflicts and for solving them.

When the organization of such States becomes powerful enough, their combined moral pressure on isolated power-blocs which are always on the brink of war is likely to be effective. Of course, the sanction behind such moral power of the non-aligned States would be the peaceful weapons of complete noncooperation, economic and other nonviolent boycotts and so on. All this, if fully effective, would lead ultimately to total disarmament and to a world government. Then the only central authority wielding physical power would be the World Government. The States would then have only municipal, judicial and administrative powers and would have no military sanctions either for defensive or offensive purposes. Attempts such as the League of-Nations, the United Nations Organization and disarmament conferences are all leading us in that direction. While this would no doubt be a great achievement, the world would still continue to be ruled by violent and coercive sanctions rather than by love and nonviolence, and there would still persist the need to preach and practise Satyagraha as conceived by Gandhi, until such time as the rule of truth, friendliness and mutual cooperation is established throughout humanity.

Since wars begin in the minds and hearts of men and since the substitute for war also has to take root and grow there only, educating the people along those lines is essential as the very first step. This has been rendered easier now, since the evil not only of atomic war but even of atomic tests has come home to the people.

Today it is a well-known fact that the world is war-weary, that while the governments concerned are preparing for war, the people not only do not want war but definitely want peace. But at the same time they are afraid of aggression, of being conquered by "others", by foreigners; they are afraid o£ losing their freedom. Obviously slavery is a continuous violence against the very soul of a people. It is natural that a people should prefer using violence to losing their freedom. It is therefore that they allow their governments to prepare for oar while they themselves are hankering for peace. They realize that at best, war is a counsel of despair and at worst an invitation to death and destruction. But they have no effective alternative to offer to their governments. If we know how to organize nonviolent and peaceful forces in our own country and in the world, there is every hope that the organization of violent forces would break down. Nobody wants violence nor its triumph. There are no advocates for war as such. Even the worst war-mongers would say that war is but a necessary evil. They would avoid it if they could but they cannot, being caught up in a vicious circle.

When such is the situation, it is the moral duty of every individual and every citizen to line himself up on the side of "no-war" and see that he supports by some intelligent action the organization of nonviolent forces. Only sentimental revulsion from war would not be very helpful. Mere lip-sympathy or intellectual appreciation of peace efforts is no longer enough. It should, however, be very clearly understood that there cannot be nonviolent action only by a single nation or its people. It has to be an international mass movement on the basis of "Peace workers of the world unite". Otherwise there is danger of subjugation by armed neighbours, which is worse than violence in defence of one's freedom. The basic need of various peace-movements today, by whatever name they might be called, is of an organized and dedicated army of workers in all countries, of the type of the satyagrahis who enrolled themselves under Gandhi's leadership in India. The next step can be taken only when there is such an army to take that first step. The quality of the army is of very great importance more than its number. The time for action would come when there shall be an army of men and women who are willing to act; then the technique of international action may be found along the lines of Satyagraha. This would include passive as well as aggressive resistance to all those agencies which today directly or indirectly promote war and violence in the various States. Of course, such resistance should start only after all other types of persuasion have failed. Such resistance may take any form, from simple noncooperation to aggressive picketing even at the risk of being shot. This may include non-payment of taxes, boycott, social boycott of people who are ordering or directly manufacturing weapons of destruction, and so on. All these would depend upon the circumstances and the skill and tact of the local leaders.

But under all circumstances, nonviolence has to be strictly adhered to and the distinction between the evil and the evildoer has to be scrupulously borne in mind. There should be the utmost readiness to suffer cheerfully the highest punishment and death, in the buoyant faith that truth-in this case the cause of non-violence-will triumph. This is a nonviolent war against war and all the courage to face the worst has to be readily in evidence. That is the true spirit of Satyagraha, the weapon of the brave against all evil.

POWER OF SATYAGRAHA

Victory of Satyagraha

A clear victory of Satyagraha is impossible so long as there is ill-will. But those who believe themselves to be weak are incapable of loving. Let, then, our first act every morning be to make the following resolve for the day: 'I shall not fear any one on earth. I shall fear God only; I shall not bear ill-will towards any one. I shall not submit to injustice from any one. I shall conquer untruth by truth and in resisting untruth I shall put up with all suffering. (SL NO. 14, 4-5-1919)

There is no time-limit for a Satyagrahi nor is there a limit to his capacity for suffering. Hence there is no such thing as defeat in Satyagraha. (YI, 19-2-1925, p.61)

It is not because I value life low that I countenance with joy thousands voluntarily losing their lives for Satyagraha, but because I know that it results, in the long run, in the least loss of life and, what is more, it ennobles those who lose their lives and morally enriches the world for their sacrifice. (YI, 8-10-1925, p. 345)

And when once it is set in motion, its effect, if it is intensive enough, can overtake the whole universe. It is the greatest force because it is the highest expression of the soul. (YI, 23-9-1926, p. 332)

My experience has taught me that a law of progression applies to every righteous struggle. But in the case of Satyagraha the law amounts to an axiom. As a Satyagraha struggle progresses onward, many another element helps to swell its current and there is a constant growth in the results to which it leads. This is really inevitable, and is bound up with the first principles of Satyagraha. For in Satyagraha the minimum is also the maximum, and as it is the irreducible minimum, there is no question of retreat, and the only movement possible is an advance. In other struggles, even when they are righteous, the demand is first pitched a little higher so as to admit of future reduction, and hence the law of progression does not apply to all of them without exception. (S, p. 319)

To me it is one of the most active forces in the world, It is like the sun that rises upon us unfailingly from day to day. Only if we would but understand it, it is infinitely greater than a million suns put together. It radiates life and light and peace and happiness. (YI, 18-4-1929, p. 126)

One True Satyagrahi

If a single Satyagrahi holds out to the end, victory is certain. (SSA, p. xiv)

Self-sacrifice of one innocent man is a million times more potent than the sacrifice of a million men who die in the act of killing others. The willing sacrificed of the innocent is the most powerful retort to insolent tyranny that has yet been conceived by God or man. (YI, 12-2-1925, p. 60)

I have maintained that, even if there is one individual who is almost completely nonviolent, he can put out the conflagration...In this age of democracy, it is essential that desired results are achieved by the collective effort of the people. It will no doubt be good to achieve an objective through the effort of a supremely powerful individual, but it can never make the community conscious of its corporate strength. (H, 8-9-1940, p. 277)

I believe in walking alone. I came alone in this world, I have walked alone in the valley of the shadow of death and I shall quit alone when the time comes. I know I am quite capable of launching Satyagraha even if I am all alone. I have done so before. (YI, 21-7-1946, p. 227)

Application of Satyagraha

It is a force that may be used by individuals as well as by communities. It may be used as well in political as in domestic affairs. Its universal applicability is a demonstration of its permanence and invincibility. It can be used alike by men, women and children.

It is totally untrue to say that it is a force to be used only by the weak so long as they are not capable of meeting violence by violence.... This force is to violence and, therefore, to all tyranny, all injustice, what light is to darkness. In politics, its use is based upon the immutable maxim that government of the people is possible only so long as they consent either consciously or unconsciously to be governed. (YI, 3-11-1927, 369)

I have never claimed to be the one original Satyagrahi. What I have claimed is the application of that doctrine on an almost universal scale, and it yet remains to be seen and demonstrated that it is a doctrine which is capable of assimilation by thousands upon thousands of peoples in all ages and climes. (YI, 22-9-1927, p. 317)

The Nonviolent Sanction

Satyagraha is a law of universal application. Beginning with the family, its use can be extended to every other circle.

Supposing a landowner exploits his tenants and mulcts them of the fruit of their toil by appropriating it to his own use. When they expostulate with him he does not listen and raises objections that he requires so much for his wife, so much for his children and so on. The tenants or those who have espoused their cause and have influence will make an appeal to his wife to expostulate with her husband. She would probably say that for herself she does not need his exploited money. The children will say likewise that they would earn for themselves what they need.

Supposing further that he listens to nobody or that his wife and children combine against the tenants, they will not submit. They will quit if asked to do so, but they will make it clear that the land himself and he will have to give in to their just demands.

It may, however, be that the tenants are replaced by others. Agitation short of violence will then continue till the replacing tenants see their error and make common cause with the evicted tenants.

Thus Satyagraha is a process of educating public opinion, such that it covers all elements of society and in the end makes itself irresistible. Violence interrupts the process and prolongs the real revolution of the whole social structure. The conditions necessary for the success of Satyagraha are: (1) The Satyagrahi should not have any hatred in his heart against the opponent. (2)

The issue must be true and substantial. (3) The Satyagrahi must be prepared to suffer till the end for his cause. (H, 31-3-1946, p. 64)

Training for Self-defence

I believe that every man and woman should learn the art of self-defence in this age. This is done through arms in the West. Every adult man is conscripted for army training for a definite period. The training for Satyagraha is meant for all, irrespective of age or sex. The more important part of the training here is mental, not physical. There can be no compulsion in mental training. The surrounding atmosphere no doubt acts on the mind, but that cannot justify compulsion...

Satyagraha is always superior to armed resistance. This can only be effectively proved by demonstration, not by argument. It is the weapon that adorns the strong. It can never adorn the weak. By weak is meant the weak in mind and spirit, not in body. That limitation is a quality to be prized and not defect to be deplored.

One ought also to understand one of its other limitations. It can never be used to defend a wrong cause.

Satyagraha brigades can be organized in every village and in every block of buildings in the cities. Each brigade should be composed of those persons who are well-known to the organizers. In this respect Satyagraha differs from armed defence. For the latter the State impresses the service of everybody. For a Satyagraha brigade only those are eligible who believe in ahimsa and satya. Therefore, an intimate knowledge of the persons enlisted is necessary for the organizers. (H, 17-3-1946, pp. 45-46)

Duragraha

I can see nothing but catastrophe for India from methods of violence. Workmen would be committing suicide and India would have to suffer indescribable misery if workingmen were to vent their anger by criminal disobedience of the laws of the land.... When I began to preach Satyagraha and civil disobedience, it was never meant to cover criminal disobedience. My experience teaches me that truth can never be propagated by doing violence.

Those who believe in the justice of their cause need to possess boundless patience, and those alone are fit to offer civil disobedience who are above committing criminal disobedience or doing violence.

A man cannot commit both civil and criminal disobedience at the same time, even as he cannot be both temperate and furious at the same time, and just as self-restraint is acquired only after one has been able to master his passions, so is the capacity for civil disobedience acquired after one has disciplined oneself in complete and voluntary obedience of the laws of the land.

Again, just as he alone can be said to be proof against temptations who, having been exposed to them, has succeeded in resisting them, so may we be said to have conquered anger when, having sufficient cause for it, we have succeeded in controlling ourselves. (YI, 28-4-1920, pp. 7-8)

Some students have revived the ancient form of barbarity in the form of 'sitting dhurna'...I call it 'barbarity' for it is a crude way of using coercion. It is also cowardly, because one who sits dhurna knows that he is not going to be trampled over. It is difficult to call the practice violent, but it is certainly worse.

If we fight our opponent, we at least enable him to return the blow. But when we challenge him to walk over us, knowing that he will not, we place him in a most awkward and humiliating position. I know that the over-zealous students who sat dhurna never thought of the barbarity of the deed. But one who is expected to follow the voice of conscience and stand even single-handed in the face of odds cannot afford to be thoughtless.

There must be no impatience, no barbarity, no insolence, no undue pressure. If we want to cultivate a true spirit of democracy, we cannot afford to be intolerant. Intolerance betrays want of faith in one's cause. (YI, 2-2-1921, p. 33)

I have not been able to understand the cause of so much excitement and disturbance that followed my detention. It is not Satyagraha. It is worse than Durgraha.

Those who join Satyagraha demonstrations were bound one and all to refrain at all hazard from violence, not to throw stones or in anyway whatever to injure anybody. But in Bombay we have been throwing stones. We have obstructed tram-cars by putting obstacles in the way. This is not Satyagraha. We have demanded the release of about 50 men who had been arrested for deeds of violence. Our duty is chiefly to get ourselves arrested. It is breach of religious duty to endeavour to secure the release of those who have committed deeds of violence. (SW, p. 474)

I have said times without number that Satyagraha admits of no violence, no pillage, no incendiarism; and still, in the name of Satyagraha, we have burnt buildings, forcibly captured weapons, extorted money, stopped trains, cut off telegraph wires, killed innocent people and plundered shops and private houses. If deeds such as these could save me from the prison-house or the scaffold, I should not like to be so saved. (ibid, p. 476)

....Heroism and sacrifice in a bad cause are so much waste of splendid energy and hurt the good cause by drawing away attention from it by the glamour of the misused heroism and sacrifice in a bad cause. (YI, 12-12-1925, p. 60)

....Indiscriminate resistance to authority must lead to lawlessness and unbridled license and consequent self-destruction. (YI, 2-4-1931, p. 58)

TRUTH IS GOD

There is an indefinable mysterious Power that pervades everything. I feel it, though I do not see it. It is this unseen Power which makes itself felt and yet defies all proof, because it is so unlike all that I perceive through my senses. It transcends the senses. But it is possible to reason out the existence of God to a limited extent.

I do dimly perceive that whilst everything around me is ever changing, ever-dying, there is underlying all that change a Living Power that is changeless, that holds all together, that creates, dissolves, and recreates. That informing Power or Spirit is God. And since nothing else I see merely through the senses can or will persist, He alone is.

And is this Power benevolent or malevolent? I see it as purely benevolent. For I can see, that in the midst of death life persists, in the midst of untruth truth persists, in the midst of darkness light persists. Hence I gather that God is Life, Truth, Light. He is Love. He is the Supreme Good.

I confess… that I have no argument to convince… through reason. Faith transcends reason. All I can advise… is not to attempt the impossible. I cannot account for the existence of evil by any rational method. To want to do so is to be co-equal with God. I am, therefore, humble enough to recognize evil as such; and I call God long-suffering and patient precisely because He permits evil in the world. I know that He has no evil in Him and yet if there is evil, He is the author of it and yet untouched by it.

I know, too, that I shall never know God if I do not wrestle with and against evil even at the cost of life itself. I am fortified in the belief by my own humble and limited experience. The purer I try to become the nearer to God I feel myself to be. How much more should I be near to Him when my faith is not a mere apology, as it is today, but has become as immovable as the Himalayas and as white and bright as the snows on their peaks? (YI, 11-10-1928, pp340-1)

My Faith

I can easily put up with the denial of the world, but any denial by me of my God is unthinkable. (YI, 23-2-1922, p112)

I know that I can do nothing. God can do everything. O God, make me Thy fit instrument and use me as thou wilt! (YI, 9-10-1924, p329)

I have not seen Him, neither have I known Him. I have made the world's faith in God my own and as my faith is ineffaceable, I regard that faith as amounting to experience. However, as it may be said that to describe faith as experience is to tamper with truth, it may perhaps be more correct to say that I have no word for characterizing my belief in God. (A, p206)

I am surer of His existence than of the fact that you and I are sitting in this room. Then I can also testify that I may live without air and water but not without Him. You may pluck out my eyes, but that cannot kill me. You may chop off my nose, but that will not kill me. But blast my belief in God, and I am dead.

You may call this a superstition, but I confess it is a superstition that I hug, even as I used to hug the name of Rama in my childhood when there was any cause of danger or alarm. That was what an old nurse had taught me. (H, 14-5-1938, p109)

I believe that we can all become messengers of God, if we cease to fear man and seek only God's Truth. I do believe I am seeking only God's Truth and have lost all fear of man.

...I have no special revelation of God's will. My firm belief is that He reveals Himself daily to every human being, but we shut our ears to the 'still small voice'. We shut our eyes to the Pillar of Fire in front of us. I realize His omnipresence. (YI, 25-5-1921, pp161-2)

Some of my correspondents seem to think that I can work wonders. Let me say as a devotee of truth that I have no such gift. All the power I may have comes from God. But He does not work directly. He works through His numberless agencies. (H, 8-10-1938, p285)

Nature of God

To me God is Truth and Love; God is ethics and morality; God is fearlessness. God is the source of Light and Life and yet He is above and beyond all these. God is conscience. He is even the atheism of the atheist. For in His boundless love God permits the atheist to live. He is the searcher of hearts. He transcends speech and reason. He knows us and our hearts better than we do ourselves. He does not take us at our word, for He knows that we often do not mean it, some knowingly and others unknowingly.

He is a personal God to those who need His personal presence. He is embodied to those who need His touch. He is the purest essence. He simply is to those who have faith. He is all things to all men. He is in us and yet above and beyond us...

He cannot cease to be because hideous immoralities or inhuman brutalities are committed in His name. He is long-suffering. He is patient but He is also terrible. He is the most exacting personage in the world and the world to come. He metes out the same measure to us that we mete out to our neighbors-men and brutes.

With Him ignorance is no excuse. And withal He is ever forgiving, for He always gives us the chance to repent.

He is the greatest democrat the world knows, for He leaves us 'unfettered' to make our own choice between evil and good. He is the greatest tyrant ever known, for He often dashes the cup from our lips and under cove of free will leaves us a margin so wholly inadequate as to provide only mirth for Himself at our expense.

Therefore it is that Hinduism calls it all His sport-lila, or calls it all an illusion-maya. We are not, He alone Is. And if we will be, we must eternally sing His praise and do His will. Let us dance to the tune of His bansi-lute, and all would be well. (YI, 5-3-1925, p81)

God is the hardest taskmaster I have known on this earth, and He tries you through and through. And when you find that your faith is failing or your body is failing you and you are sinking, He comes to your assistance somehow or other and proves to you that you must not lose your faith and that He is always at your beck and call, but on His terms, not on your terms. So I have found. I cannot really recall a single instance when, at the eleventh hour, He has forsaken me. (SW, p1069)

In my early youth I was taught to repeat what in Hindu scriptures are known as one thousand names of God. But these one thousand names of God were by no means exhaustive. We believe-and I think it is the truth-that God has as many names as there are creatures and, therefore, we also say that God is nameless and, since God has many forms, we also consider Him formless, and since He speaks to us through many tongues, we consider Him to be speechless and so on.

And so when I came to study Islam, I found that Islam too had many names for God.

I would say with those who say God is Love, God is Love. But deep down in me I used to say that though God may be Love, God is Truth, above all. If it is possible for the human tongue to give the fullest description of God, I have come to the conclusion that, for myself, God is Truth.

But two years ago I went a step further and said that Truth is God. You will see the fine distinction between the two statements, viz., that God is Truth and Truth is God. And I came to the conclusion after a continuous and relentless search after Truth which began nearly fifty years ago.

I then found that the nearest approach to Truth was through love. But I also found that love has many meanings in the English language at least and that human love in the sense of passion could become a degrading thing also. I found too that love in the sense of ahimsa had only a limited number of votaries in the world. But I never found a double meaning in connection with truth and not even atheists had demurred to the necessity or power of truth.

But, in their passion for discovering truth, the atheists have not hesitated to deny the very existence of God-from their own point of view, rightly. And it was because of this reasoning that I saw that, rather than say that God is Truth, I should say that Truth is God. (YI, 31-12-1931, p427-8)

God is Truth, but God is many other things also. That is why I say Truth is God.... Only remember that Truth is not one of the many qualities that we name. It is the living embodiment of God, it is the only Life, and I identify Truth with the fullest life, and that is how it becomes a concrete thing, for God is His whole creation, the whole Existence, and service of all that exists-Truth-is service of God. (H, 25-5-1935, p115)

Perfection is the attribute of the Almighty, and yet what a great democrat He is! What an amount of wrong and humbug He suffers on our part! He even suffers us insignificant creatures of His to question His very existence, though He is in every atom about us, around us and within us. But He has reserved to Himself the right of becoming manifest to whomsoever He chooses. He is a Being without hands and feet and other organs, yet he can see Him to whom He chooses to reveal Himself. (H, 14-11-1936, p314)

God Through Service

If I did not fee the presence of God within me, I see so much of misery and disappointment every day that I would be a raving maniac and my destination would be the Hooghli. (YI, 6-8-1925, p275)

If I am to identify myself with the grief of the least in India, aye, if I have the power, the least in the world, let me identify myself with the sins of the little ones who are under my care. And so doing in all humility, I hope some day to see God-Truth-face to face. (YI, 3-12-1925, p422)

I am endeavoring to see God through service of humanity, for I know that God is neither in heaven, nor down below, but in every one. (YI, 4-8-1927, p247-8)

I am a part and parcel of the whole, and I cannot find Him apart from the rest of humanity. My countrymen are my nearest neighbors. They have become so helpless, so resourceless, so inert that I must concentrate on serving them. If I could persuade myself that I should find Him in a Himalayan cave, I would proceed there immediately. But I know that I cannot find Him apart from humanity. (H, 29-8-1936, p226)

I claim to know my millions. All the 24 hours of the day I am with them. They are my first care and last because I recognize no God except the God that is to be found in the hearts of the dumb millions. They do not recognize His presence; I do. And I worship the God that is Truth or Truth which is God through the service of these millions. (H, 11-3-1939, p44)

Guide and Protector

I must go... with God as my only guide. He is a jealous Lord. He will allow no one to share His authority. One has, therefore, to appear before Him in all one's weakness, empty-handed and in a spirit of full surrender, and then He enables you to stand before a whole world and protects you from all harm. (YI, 3-9-1931, p247)

I have learned this one lesson-that what is impossible with man is child's play with God and if we have faith in that Divinity which presides on the destiny of the meanest of His creation, I have no doubt that all things are possible; and in that final hope, I live and pass my time and endeavor to obey His will. (YI, 19-11-1931, p361)

Even in darkest despair, where there seems to be no helper and no comfort in the wide, wide world, His Name inspires us with strength and puts all doubts and despairs to flight. The sky may be overcast today with clouds, but a fervent prayer to Him is enough to dispel them. It is because of prayer that I have known no disappointment.

...I have known no despair. Why then should you give way to it? Let us pray that He may cleanse our hearts of pettiness, meanness and deceit and He will surely answer our prayers. Many I know have always turned to that unfailing source of strength. (H, 1-6-1935, p123)

I have seen and believe that God never appears to you in person, but in action which can only account for your deliverance in your darkest hour. (H, 10-12-1938, p373)

Individual worship cannot be described in words. It goes on continuously and even unconsciously. There is not a moment when I do not feel the presence of a Witness whose eye misses nothing and with whom I strive to keep in tune.

I have never found Him lacking in response. I have found Him nearest at hand when the horizon seemed darkest in my ordeals in jails when it was not all-smooth sailing for me. I cannot recall a moment in my life when I had a sense of desertion by God. (H, 24-12-1938, p395)

Self-realization

I believe it to be possible for every human being to attain to that blessed and indescribable, sinless state in which he feels within himself the presence of God to the exclusion of everything else. (YI, 17-11-1921, p368) What I want to achieve, what I have been striving and pining to achieve..., is self-realization, to see God face to face, to attain moksha. I live and move and have my being in pursuit of this goal. All that I do by way of speaking and writing and all my ventures in the political field are directed to this same end. (A, p xiv)

For it is an unbroken torture to me that I am still so far from Him, who, as I fully know, governs every breath of my life, and whose offspring I am. I know that it is the evil passions within that keep me so far from Him, and yet I cannot get away from them. (ibid, p xvi)

This belief in God has to be based on faith, which transcends reason. Indeed, even the so-called realization has at bottom an element of faith without which it cannot be sustained. In the very nature of things it must be so. Who can transgress the limitations of his being? I hold that complete realization is impossible in this embodied life. Nor is it necessary. A living immovable faith is all that is required for reaching the full spiritual height attainable by human beings. God is not outside this earthly case of ours. Therefore, exterior proof is not of much avail, if any at all. We must ever fail to perceive Him through the senses, because He is beyond them. We can feel Him if we will but withdraw ourselves from the senses. The divine music is incessantly going on within ourselves, but the loud senses drown the delicate music, which is unlike and infinitely superior to anything we can perceive or hear with our senses. (H, 13-6-1936, pp140-1)

THE ROOTS OF TRUTH

Among the delusions which at different periods have afflicted mankind, perhaps the gretest-certainly the least creditable-is modern economics based on the idea that an advantageous code of action may be determined irrespectively of the influence of social affection. Of course, as in the case of other delusions, political economy has a plausible idea at the root of it. 'The social affections,' says the economist, 'are accidental and disturbing elements in human nature ; but avarice and the desire for progress are constant elements. Let us eliminate the inconstants, and considering man merely as a money-making machine, examine by what laws of labour, purchase and sale, the greatest amount of wealth can be accumulated. Those laws once determined, it will be for each individual afterwards to introduce as much of the disturbing affectionate element as he chooses.'

This would be a logical method of analysis if the accidentals afterwards to be introduced were of the same nature as the powers first examined. Supposing a body in motion to be influenced by constant and inconstant forces, it is the simplest way of examining its course to trace it first under the persistent conditions and afterwards introduce the causes of variation. But the disturbing elements in the social problem are not of the same nature as the constant ones; they alter the essence of the creature under examination the moment they are added. They operate not mathematically but chemically, introducing conditions which render all our previous knowledge unavailable.

I do not doubt the conclusions of the science of its terms are accepted. I am simply uninterested in them, as I should be in those of a science of gymnastics which assumed that men had no skeletons. It might be shown on that supposition that it would be advantageous to roll the students up into pellets, flatten them into cakes, or stretch them into cables; and that when these results were effected, the reinsertion of the skeleton would be attended with various inconveniences to their constitution. The reasoning might be admirable, the conclusions true, and the science deficient only in applicability. Modern political economy stands on a precisely similar basis. It imagines that man has a body but no soul to be taken into account and frames its laws accordingly. How can such laws possibly apply to man in whom the soul is the predominant element?

Political economy is no science at all. We see how helpless it is when labourers go on a strike. The masters take one view of the matter, the operatives another; and no political economy can set them at one. Disputant after disputant vainly strives to show that the interests of the masters are not antagonistic to those of the men.

In fact it does not always follow that the persons must be antagonistic because their interests are. If there is only a crust of bread in the house, and mother and children are starving, their interests are not the same. If the mother eats it, the children want it; if the children eat it, the mother must go hungry to her work. Yet it does not follow that there is antagonism between them, that they will fight for the crust, and the mother, being strongest, will get it and eat it. Similarly it cannot be assumed that because their interests are diverse, persons must regard one another with hostility and use violence or cunning to obtain the advantage.

Even if we consider men as actuated by no other moral influences than those which affect rats or swine, it can never be shown generally either that the interests of master and labourer are alike or that they are opposed; for according to circumstances they may be either. It is indeed the interest of both that the work should be rightly done and a just price obtained for it ; but in the division of profits, the gain of the one may or may not be the loss of the other. It is not the master's interest to pay wages so low as to leave the men sickly and depressed, nor the workman's interest to be paid high wages if the smallness of the master's profit hinders him from conducting it in a safe and liberal way. A stoker ought not to desire high pay if the company is too poor to keep the engine-wheels in repair.

All endeavour, therefore, to deduce rules of action from balance of expediency is in vain. And it is meant to be in vain. For no human actions ever were intended by the Maker of men to be guided by balances of expediency but by balances of justice. He has therefore rendered all endeavours to determine expediency futile for evermore. No man can know what will be the ultimate result to himself or others of any given line of conduct. But every man may know and most of us do know what is a just and unjust act. And all of us may know also that the consequences of justice will be ultimately the best possible, both to others and ourselves, though we can neither say what is best, or how it is likely to come about.

I have meant in the term justice to include affection-such affection as one man owes to another. All right relations between master and operative ultimately depend on this.

As an illustration let us consider the position of domestic servants.

We will suppose that the master of a household tries only to get as much work out of his servants as he can, at the rate of wages he gives. He never allows them to be idle ; feeds them as poorly and lodges them as ill as they will endure. In doing this, there is no violation on his part of what is commonly called 'justice'. He agrees with the domestic for his whole time and service and takes them, the limits of hardship in treatment being fixed by the practice of other masters in the neighbourhood. If the servant can get a better place, he is free to take one.

This is the politico-economical view of the case according to the doctors of that science who assert that by this procedure the greatest average of work will be obtained from the servant, and therefore the greatest benefit to the community, and through the community, to the servant himself.

That however is not so. It would be so if the servant were an engine of which the motive power was steam, magnetism or some such agent of calculable force. But on the contrary he is an engine whose motive power is the Soul. Soul force enters into all the economist's equations without his knowledge and falsifies every one of their results.

The largest quantity of work will not be done by this curious engine for pay or under pressure. It will be done when the motive force, that is to say, the will or spirit of the creature, is brought to its greatest strength by its own proper fuel, namely by the affections. It does happen often that if the master is a man of sense and energy, much material work may be done under pressure ; also it does happen often that if the master is indolent and weak, a small quantity of work, and that bad, may be produced by his servant. But the universal law of the matter is that, assuming any given quantity of energy and sense in master and servant, the greatest material result obtainable by them will be not through antagonism to each other, but through affection for each other.

Nor is this one whit less generally true because indulgence will be frequently abused, and kindness met with ingratitude. For the servant who, gently treated, is ungrateful, treated ungently, will be revengeful ; and the man who is dishonest to a liberal master will be injurious to an unjust man.

In any case and with any person, this unselfish treatment will produce the most effective return. I am here considering the affections wholly as a motive power ; not at all as things in themselves desirable or noble. I look at them simply as an anomalous force, rendering every one of the ordinary economist's calculations nugatory. The affections only become a true motive power when they ignore every other motive and condition of economics. Treat the servant kindly with the idea of turning his gratitude to account, and you will get, as you deserve, no gratitude nor any value for your kindness ; but treat him kindly without any economical purpose, and all economical purposes will be answered ; here as elsewhere whoever will save his life shall lose it, whoso loses it shall find it.

The next simplest example of relation between master and operative is that which exists between the commander of a regiment and his men.

Supposing the officer only desires to apply the rules of discipline so as, with least trouble to himself, to make the regiment most effective, he will not be able, by any rules, on this selfish principle, to develop the full strength of his subordinates. But if he has the most direct personal relations with his men, the most care for their interests, and the most value for their lives, he will develop their effective strength, through their affection for his own person and trust in his character, to a degree wholly unattainable by other means. This applies more stringently as the numbers concerned are larger : a charge may often be successful though the men dislike their officers ; a battle has rarely been won, unless they loved their general.

A body of men associated for the purposes of robbery (as a Highland clan in ancient times) shall be animated by perfect affection, and every member of it be ready to lay down his life for the life for the life of his chief. But a band of men associated for purpose of legal production is usually animated by no such emotions, and none of them is willing to give his life for the life of his chief. For a servant or a soldier is engaged at a definite rate of wages for a definite period ; but a workman at a rate of wages variable according to the demand for labour, and with the risk of being at any time thrown out of employment by chances of trade. Now as under these conditions no action of the affections can take place, but only an explosive action of disaffections, two points offer themselves of consideration in the matter :

1. How far the rate of wages may be so regulated as not to vary with the demand for labour ;
2. How far it is possible that bodies of workmen may be engaged and maintained at such fixed rate of wages (whatever the state of trade may be), without enlarging or diminishing their number, so as to give them permanent interest in the establishment with which they are connected, like that of the domestic servants in an old family, or an esprit de corps, like that of the soldiers in a crack regiment.

A curious fact in the history of human error is the denial by the economist of the possibility of so regulating wages as not to vary with the demand for labour.

We do not sell our prime-minister by Dutch auction. Sick, we do not inquire for a physician who takes less than a guinea ; litigious, we never think of reducing six-and-eightpence to four-and-sixpence ; caught in a shower we do not canvass the cabmen to find one who value his driving at less than sixpence a mile.

The best labour always has been, and is, as all labour ought to be, paid by an invariable standard.

'What !' the reader perhaps answers amazedly : 'to pay good and bad workman alike ?'

Certainly. You pay with equal fee, contentedly, the good and bad preachers (workmen upon your soul) and the good and bad physicians (workmen upon your body) ; much more may you pay, contentedly, with equal fees, the good and bad workmen upon your house.

'Nay, but I choose my physician, thus indicating my sense of the quality of their work.' By all means choose your bricklayer ; that is the proper reward of the good workman, to be 'chosen'. The right system respecting all labour is, that it should be paid at a fixed rate, but the good workman employed, and the bad workman unemployed. The false system is when the bad workman is allowed to offer his work at half-price, and either take the place of the good or to force him by his competition to work for an inadequate sum. This equality of wages, then, being the first object towards which we have to discover the road, the second is that of maintaining constant numbers of workmen in employment, whatever may be the accidental demand for the article they produce.

The wages which enable any workman to live are necessarily higher if his work is liable to intermission, than if it is assured and continuous. In the latter case he will take low wages in the form of a fixed salary. The provision of regular labour for the workman is good for him as well as for his master in the long run, although he cannot then make large profits or take big risks or indulge in gambling. The soldier is ready to lay down his life for his chief and therefore he is held in greater honour than an ordinary workman. Really speaking, the soldier's trade is not slaying, but being slain in the defence of others. The reason the world honours the soldier is, because he holds his life at the service of the State.

Not less is the respect we pay to the lawyer, physician and clergyman, founded ultimately on their self-sacrifice. Set in a judge's seat, the lawyer will strive to judge justly, come of it what may. The physician will treat his patients with care, no matter under what difficulties. The clergyman will similarly instruct his congregation and direct it to the right path.

All the efficient members of these so-called learned professions are in public estimate of honour preferred before the head of a commercial firm, as the merchant is presumed to act always selfishly. His work may be very necessary to the community ; but the motive of it is understood to be wholly personal. The merchant's first object in all his dealings must be (the public believe) to get as much for himself and leave as little to his customer as possible. Enforcing this upon him, by political statute, as the necessary principle of his action ; recommending it to him, and themselves reciprocally adopting it, proclaiming for law of the universe that a buyer's function is to cheapen, and a seller's to cheat,-the public, nevertheless, involuntarily condemn the man of commerce for his compliance with their own statement, and stamp him for ever as belonging to an inferior grade of human personality.

This they must give up doing. They will have to discover a kind of commerce which is not excluselfish. Or rather they must discover that there never was or can be any other kind of commerce ; and that this which they have called commerce was not commerce at all but cozening. In true commerce, as in true preaching or true fighting, it is necessary to admit the idea of occasional voluntary loss ;-that sixpences have to be lost, as well as lives, under a sense of duty ; that the market may have its martyrdoms as well as the pulpit ; and trade its heroism as well as war.

Five great intellectual professions exist in every civilized nation :

The Soldier's profession is to defend it.

The Pastor's to teach it.

The Physician's to keep it in health.

The Lawyer's to enforce justice in it.

The Merchant's to provide for it.

And the duty of all these men is on due occasion to die for it. For truly the man who does not know when to die does not know how to live.

Observe, the merchant's function is to provide for the nation. It is no more his function to get profit for himself out of that provision than it is a clergyman's function to get his stipend. This stipend is a necessary adjunct but not the object of his life if he be a true clergyman, any more than his fee (or honorarium) is the object of life to a true physician. Neither is his fee the object of life to a true merchant. All three, if true men, have a work to be done irrespective of fee-to be done even at any cost, or for quite thc contrary of fee ; the pastor's function being to teach, the physician's to heal and the merchant's to provide. That is to say, he has to apply all his sagacity and energy to the producing the thing he deals in perfect state and distributing it at the cheapest possible price where it is most needed.

And because the production of any commodity involves the agency of many lives and hands, the merchant becomes in the course of his business the master and governor of large masses of men in a more direct way than a military officer or pastor, so that on him falls, in great part, the responsibility for the kind of life they lead ; and it becomes his duty not only to produce goods in the purest and cheapest forms, but also to make the various employments involved in the production most beneficial to the men employed.

And as into these two functions, requiring for their right exercise the highest intelligence as well as patience, kindness and tact, the merchant is bound to put all his energy, so for their just discharge he is bound, as solier or physican is to give up, if need be, his life, in such way as it may be demanded of him.

Two main points he has to maintain ; first his engagement ; and secondly the perfectness and purity of the thing provided by him ; so that rather than fail in any engagement or consent to any deterioration, adulteration, or unjust or exorbitant price of that which he provides, he is bound to meet fearlessly any form of distress, poverty or labour which may through maintenance of these points come upon him.

Again in his office as governor of the men employed by him, the merchant is invested with a paternal authority and responsibility. In most cases a youth entering a commercial establishment is withdrawn altogether from home influence ; his master must become his father; else he has, for practical and constant help, no father at hand. So that the only means which the master has of doing justice to the men employed by him is to ask himself sternly whether he is dealing with such subordinate as he would with his own son, if compelled by circumstances to take such a position.

Supposing the captain of a frigate were obliged to place his own son in the position of a common sailor ; as he would then treat his son, he is bound always to treat every one of the men under him. So also supposing the master of a factory were obliged to place his own son in the position of an ordinary workman ; as he would then treat his son, he is bound always to treat every one of his men. This is the only effective, true or practical Rule which can be given in this point of economics.

And as the captain of a ship is bound to be the last man to leave his ship in case of wreck and to share his last crust with the sailors in case of famine, so the manufacturer, in any commercial crisis, is bound to take the suffering of it with his men, and even to take more of it for himself than he allows his men to feel ; as a father would in a famine, shipwreck or battle, sacrifice himself for his son.

All this sounds very strange; the only real strangeness in the matter being, nevertheless, that it should so sound. For all this is true everlastingly and practically ; all other doctrine than this being impossible in practice, consistently with any progressive state of national life ; all the life which we now possess as a nation showing itself in the denial by a few strong minds and faithful hearts of the economic principles taught to our multitudes, which principles, so far as accepted, lead straight to national destruction.

The Technique of Satyagraha

Not to yield your soul to the conqueror means that you will refuse to do that which your conscience forbids you to do. Suppose the 'enemy' were to ask you to rub your nose on the ground or to pull your ears or to go through such humiliating performances, you would not submit to any of these humiliations. But if he robs you of your possessions, you will yield them because, as a votary of ahimsa, you have from the beginning decided that earthly possessions have nothing to do with your soul. That which you look upon as your own you may keep only so long as the world allows you to own it.

Not to yield your mind means that you will not give way to any temptation. Man is oftentimes weak-minded enough to be caught in the snare of greed and honeyed words. We see this happening daily in our social life. A weak-minded man can never be a Satyagrahi. The latter's 'no' is invariably a 'no' and his 'yes' an eternal 'yes'. Such a man alone has the strength to be a devotee of truth and ahimsa. But here one must know the difference between steadfastness and obstinacy. If, after having said 'yes' or 'no', one finds out that the decision was wrong and in spite of that knowledge clings to it, that is obstinacy and folly. It is necessary to think things out carefully and thoroughly before coming to any decision. The meaning of refusal to own allegiance is clear. You will not bow to the supremacy of the victor, you will not help him to attain his object. Herr Hitler has never dreamt of possessing Britain. He wants the British to admit defeat. The victor can then demand anything he likes from the vanquished, and the latter has perforce to yield. But if defeat is not admitted, the enemy will fight until he has killed his opponent. A Satyagrahi, however, is dead to his body even before the enemy attempts to kill him, i.e., he is free from attachment to his body and only lives in the victory of the soul.

Therefore, when he is already thus dead, why would be yearn to kill anyone? To die in the act of killing is in essence to die defeated. Because, if the enemy is unable to get it after killing you. If, on the other hand, he realizes that you have not the remotest thought in your mind of raising your hand against him even for the sake of your life, he will lack the zest to kill you. Every hunter has had this experience. No one has ever heard of anyone hunting cows. (H, 18-8-1940, pp. 253-4)

Power of Suffering

The hardest heart and the grossest ignorance must disappear before the rising sun of suffering without anger and without malice. (YI, 19-2-1925, p. 61)

Suffering has its well-defined limits. Suffering can be both wise and unwise, and when the limit is reached, to prolong it would be not unwise but the height of folly. (YI, 12-3-1931, p. 30)

True suffering does not know itself and never calculates. It brings its own joy which surpasses all other joys. (YI, 19-3-1931, p. 41)

The conviction has been growing upon me that things of fundamental importance to the people are not secured by reason alone, but have to be purchased with their suffering. Suffering is the law of human beings; war is the law of the jungle. But suffering is infinitely more powerful than the law of the jungle for converting the opponent and opening his ears, which are otherwise shut, to the voice of reason. (YI, 5-11-1931, p. 341)

THE GOSPEL OF SATYAGRAHA

Condition Precedent: The first indispensable condition precedent to any civil resistance is that there should be surety against any outbreak of violence, whether on the part of those who are identified with civil resistance or on the part of the general public. It would be no answer in the case of an outbreak of violence that it was instigated by the State or other agencies hostile to civil resisters. It should be obvious that civil resistance cannot flourish in an atmosphere of violence. This does not mean that the resources of a satyagrahi have come to an end. Ways other than civil disobedience should be found out. (H, 18-3-1939, p. 53)

Civil Disobedience: Disobedience to be civil must be sincere, respectful, restrained, never defiant, must be based upon some well-understood principle, must not be capricious and, above all, must have no ill-will or hatred behind it. (YI, 24-3-1920, p. 4)

I hold the opinion firmly that civil disobedience is the purest type of constitutional agitation. Of course, it becomes degrading and despicable, if its civil, *i.e.,* nonviolent character is a mere camouflage. If the honesty of nonviolence be admitted, there is no warrant for condemnation even of the fiercest disobedience, because of the likehood of its leading to violence. No big or swift movement can carried on without bold risks, and life will not be worth living if it is not attended with large risks. Does not the history of the world show that there would have been no romance in life if there had been no risks? (YI, 15-12-1921, p. 419)

Civil disobedience is the inherent right of a citizen. He dare not give it up without ceasing to be a man. Civil disobedience is never followed by anarchy. Criminal disobedience can lead to it. Every state puts down criminal disobedience by force. It perishes if it does not. (YI, 5-1-1922, p. 5)

A Satyagrahi obeys the laws of society intelligently and of his own free will, because he considers it to be his sacred duty to do so. It is only when a person has thus obeyed the laws of society scrupulously that he is in a position of judge as to which particular laws are good and just and which unjust and iniquitous.

Only when does the right accrue to him of civil disobedience of certain laws in well-defined circumstances. (A, p. 347)

Character of Satyagraha: That is the beauty of Satyagraha. It comes up to oneself, one has not to go out in search for it.

That is a virtue inherent in the principle itself. A dharmayuddha, in which there are no secrete to be guarded, no scope for canning and no place for untruth, comes unsought; and a man of religion is ever ready for it. A struggle which has to be previously planned is not and it is only when the Satyagrahi feels quite helpless, is apparently on his last legs and finds utter darkness all around him, that God comes to the rescue. (SSA, p. xiv)

In the application of Satyagraha, I discovered, in the earliest stages, that pursuit of Truth did not admit of violence being inflicted on one's opponent, but that he must be weaned from error by patience and sympathy. For, what appears to be truth to the one may appear to be error to the other. And patience means self-suffering. So the doctrine came to mean vindication of Truth, not by infliction of suffering on the opponent but one's own self. (RCPS)

Satyagraha and its off-shoots, noncooperation and civil resistance, are nothing but new names for the law of suffering. (YI, 11-8-1920, p. 3)

With satya combined with ahimsa, you can bring the world to your feet. Satyagraha in its essence is nothing but the introduction of truth and gentleness in the political, *i.e.*, the national, life. (YI, 10-3-1920, p. 3)

Satyagraha is utter self-effacement, greatest humiliation, greatest patience and brightest faith. It is its own reward. (YI, 26-2-1925, p. 73)

Satyagraha is a relentless search for truth and a determination to reach truth. (YI, 19-3-1925, p. 95)

It is a force that works silently and apparently slowly. In reality, there is no force in the world that is so direct or so swift in working. (YI, 4-6-1925, p. 189)

The word Satyagraha is often most loosely used and is made to cover veiled violence. But, as the author of the word, I may be allowed to say that it excludes every form of violence, direct or indirect, veiled or unveiled, and whether in thought, word or deed. It is breach of Satyagraha to with ill to an opponent or to say a harsh word to him or of him with the intention of harming him... Satyagraha is gentle, it never wounds. It must not be the result of anger or malice. It is never fussy, never impatient, never vociferous. It is the direct opposite of compulsion. It was conceived as a complete substitute for violence. (H, 15-4-1933, p. 8)

The fight of Satyagraha is for the strong in spirit, not the doubter or the timid. Satyagraha teaches us the art of living as well as dying. Birth and death are inevitable among mortals. What distinguishes the man from the brute is his conscious striving to realize the spirit within. (H, 7-4-1946, p. 74)

The Technique of Satyagraha: Not to yield your soul to the conqueror means that you will refuse to do that which your conscience forbids you to do. Suppose the 'enemy' were to ask you to rub your nose on the ground or to pull your ears or to go through such humiliating performances, you would not submit to any of these humiliations. But if he robs you of your possessions, you will yield them because, as a votary of ahimsa, you have from the beginning decided that earthly possessions have nothing to do with your soul. That which you look upon as your own you may keep only so long as the world allows you to own it.

Not to yield your mind means that you will not give way to any temptation. Man is oftentimes weak-minded enough to be caught in the snare of greed and honeyed words. We see this happening daily in our social life. A weak-minded man can never be a Satyagrahi. The latter's 'no' is invariably a 'no' and his 'yes' an eternal 'yes'. Such a man alone has the strength to be a devotee of truth and ahimsa.

But here one must know the difference between steadfastness and obstinacy. If, after having said 'yes' or 'no', one finds out that the decision was wrong and in spite of that knowledge clings to it, that is obstinacy and folly. It is necessary to think things out carefully and thoroughly before coming to any decision.

The meaning of refusal to own allegiance is clear. You will not bow to the supremacy of the victor, you will not help him to attain his object. Herr Hitler has never dreamt of possessing Britain. He wants the British to admit defeat. The victor can then demand anything he likes from the vanquished, and the latter has perforce to yield.

But if defeat is not admitted, the enemy will fight until he has killed his opponent. A Satyagrahi, however, is dead to his body even before the enemy attempts to kill him, *i.e.*, he is free from attachment to his body and only lives in the victory of the soul. Therefore, when he is already thus dead, why would be yearn to kill anyone? To die in the act of killing is in essence to die defeated. Because, if the enemy is unable to get it after killing you. If, on the other hand, he realizes that you have not the remotest thought in your mind of raising your hand against him even for the sake of your life, he will lack the zest to kill you. Every hunter has had this experience. No one has ever heard of anyone hunting cows. (H, 18-8-1940, pp. 253-4)

Evolving Science: I am myself daily growing in the knowledge of Satyagraha. I have no text-book to consult in time of need, not even the Gita which I have called my dictionary. Satyagraha as conceived by me is a science may prove to be no science at all and well prove to be the musings and doings of a fool, if not a madman. It may be that what is true in Satyagraha is as ancient as the hills. But it has not yet been acknowledged to be of any value in the solution of world problems or, rather, the one supreme problem or war. It may be that what is claimed to be new in it will prove to be really of no value in terms of that supreme problem. It may be that what are claimed to be victories of Satyagraha *i.e.*, ahimsa, were really victories not of truth and nonviolence but of fear of violence. These possibilities have always been in front of me. I am helpless. All I present to the nation for adoption is an answer to prayer or, which is the same thing, constantly waiting on God. (H, 24-9-1938, p. 266)

Code of Satyagraha: A Satyagrahi bids good-bye to fear. He is therefore, never afraid of trusting the opponent. Even if the opponent plays him false twenty times, the Satyagrahi is ready to trust him the twenty-first time, for an implicit trust in human nature is the very essence of his creed. (SSA, p. 159)

A Satyagrahi is nothing if not instinctively law-abiding, and it is his law-abiding nature which exacts from him implicit obedience to the highest law, that is the voice of conscience which overrides all other laws. (SW, p. 465)

Since Satyagraha is one of the most powerful methods of direct action, a Satyagrahi exhausts all other means before he resorts to Satyagraha. He will, therefore, constantly and continually approach the constituted authority, he will appeal to public opinion, educate public opinion, state his case calmly and coolly before everybody who wants to listen to him, and only after he has exhausted all these avenues will he resort to Satyagraha. But when he has found the impelling call of the inner voice within him and launches out upon Satyagraha, he has burnt his boats and there is no receding. (YI, 20-10-1927, p. 353)

The Satyagrahi, whilst he is ever ready for fight, must be equally eager for peace. He must welcome any honourable opportunity for peace. (YI, 19-3-1931, p. 40)

My advice is Satyagraha first and Satyagraha last. There is no other or better road to freedom. (H, 15-9-1946, p. 312)

In the code of the Satyagrahi there is no such thing as surrender to brute force. Or the surrender then is the surrender of suffering and not to the wielder of the bayonet. (YI, 30-4-1931, p. 93)

As a Satyagrahi I must always allow my cards to be examined and re-examined at all times and make reparation if an error is discovered. (H, 11-3-1939, p. 44)

FASTING AND SATYAGRAHA

Weapon of Satyagraha

Fasting is a potent weapon in the Satyagraha armoury. It cannot be taken by every one. Mere physical capacity to take it is no qualification for it. It is of no use without a living faith in God. It should never be a mechanical effort or a mere limitation. It must come from the depth of one's soul. It is, therefore, always rare. (H, 18-3-1939, p. 56)

There can be no room for selfishness, anger, lack of faith or impatience in a pure fast....Infinite patience, firm resolve, single-mindedness of purpose, perfect calm, and no anger must of necessity be there. But since it is impossible for a person to develop all these qualities all at once, no one who has not devoted himself to following the laws of ahimsa should undertake a Satyagrahi fast. (H, 13-10-1940, p. 322)

[Fasting] is...fierce and not altogether free from danger. I myself have before condemned fasting when it seemed to me to be wrong or morally unjustified. But to shirk a fast where there is a clear moral indication is a dereliction of duty. Such a fast has to be based on unadulterated truth and ahimsa. (H, 28-7-1946, p. 235)

Fasting and Death

Fasting unto death is the last and the most potent weapon in the armoury of Satyagraha. It is a sacred thing. But it must be accepted with all its implication. It is not the fast itself, but what it implies that matters. (H, 18-8-1846, p. 262)

Fasting and the Way of Christ

Fasting cannot be undertaken mechanically. It is a powerful thing but a dangerous thing, if handled amateurishly. It requires complete self-purification, much more than what is required in facing death with retaliation even in mind. One such act of perfect sacrifice would suffice for the whole world. Such is held to be Jesus' example. (H, 27-10-1946, p. 272)

Of course, it is not to be denied that fasts can be really coercive. Such are fasts to attain a selfish object. A fast undertaken to wring money from a person or for fulfilling some such personal end would amount to the exercise of coercion or undue influence. I would unhesitatingly advocate resistance of such undue influence. I have myself successfully resisted it in the fasts that have been undertaken or threatened against me.

And if it is argued that the dividing line between a selfish and unselfish end is often very thin, I would urge that a person who regards the end of a fast to be selfish or otherwise base should resolutely refuse to yield to it, even though the refusal may result in the death of the fasting person.

If people will cultivate the habit of disregarding fasts which, in their opinion, are taken for unworthy ends, such fasts will be robbed of the taint of coercion and undue influence. Like all human institutions, fasting can be both legitimately and illegitimately used. (H, 9-9-1931, p. 5)

If a man, however popular and great he may be, takes up an improper cause and fasts in defence of the impropriety, it is the duty of his friends (among whom I count myself), fellow-workers and relatives to let him die rather than that an improper cause should triumph so that he may live. Fairest means cease to be fair when the end sought is unfair. (H, 17-3-1946, p. 43)

Last Resort

One general principle, however, I would like to enunciate. A Satyagrahi should fast only as a last resort when all other avenues of redress have been explored and have failed. There is no room for imitation in fasts. He who has no inner strength should not dream of it, and never with attachment to success.

But if a Satyagrahi once undertakes a fast from conviction, he must stick to his resolve whether there is a chance of his action bearing fruit or not. This does not mean that fasting cannot or can bear fruit. He who fasts in the expectation of fruit generally fails. And even if he does not seemingly fail, he loses all the inner joy which a true fast holds...

Ridiculous fasts spread like plague and are harmful. But, when fasting becomes a duty, it cannot be given up. Therefore, I do fast when I consider it to be necessary and cannot abstain from it on any score. What I do myself I cannot abstain from it on any score. What I do myself I cannot prevent others from doing under similar circumstances. It is common knowledge that the best of good things are often abused. We see this happening every day. (H, 21-4-1946, p. 93)

...When human ingenuity fails, the votary fasts. This fasting quickens the spirit of prayer, that is to say, the fasting is a spiritual act, and therefore, addressed to God. The effect of such action on the life of the people is that, where the person fasting is at all known to them, their sleeping conscience is awakened.

But there is the danger that the people through mistaken sympathy may act against their will in order to save the life of the loved one. This danger has got to be faced. One ought not to be deterred from right action when one is sure of the rightness. It can best promote circumspection. Such a fast is undertaken in obedience to the dictates of the inner voice and, therefore, prevents haste. (H, 21-12-1947, p. 476)

8

Gandhian Social and Cultural Philosophy

Gandhi is a world-historical figure. Though he refused to formulate a religious or philosophical system, he did stand, throughout his life, for certain ideas, which are nothing if not of universal significance. In order to see this clearly, let us review, very briefly, the nature and context of the challenge to which his life and thought were a dedicated response.

Within the limited scope of this essay, it is not possible to begin at the beginning of Gandhi's political career in South Africa; we cannot even review his role in the Indian independence movement in any systematic way. All that can be done here is to indicate some salient features of India's freedom struggle at the time Gandhi entered the scene as a major figure after World War I.

The Indian freedom movement was a number of different things at the same time. It was a reform, a renaissance and a nationalist movement. At the same time it was also a movement for religious revivalism under the name of Hindu nationalism. At the time Gandhi came on the Indian political scene, it was dominated by Gokhale and Tilak: Gokhale leading the reformist and secularist or non-religious form of nationalism and Tilak leading the religio-social revivalist interpretation of the nationalist movement. The tension that developed between Gokhale and Tilak, as leaders of the Indian freedom struggle, reflected something far deeper than a clash of personalities. It signified the essential incompatibility between the idea of nationalism and Hinduism, and for that matter, Islam. In other words, while Hindu nationalism or Islamic nationalism is a contradiction in terms, both nationalism and Hinduism had necessarily to be emphasized by the anti-Imperialist forces in the Indian political and social movement. At one level, Hinduism and Hindu society are inseparable and hence to strengthen or weaken the one has profound significance for the other. Now Hindu society being a caste society, an outcaste, though a Hindu is really an outsider and hence he can be easily lured into other religions.

For this reason certain reforms became necessary and urgent, for Hinduism at this time was being threatened not only by Christianity and Islam, but also by Western rationalism. But this reform of Hinduism had at the same time to be a kind of revivalism, for that was the only way to unify, to get a collective identity and to rouse and gear the society to act against foreign rule. In other words, in the specific historical context of India under modern Western imperial rule Reformist and Modernist forces could work only within very narrow limitations. Thus Gokhale's correct non-religious interpretation of nationalism was bound to develop serious inner tensions in the Indian situation—for given the history of Hindu-Muslim relations, it was impossible to forge a truly national identity in terms of a common historical past. Hence there was not only the appeal, but a kind of irrefutability in Tilak's idea of nationalism as the completion of Sivaji's task—an interpretation, however, which can have meaning only within Hinduism and must be rejected by the Muslims. This inner schism in the freedom-cum-nationalist movement of India has persisted all the way down to our time. After Gokhale and Tilak, the two inconsistent aspects of the nationalist movement were represented by Nehru and Patel, and even though Patel died in 1950 the idealogical forces which he represented are very much alive and strong.

The immediate successor of both Gokhale and Tilak was, of course, Gandhi. How did he heal, or at any rate, deal with this inner schism? Gandhi's response to this crucial challenge was threefold. He radically changed the basis, the scope and the nature of the Indian freedom movement.

Basis: With Gandhi the Indian National Congress became a people's party. At any rate, it ceased to be confined to upper and middle educated classes.

Scope: He universalized the scope of Indian politics, emphasizing the world-historical character of the Indian struggle as representing the struggle of the oppressed and the exploited against all oppressors and exploiters. He thought of himself as fighting for a better world-order and not simply for a free India. Indeed, until comparatively late in his political career, he did not emphasize so much the freedom of India, as he did a reformed British Commonwealth in which India could be a self-respecting and valuable partner. In his own view, the Indian movement was not national but universal-human—one global in scope and paralleling the Marxist movement.

Nature: Gandhi changed the nature of Indian politics by spiritualizing it. By this I refer to the Gandhian principles of Truth and Non-violence as the basis of social order and the instruments of socio-political dynamics. In other words, Gandhi stood for the substitution of Power politics by Goodness politics in terms of his doctrine of the integrality and symmetry of ends and means. Gandhi repudiated the idea that morality is simply an individual affair; on the contrary he emphasized the idea that a moral and spiritual social order was a *sine qua non* for human life at its proper level. Accordingly, he firmly believed in and straightforwardly advocated a socio-economic order and a political system based on the traditional virtues: *Satya* (Truth), *Ahimsa* (Non-violence), *Aparigraha* (non-possession), *Asteya* (Non-covetousness), and *Brahmacharya* (Self-control of the senses and the sex impulse particularly).

The significance of this threefold Gandhian revolution can hardly be exaggerated. It is crucial not only for understanding the nature, the success and the failure of the Indian freedom movement but also and no less importantly, for understanding the relevance of Gandhism to contemporary India and the world. Suffer me to offer a brief analysis of this Gandhian revolution:

First, by emphasizing the people, their needs and aspirations, he at one stroke cut through the Gokhale/Tilak or the Rationalism/Tradition, or the Reform/Revival antitheses. To the masses Hindu or Muslim or Sikh or Buddhist or Christian religion was real and meaningful: thus by emphasizing the truth in Hinduism and Islam, indeed in all religions, and by extending political thought and action from the classes to the common people, the peasantry, he modified in a major way the nature of both Indian Nationalism and Hindu revivalism. He sought to accomplish the dual transformation by taking the religiousness and misery of the Indian common people as the given basis for a

community of fate; the specific religious differences between Hinduism and Islam he attempted to resolve by a transcendent religion, or rather by a spiritual catholicism. In effect, Gandhi sought to minimize the twin problems of unity and identity of India which, he rightly thought, were at the root of the tension between nationalism and revivalism. His method was to universalize the perspective for the identity problem, so that the specific burden of India's history would not be felt as a dead weight. This was reinforced by the effect of his second revolution, namely the universalization of the freedom struggle, making his ideal essentially the foundation of a new stage in human history. It thus undermines the idea of nationalism which is both parochial and retrograde when viewed independently of its colonial or anti-imperialist context.

The viability of the second revolution depends in fact on his third revolution: the spiritualisation of politics. This is the foundation of Gandhi's thought. If there can be a goodness politics, then the idea of nation-states can be used creatively: in the absence of a spiritual social-political order, as distinguished from a religious one, the concept of nation must be maintained for the solution of the identity problem, that is if a universal context is not found, one able to replace the imperial context. Religion and Communism have supplied so far the supra-national context for unity and identity. In his idea of spiritualization of politics Gandhi seeks to provide a renewal and a reinterpretation of the religious context which will at the same time supersede the Communist context. He attempted to do this by going beyond both the modern Western theory of the State as the embodiment of the will of the people, and the Hindu theory of State as the embodiment of the Dharma. He thought of non-violence and truth as the foundation of State as well as of social order, interpreting these as universal spiritual principles independent of all formulated religions. The idea, however, led him ultimately to the theory of a stateless society—a development that paralleled the Marxist theory of the withering away of the state.

Though Gandhi was never a Marxist, this parallelism is not a mere chance convergence: it is inherent in all universalization of politics. Another concept that Gandhi evolved in his effort to provide a non-Marxian solution to the inherent problems of modern politico-social theory is that of trusteeship. In Gandhian thinking it has two fundamental roles: socio-economically, the concept of trusteeship is designed to prevent a productive society from becoming acquisitive and exploitative, and politically it is meant to resolve a major difficulty in the modern Western theory of democracy.

The difficulty is this: the relationship between the State (Ruler) and the People (Ruled) in a democratic socio-political system ought not to be that of guardian and ward, doctor-patient, educator-educated. However, in modern democratic societies this is precisely the nature of the relation between the State and the people. Indeed the key institution of modern democratic process, viz. leadership may, strictly speaking, be said to be undemocratic, a point often indirectly conceded through opposition to what is called the cult of personality and through proposals for collective leadership. Indeed, the more technologically advanced a society is, the more have the people to be managed, the greater the need for protection, and thus the relation between the people and the State tends to be increasingly that of ward and guardian.

The Gandhian theory of trusteeship tries to resolve this dilemma by replacing the concept of representation by that of trusteeship. However, for this change of concepts to have more than a terminological significance it is necessary that the idea of trusteeship be an organic part of the Gandhian theory of a society based both individually and collectively on the virtues of self-suffering and non-possession. This approach was profound, broad-based, farsighted, and a failure. Gandhi himself was the most self-aware, anguished and undespairing witness to the grandeur and misery of his life's work: the grandeur, transfer of power to India, largely through a non-violent freedom struggle; the misery, the communal disharmony culminating in the partition of India.

Gandhi wanted two things: the restoration of a spiritual or normal social order in India and by extension in the world, and secondly to free India from foreign rule; this freedom according to Gandhi was a pre-condition for his first goal.

He did not succeed. For Gandhi the partition robbed India's freedom of its full truth and the socio-historical process culminating in the post-independence Indian society signified the failure of his main mission: the spiritual renewal of man.

Too saintly to lose faith and too great to feel frustrated, Gandhi nevertheless knew that his vision had suffered a great setback; indeed, he knew this with a clarity rare among the great.

If Gandhi was simply a survival produced by the liberal, civilized British rule in India, if his cardinal spiritual quest and mission were in the last analysis a clever Hindu's embellishments of his political struggle and hence a distraction for the social scientist, if Gandhi was just a parochial figure trying to do something good to the Hindu character under colonial rule—in a word, if the failure of Gandhi and the failure of the Gandhian idea are synonymous, then Gandhi's life and thought are irrelevant to our times. And if I, for one, believed this, I would see no reason to be interested in talking at all about Gandhi or Gandhism.

If, however, the threefold Gandhian revolution about which we have been speaking constitutes a real revolution with world-historical significance, if Gandhi was *not* just a colonial leader who happened to achieve some kind of world fame, but, on the contrary, is a universal figure with relentless and steadfast concern with the destiny of man, then the central question raised by Gandhi, his thought, life and work, is the question of its relevance to our times and this is nothing else or no less than this: Has the voice of sanity any chance at all against the dark, demonic powers of our times? It is a terrible question. Apart from the fact that like everybody else I am deeply involved in the question, I have no competence to answer it. What I have to say in the rest of the space available to me is nothing more than an analysis of the question itself. Let me repeat, the observations that follow make no claim to answering the question that has just been put. All I attempt to do is to explore a little the implications of this question from the Gandhian standpoint. I said that to ask the question of the contemporary relevance of Gandhism is really to ask the question about society and survival. To see this, and to understand the question of Gandhism's contemporary relevance in its proper perspective, it is essential to speak briefly about the Gandhian vision of a normal society—the kind of society for which Gandhi lived and died.

Gandhi did not believe in the coexistence of moral man and immoral society. In fact, one of his most important contributions to political thought and action is the idea that ways of moral action and resistance could be transferred from the individual to the collective plane and be used as powerful forms of political action. Indeed, the technique of *Satyagraha* (fast, civil disobedience, *dharna* and other variants) presuppose this basic idea. Gandhi believed that Society could be, and should be moral. Did he also hold that man as an individual needed a moral society in order to be moral himself? I think this is a fundamental point in understanding Gandhi's sociological thought. Let us therefore ponder it a moment.

Gandhi was a great believer in the virtues of compromise, not only in the political but in almost all spheres; it was part of his political theory and practice to lay the greatest stress on sincerity and the purity of the personal lives of every political actor. In a more general way, too, he gave all possible emphasis and attention to political participants as persons. Looking at his thought and practice from this point of view, it may look as if Gandhi did not rule out the possibility of moral men in a not-so-moral society. In further support of such an interpretation of Gandhi's thought, it could be pointed out that the ultimate orientation of Gandhi's political action was towards effecting a change of heart of the other party. Both his thinking and the forms of political action that he developed imply, it may be argued, a cumulative process of social change.

All this is correct. However, I would like to argue that this does not invalidate my thesis that Gandhi did not think that individually man could be moral in a non-moral, immoral or unjust society, that is, he did not believe in the Niebuhrian antithesis of moral man and immoral society. I want to show that in any analysis of his thought and work the coexistence (of moral man and immoral society) theory would be seriously misleading.

Gandhi did place man as person in the forefront. But this was only a powerful and realistic way of focussing attention on what may be called the principle of normalcy. A normal society is simply a society. Opposed to it are what have been called mass-society and mass man—and mass—or what is currently called "pop" culture. The mass and the society used to be contrary to each other. They have been hyphenated today.

A society has an intelligible order and an overall purpose. A mass lacks both. It follows that members of a society have their own place and function in it. Not so in a mass. A society whose members are humans is a human society. When man is called a social animal, the reference obviously is to his innate love of order and purpose and not to any "herd" instinct or some "natural" inclination for the company of his own kind. For these propensities are by no means exclusively human. Man, unlike many other animals, cannot suffer to live merely as a unit, for the love of order *and* Purpose are given to him in his self-consciousness.

Those who talk of mass-society certainly recognize the distinction between mass and society. They are often aware—implicitly, if not always explicitly,—that mass undermines society. They understand that the mass-man is not human—at least not fully human. They had learnt to admire certain things, certain states of affairs, certain states of mind which they conceptualized as civilization. They now realize that the mass will destroy this civilization more effectively, in fact, than any barbarian onslaught could ever do. They are not unaware that the barbarian has entered the soul. Somewhere at some time modern man was lured into the magician's bargain: Give up your soul, get power over everything in return. Anxiously aware of the deadening influence of this demonic deal, modern thinkers are nonetheless too much under its spell to believe in the possibility of its total repudiation. Through a variety of ideas they search for a synthesis of mass and society, that is, of the infra-human and the human: they are exploring the possibility of a mass that will have just enough of the social to save it from withering away.

Gandhi wanted to break the spell. He would disown and destroy this diabolic bond. Herein lies the basic difference between Gandhi's critique of modern society and those of most other modern thinkers. And what is even more important, this also defines the difference between Gandhi and Gandhism in India today. Gandhi was against "mass-society". He was uncompromisingly opposed to the modern industrial technological society and civilization. He knew what forces, what propensities underlie such a socio-cultural system; and unlike most contemporary thinkers and leaders, he remained relentlessly consistent and thoroughgoing in his opposition to these forces.

He went to the root of the matter and attacked the very concept of a rising standard of living. He could see most clearly what this really meant, viz., a continually rising standard of consumption even to the point when rapid, built-in obsolescence and wanton destruction become the controlling principles of the economy. In opposition to this economic theory, he boldly set up the theory of *Aparigraha* (non-possession, non-acquisitiveness) and the minimisation of wants. The principle of Aparigraha, it is to be noted, is one that emphasizes the present and hence it severely limits the cumulative process and thus undermines a capitalist as well as a State-planned 'Socialist' production system.

Indeed, the ideas of minimal wants and of non-possession pre-suppose a world outlook that is quite incompatible with the currently accepted ideology for a planned society.

It is in this context that Gandhi's emphasis on the individual person should be understood. From the Gandhian point of view the modern industrial-technological mass-society is really a collectivity of sub-humans. Gandhi thought steadfastly in terms of a society of men: a society in which there will be no mechanical equality, but at the same time nobody will be forced to live at a subhuman level; a society in which every member will be a full member according to his own place and specific competence.

Contrary to a prevalent interpretation, I think that Gandhi did not believe in the individual as the source of social change. Absolutely believing in God and Providential guidance, Gandhi thought that man could only be an instrument of God's will. He emphasized purity of heart and mind so that one could attain to the highest point of human creativity and get a correct intimation of the divine will and act efficiently according to it.

Gandhi believed that a suprahuman order was the common ground of both man and society. Given this frame of reference, the antithesis of man and society could not arise, unless one held, as Gandhi *did not,* that a social order could not be built on moral and metaphysical principles like truth and non-violence. In fact, a whole social order based on truth and non-violence—and not merely individual truthfulness and non-violence—is the very cornerstone of Gandhian sociology.

In summary form, the Gandhian socio-economic system can be described in terms of the following ideas and principles: Means and ends should be seen as parts of a whole which has a transcendental reference.

The productive system should be based on the principle of optimal minimisation of needs (and not on that of multiplication of wants). The economy should be life-centred (and not one that is oriented to commodity-production). This means that the socio-economic system should operate on the principle of a metaphysically grounded optimum (and not on the principle of maximisation). Consequently, it is to be a non-exploitative economy based on simple and limited technology. Social and economic organization should be decentralized based on the principle of optimum autonomy. Truth and non-violence should form the foundation of the political order.

Satyagraha (the determined pursuit of truth or the right path) should be the chief form of political vigilance and protest. Both the social and economic systems should be hierarchical, non-competitive and non-acquisitive, based on the principle of trusteeship. Ideally it should be a stateless society. What has been the impact on our times of Gandhian economics and sociology, or better, of Gandhi's life and thought as a whole? The question has two parts, the first about the role of Gandhi's ideas in the independence movement of India and the second about the relevance of Gandhism to Free India and to our times in general.

The role of Gandhi and his ideas in the Indian freedom movement is greatly important; however to determine the precise nature of his role and its relation with other factors and forces operating to shape that movement is by no means an easy task. It requires difficult and careful analysis which I cannot attempt here.

However, it must be pointed out that even though throughout his life Gandhi thought and worked in the context of a relentless struggle against imperialist forces, the question of the contemporary relevance of his thought is not bound by this historical context. In other words, the question of the validity of Gandhism is inseparable from that of its universality.

I say this for two closely related reasons. First, Gandhi's thought and work developed in the context of an encounter between India and the West, tradition and modernity, and his stand was not simply that the Indians should not be forced to accept Western civilisation through British rule; much more important was his conviction that the modern industrial-technological civilisation is not good for man, Eastern or Western.

He increasingly made India's freedom struggle something subsidiary to a struggle and movement for a normal world society. Second, the principles on which he based his political action as well as those in terms of which he constructed his vision of free India were universal by their very nature; and Gandhi always made it clear that he did not regard his fundamental ideas as merely matters of policy or suitable strategy in the Indian freedom struggle.

To return to the question of the impact of Gandhism. In my opinion, Gandhi's life and thought were completely repudiated by Independent India. I am aware that Nehru often denied this but I do not know what he was talking about. If the present interpretation of the essentials of Gandhi's social, political and economic thought is correct, the state-planned centralized industrial-technological society which India adopted as her goal is quite contrary to Gandhi's vision of free India. As to the political order, non-violence and truth have not at all been accepted as its foundation.

In fact, today there is a great deal of violence simply in running the Government: much more than any democratic people should tolerate, whether or not they believe in non-violence. Gandhi would not have supported a government which needed this kind of violence as its sanction not only in extreme situations, but for its day-to-day running. And, in the so-called conquest of Goa, the Government of India explicitly, though unnecessarily, repudiated truth and non-violence as principles of state policy.

It is often said that Gandhi was not wholly uncompromising in his doctrine of non-violence, that he would make exceptions, that, in fact, he did not oppose the Kashmir war in 1947. Such a view rests on a complete misunderstanding. I think it can be confidently stated that Gandhi made no exceptions whatsoever to his doctrine of truth and non-violence. A full defence of the above statement will need another article; however a brief explanation may be attempted here.

Non-violence sounds as if it were a negative concept, but it is not. It is violence that is negative in nature; for essentially every violent act or thought violates reality. All violence is fundamentally violence against reality. Non-violence is thus acceptance of reality as it is. This is why Gandhi always emphasizes the equation—indeed, the essential synonymy—of non-violence and truth.

In the sphere of human relationship—leaving aside for the moment that of man-nature relationship—violence arises only when there is a failure of rational communication: it is one of the forms of infra-rational communication. So, in all such situations, instead of violence, Gandhi recommended, without exception, resort to non-violence.

What does this mean? It means this: that when parties to a situation do not see the relevant reality in a mutually acceptable way, the believer in non-violence, that is one who wants to accept reality-as-it-is, will voluntarily undertake to suffer for his vision of reality. (That is, instead of trying forcibly to impose it on the other party, he will accept temporarily the other party's view of reality under protest and on pain of self-suffering).

This will bring about a change of heart and mind in the other party, or in the sufferer, or in both: and thus a common vision of reality will emerge eliminating any imposition of a supervening reality by the use of superior physical force.

This implies that non-violence can only be an expression of the inner truth of the non-violent actor. Otherwise, his suffering cannot be said to be really voluntary, for if it (non-violence) is not the externalization of his inner vision, it can only be something forced upon him by external and even extraneous circumstances.

This is why Gandhi said that when non-violence does not express the inner truth of the person, it will be cowardly to stick to it. If the unity of truth and non-violence is disrupted and a choice is to be made between the two, Gandhi would be for truth. In other words, he preferred a straightforward and honest rejection of a fundamental principle to

its half-hearted or insincere acceptance and lukewarm, opportunistic or compulsive application.

By the dictum, "rather kill than be a coward", Gandhi expressed his refusal to compromise with the purity of non-violence. He did not mean any approval of violence in assorted situations. This is why he stood steadfastly for a non-exploitative socio-economic order, for he understood perfectly well that violence is built into an exploitative social system. And holding fast to the doctrine of integrality of means and ends, he adhered throughout to the view that a technology-centred socio-economic system could not but be exploitative.

Do Vinoba Bhave and his movement represent the Gandhian spirit today? I wish it were possible to answer this question with a plain "yes" or "no". Unfortunately, the position is complicated. Even though in his vision of a normal human society Vinoba seems committed to the Gandhian principles, I think there are crucial differences between his thinking and that of Gandhi. In his later thinking Vinoba has been inclined to emphasize the purely instrumental nature of technology and modern natural science.

He distinguishes extensive, constructive and destructive types of technology and is really opposed only to the last type. He believes in the well-known argument that technology by itself is just a set of means; hence everything depends upon how and for what ends it is used.

He also believes that man can develop the kind of spiritual power that can contain and control technology and technological power. He thinks that the Hindu tradition (in fact, all traditions) is not yet complete in its development. He hopes for a future develop-ment of metaphysics and religion which will be a synthesis of spirituality, science and technology.

In this article I cannot examine this theory in any systematic manner. It may be pointed out, however, that Vinoba's thinking is inconsistent here, for its violates the principle of the integrality of means and ends which he does accept.

In other words, Vinoba fails to see that a technological system is not a free gift from Above or from the U.S.A., to be used in the chosen manner; it has to be produced by the society which uses it, and its *production,* apart from *use,* alters the nature of that society. A society based on the principles of the minimization of wants and non-possession is a society with a low level of technological development; it cannot be otherwise. By the same token, if one wants a Gandhian society, one has to be opposed to the development and production of technology beyond a certain fairly low level.

In talking about spirituality, natural science and technology, we must remember that the essential (spiritual) question is not, How and for what purpose is technological power to be used? The crucial question is: What kind of power and in what measure ought Man to acquire it? It seems to me that Vinoba's views on modern natural science and technology are not sufficiently sensitive to the traditional principle that man's knowledge must never exceed his being.

The other fundamental departure from Gandhian principles is Vinoba's support for a government which bases itself on a fundamental. negation of the principles of Gandhism and *Sarvodaya.* Whether the revolution for which Vinoba is working should necessarily involve a large-scale non-violent movement aiming at the complete overthrow of the present government is an open question. In any case, it can certainly be argued that it is not the only alternative in the present situation.

However, what cannot be justified, I think, is the open and positive support Vinoba gave to the government over the Indo-Pakistan War (1965). Nor is it possible to understand why Vinoba and other Sarvodaya leaders have not yet straightforwardly rejected and opposed the government's socio-economic principles and plans.

I can only briefly touch upon the question of the impact of Gandhism on the contemporary Western world. I think the most important thing to note here is the general narrowness of the Western response. Gandhism calls for a radical revolution, for a complete transformation of man's thinking and way of life, social as well as individual. In a word, it aims at *metanoia.* But apart from the theoretical interest of certain European philosophers like Arne Naess, the major western interest in Gandhi, when it is not historical or aesthetic, is predominantly in Gandhian techniques that may be tried for resolving certain problems and tensions of the modern society for which local methods have been proving increasingly inadequate.

With Gandhism as a way of life, that is, with a Gandhian socio-economic system, the West so far has been concerned only rarely. By and large, its interest in Gandhism and non-violent techniques has been experimental in nature and approach.

By virtue of its all-embracing scope and radical nature, the Gandhian vision is an alternative to the two dominant world-views today: the liberal democratic and the Marxian. The one question about Gandhism and our times is, therefore, simply this: Can Gandhism work as the new world-view? Is there a possibility of a radical change in the orientation and structure of contemporary society? Can we hope for *metanoia?*

UNDERSTANDING GANDHIAN PHILOSOPHY

Gandhi, it is true, was not concerned with constructing a system of philosophy, but mainly with applying the ideals and principles that had become a part of his life. Therefore, we do not find the distinction between the ideal and the actual explicitly stated.

One discovers this only when studying his ideas in the context of his background, which was essentially that of Hindu philosophy. Cut off from this source, his ideas sometimes produce the impression of inconsistency; read in the context, they form a coherent whole. He may, therefore, not appear to be consistent with his previous statements, but be is, in his own words, consistent with truth as it may present itself at a given moment.

He explains it further: "Whenever I have been obliged to compare my writing even fifty years ago with the latest, I have discovered no inconsistency between the two. But friends who observe inconsistency... should try to see if there is not an underlying and abiding consistency between the two seeming inconsistencies."

Although for understanding Gandhi's philosophy it is necessary that the concepts be understood in the context of Hindu philosophy, it is equally important to bear in mind that Gandhi's connotations of terms are different from the prevalent ones. Quite often they sound national or geographical, when in fact they are universal. He never seems to have realised that this could sometimes have the effect of damaging his own purpose.

The ultimate ideal for Gandhi, as he repeated several times, is unrealised and unrealisable; its value consists in pointing out the direction. According to him, there must always be an unbridgeable gulf between the ideal and its practice. The ideal will cease to be one if it becomes possible to realise it. He argues: "Where would there be room for that constant striving, that ceaseless quest after the ideal that is the basis of all spiritual progress, if mortals could reach the perfect state while still in the body?" Striving after the ideal is the very essence of practising Gandhi's philosophy. To the extent we make this effort, to that extent we realise the ideal.

ALTERNATIVE WAY OF LIFE

Gandhi was aware of the fact that many national leaders were not convinced of the dangers of industrialization, but were fascinated by the material development of industrial societies. Gandhi was of the opinion that India could not be liberated without putting aside modern civilization. Our socio-cultural features were unique and different from those of others and we should develop means and tools indigenously in order to create a better socio-cultural situation in our society by rectifying the defects and weaknesses of our own culture. Accordingly, he suggested a non-violent model of development for India as an alternative pattern meant for the integrated development of the individual and society, which he named village *swaraj*. Such a model would look after the basic necessities of every member in the society. He specified that everybody should get a balanced diet, necessary clothing and necessary shelter. He explained the possibility of the village *swaraj* overcoming the ills of the lopsided growth of the world.

The goal of the village *swaraj* was an ordered society which could pursue the path of happiness and peace for individuals and the whole society; it was an attempt towards perfection. By *swaraj* Gandhi meant self-control and independence. The micro-aspect of *swaraj* was the realization of self-control and independence by each and every individual. It aimed at the full development of the individuals. Such mature members were the perfect volunteers who could motivate the whole community towards perfection. Thus, *swaraj* could be created by sovereign individuals whose strength was pure moral authority.

The macro aspect of *swaraj* was the realization of order, peace and independence by society. In short it was the manifestation of truth in the society. The non-violent, socio-political, economic, moral and spiritual structures provide the infrastructure necessary for an integral development of individuals in the society. In such a situation all individuals can lead a virtuous life without great hardship.

But such a social structure could be achieved only there are perfect individuals in the society who would volunteer to work for the general welfare of the community. In this sense, *swaraj* was a process towards perfection for both individuals, as well as for society.

The Significance of Swadeshi

According to Gandhi, the village *swaraj* was not simply the resurgence of the old village *panchayats*, but a fresh attempt to create independent village units on strong moral foundations. He felt that the village *swaraj* would be the most workable social system in the context of modern India. It was a non-violent structure of a society.

The village *swaraj* was a democratic unit where social, political and economic structures were methodically decentralized. *Swaraj* was not imposed from above, but emerged from the masses. It was the self-rule of persons. The *village swaraj* was envisaged as an ideal infrastructure for the integral development of the person and of society. According to Gandhi, the workability of the village *swaraj* depended on the successful implementation of the principle of *swadeshi*.

The concept of *swadeshi* was popularly understood as the expression of a citizen's love towards his nation. It is described usually as an act of patriotism. A patriotic act is mostly generated out of a person's love towards his nation and hatred towards the other competing nations. Thus, we were able to practice *swadeshi* of the most popular type with much spirit and vigor during our freedom struggle against the British dominance. Even now, a few voluntary organizations use *swadeshi* as a political weapon to fight against the economic dominance of the industrially advanced countries. This practice of *swadeshi* brings about a division between *swadeshi and videshi* or *paradeshi.*

But the Gandhian concept of *swadeshi* was not intended to create a division in the society. Gandhian *swadeshi* aimed more at the integration of the people. It was considered a virtue prescribed for the implementation of justice in a situation where one lived by paying what one owed to one's own immediate neighbours. The foundation of *swadeshi* was to be traced to a universal moral law aimed at the good of all.

How can one seek the good of all by giving what one owes only to his immediate neighbours and not to others? Can universal love be limited to one's immediate surroundings alone? According to Gandhi, *swadeshi* should not exclude individuals who are far away, but our attempt to serve them should not be to the exclusion of our immediate neighbours who need our help. We should be available to the people who are immediately near us. If an individual neglects his kith and kin, to be of service to humanity by attending to the needs of distant people he might not get a chance to serve at all, because he might not be needed there. Therefore, the motto 'one who serves his neighbor serves all the world' was considered by Gandhi as the motivating principle of *swadeshi.* Similarly, we should also seek the help we want primarily from our neighborhoods.

Gandhi tried to bring out the social implications of *swadeshi* by defining it as "that spirit in us which restricts us to the use and service of our immediate surroundings to the exclusion of the more remote." Its implications could be seen in various realms. Gandhi advised those people who were after foreign cultural and religious traditions to be contented and happy with their own heritage in which they were born and brought up. One should prefer one's own socio-cultural traditions to that of a foreign tradition. Gandhi found that many Indians were forced to leave their own Hindu traditions due to the intolerant attitudes towards low caste people. Therefore, he tried to empower the backward classes and untouchables to refine the system by purging it of its evils instead of running away from their original established culture. Similarly, he encouraged the volunteers of *swaraj* to develop a political institution based on indigenous political traditions. The concept of *swadeshi* had a deeper and longer impact on the Indian economy. According to the *swadeshi* principle, one should use only those goods which were produced by one's immediate neighbours, so that the local industries could be saved from collapse due to unhealthy foreign competition. Gandhi assumed that a non-violent social system could be established only if we followed the principles of *swadeshi.*

Non-Violent Social Order

According to Gandhi, 'the welfare of all' was the goal of an ideal social order. This could be achieved only through all-embracing, non-violent love. Violence leads to hatred and mutual distrust which is be the beginning of a war of each one against the other that leads to the end of the human species. Thus, non-violence should be the primary basis for achieving human brotherhood; it can enlighten the people and redeem them from their darkness. Because of our ignorance, we separate and segregate people in the name of nations, religions, class, caste, race, etc. The clannish tendency in us could be satisfied when we confine ourselves to our peer groups. A non-violent love is all-embracing; a non-violent society can incorporate all within itself. Everybody, without any exception, has an important place in a non-violent society: prince and peasant, Hindu and Muslim, touchable and untouchable, white and black, saint and sinner, all are treated equally without any segregation, in such a society. Physical and mental differences among the members are recognized as complementary for the development of the society. The aim of a non-violent society is not the uniformity of the people, but their unification, non-violent love is the center of human unity.

Gandhi was not satisfied by just affirming the essential likeness of human beings. All living beings should have the same status; we should establish equality between man and man and also with the whole creation. As he was influenced by the Indian religious teachings, he found no difficulty in accepting the divine presence in every being. He believed that the essence of every living being was the same. Thus, his wider concept of brotherhood could accept equal status for man and for the whole of God's creation.

Each individual was unique in his or her own way and was also different from others in many respects. In a non-violent society, differences among the members were not treated as inequalities. Gandhi blamed the vertical division of the Indian society in terms of caste, color, power, wealth, etc., and considered it an unjust social order. We should aim at a horizontal division of the society where there is no social ranking, because "all these are pervaded by God, there is none that is high and none that is low, all are absolutely equal, equal because all are the creatures of that Creator."

By equality, what Gandhi meant was equal status and not equal division of social wealth. Whenever he referred to equal wages for all services, his emphasis was not on the wage but on equal respect for all professions. As everyone should strive to fulfil only his or her needs and be satisfied with that, the distribution of wealth was not a question to be specifically considered. He emphasized the co-operative and collective use of society's wealth. Special talents of any particular member of the society should be treated as his gifts to the society for serving the poor and the needy. Thus, every member of a non-violent society should give great importance to the welfare of all. They should be ready to sacrifice their self-interests for the common interests of all. Everyone was free to choose his profession according to his aptitude and temperament to fulfil the social needs. Vocations should be chosen not for one's personal advancement, but for the good of society as a whole. On the contrary, in practice we opt for a profession that will fetch us money, power and status, which endangers society. For example, if one who does not have an aptitude for taking care of sick persons, chooses to become a doctor or a nurse, what good can the society expect?

A non-violent social organization should respect the individual's freedom: every member in society should be considered a responsible person. Thus, society should be regulated with the least external coercion. Freedom is an internal force and voluntary actions should be guided by the moral force from within. The society should make provision for the integral development of individuals by their own moral pursuits.

In contrast a violent society finds it easier to regulate society by external force. In order to establish social order it inculcates fear in the minds of its members; at the cost of human dignity, it establishes a social order.

Gandhi was of the opinion that the progress of a society is retarded by the suppression of the free expressions of the individual. Fear tends to eliminate criticism, but the absence of criticism is a sign of retardation. No society could be refined without accepting criticism. A society that suppresses public opinion becomes dogmatic and remains static. A non-violent social order should be transparent and accept freedom of expression as its moral basis.

Gandhi observed that his society was unbearably male-dominated and customs and conventions were not at all favorable to the female members of the community. On the contrary, many privileges and exceptions were given to the male members. Among high caste Hindus, widowhood was enforced, while men were allowed to remarry. Gandhi realized that the remarriage of widows was better than forcing women to suffer their bitter widowhood. Therefore, he encouraged the remarriage of widows. Women were enslaved by male chauvinistic social norms; wives were treated badly for misconduct, while that of husbands was tolerated.

Child marriage was a notorious practice. Parents gave away their girl children in marriage at a tender age. Some parents allowed aged men to marry their young daughters. Gandhi considered this abominable and questioned the authority of parents to indulge in such misdeeds. In this regard, Gandhi can be considered as a forerunner to many modern feminists. He analyzed the history of female inferiority: "The two (man and woman) live the same life, have the same feelings. Each is a complement of the other. The one cannot live without the other's active help. But somehow or other man has dominated woman from ages past, and so woman has developed an inferiority complex. She has believed in the truth of man's interested teaching that she is inferior to him." He argued for the equal rights of both sexes; treating one as superior and the other as inferior he considered an act of violence. Gandhi asserted that a non-violent India could be formed only by the elimination of untouchability and the establishment of equal status for all members of the society. He wondered how a few sparks of the same fire could be treated as outcasts. He was not satisfied with a mere friendly or sympathetic attitude towards the so-called untouchables. The village *swaraj* could be established only through selfless love and service by the leaders to every member of the society. Any form of segregation or separation of a few was against its spirit.

There was a link between untouchability and *varnadhanna* and many questioned his attempt to justify *varna.* Yet Gandhi accepted the *varna* system which divided employment according to families as a workable social system. For Gandhi, *varnasramadharma* was a functional division of the society in ancient India. Its initial purpose of it was to protect certain skills through inheritance which might have otherwise been destroyed in the course of history. It was arranged in a way that would provide livelihood to all. The noble purpose of the *Varna* system was degraded through the enslavement and exploitation of manual workers. Gandhi believed that a refined law of *varna* would be a workable principle under village *swaraj,* helping to overcome material ambitions. He also considered *varnasramadharma* to be a means for the realization of God. This he explained it in *Young India,* in 1927: "*Varnasrama Dharma* defines man's mission on this earth. He is not born day after day to explore avenues for amassing riches and to explore different means of livelihood; on the contrary man is born in order that he may utilize every atom of his energy for the purpose of knowing his Maker. It restricts him, therefore, for the purpose of holding body and soul together, to the occupation of his forefathers."

We know that his position on *varnasrama dharma* was widely criticized in India. Several movements of the backward communities have criticized the rigid laws of the *varnas* and opposed the very concept of *varna* as a systematic and concealed attempt by the upper caste people to exploit the lower caste members of the society, to torture them without applying any physical coercion. Critics questioned the wisdom of Gandhi in reviving a system which had failed even in a primitive simple society. But Gandhi stuck to his position that it ensured the survival of hereditary skills, provided livelihood to all, and reduced excessive competition and exploitation. He considered it a remedy against pauperism. But he subscribed also to the view that a rotten *dharma* was the worst *adharma.*

An analysis of Gandhi's village *swaraj,* where each member stood for the welfare of all, would help us perceive that the law of *varnasrama dharma* has no significant role to play in it. In *swaraj* the occupation of each member was not based on inheritance, but on the social need and aptitudes of each and every individual. In a multi-religious and multi-cultural society such as ours the choice of occupations could be made without any caste connotations. Above all, when we consider the negative influence of the caste system in our society, it has been pointed out by critics that it would have been better for Gandhi to think of a *swaraj* without the phenomenon of the caste system.

A non-violent society gave equal respect to all the religions. No religion was considered as specially favoured by either the state or the village *swaraj.* Gandhi advised Congress workers to cultivate the habit of building friendships with persons belonging to religions other than their own. One should develop the same regard for the other faiths as one had for one's own. Every religion attempted to realize the same reality. God expressed Himself to all, but we failed to understand Him. When His revelation was received by the human hand, our imperfections got alloyed with it. Most of us could not fully understand the Truth. Thus, we were biased towards considering other religions to be inferior. The core teachings of all religions were similar, the differences being mostly in their interpretations and rituals. Gandhi expressed this idea by using the analogy of the leaves and the tree. The leaves of a tree are separate and differ in many respects from the tree, but all are supported from the same stem and root. They do not quarrel with each other, due to their differences, instead they dance to the tune of the same breeze and play a sweet symphony together. Every religion should try to create such harmony. The task of the spiritual members of the society should not be to compare and compete, but to compare and complement each other for the full realization of Truth. The realization of the religious values was hindered due to proselytization and the related competition among many religions. The implication of *swadeshi* was that all should discover the richness of their own ancestral religion. If there were evils or defects in the teachings or practices of one's religion, one should try to purify his religion. A change of religion was not the proper method of fighting against the evils of one's own religion. Conversion of heart was the aim of every religion, if hearts were not converted, religious conversion would be superfluous and absurd. Every religion should be able to serve humanity without competing with each other.

Ever since Gandhi landed in South Africa in 1893 he was an eyewitness to the way Indians, including himself, were repressed and segregated by the white people and their regime. Along with other Indians, he developed *satyagraha* as a powerful weapon against racial separation. They courted arrest by disobeying the ordinance known as 'The Black Act,' by which all Asians in South Africa were ordered to register with authorities and carry a certificate with them at all times. He condemned such discrimination as a threat to human brotherhood and was concerned about the fate of the people of color under the dominance of the White. When Afro-Americans organized themselves against racism, they were advised to follow the non-violent political techniques for lessening racial discrimination and some were adopted by the organization called the Congress of Racial Equality-CORE. Under the leadership of Martin Luther King Jr, the Civil Rights movement in America adopted and successfully implemented the Gandhian methods.

In the same way, Gandhi very vigorously attacked the Nazi anti-Semitism. He felt that in Europe Jews were ill-treated as untouchables by the Christians. Aggression against the Jews reached its peak when German Nazism turned against them, but Gandhi did not show any sympathetic bias towards the Jews. He blamed the Jews for not asserting their citizenship in the country where they were born and brought up. He feared that their call for a homeland in Palestine would be taken as proving the Nazi argument that the Jews were exploiting Germany without loving that country. Gandhi brought to the notice of the Zionists and the world powers that their imposition of the Jews on the Arabs was wrong and inhuman. Already in 1938 Gandhi wrote in *Harijan:* "What is going on in Palestine today cannot be justified by any moral code of conduct. The mandates have no sanction but that of the last war. Surely it would be a crime against humanity to rob the proud Arabs of their land so that Palestine be given to the Jews partly or wholly as their national home." If the world powers had heeded the words of Gandhi, they could have avoided another volatile zone in the world. But their interest was not to solve the problem but to pass on the issue to somebody else. The intention of *swadeshi* was not to create a national land for any race, but to promote an attitude among people so that they could live together by appreciating the cultural and racial differences of each group.

In sum, an ideal social order was one where every member of the society could lead a happy life by pursuing his goal. In such a society everybody could enjoy freedom with a non-violent spirit. Choice, with an all-embracing non-violent love, would not contradict any collective interest. A non-violent society is an integral society which would seek the total development of every member in it. Such a society could provide sufficient job opportunities to all the individuals without any kind of discrimination. And all would use their talents and opportunities for the welfare of all.

Non-Violent Political Order

According to Gandhi an ideal political system should be a stateless democracy where social life was self-regulated. In that case, no political structure would be required to regulate or control social behaviour. But he was not such an idealist as to believe in the full realization of such an ideal. So, he suggested a political structure that would be closer to his ideal of a stateless democracy. Real democracy should aim at the integral development of the individual and of society. The state should prepare all individuals for self-regulation.

The state as externally coercive should gradually vanish by the creation of smaller units which would regulate themselves from within. Therefore, the state was considered as a temporary phenomenon that was planning for the perfection of the individual and the society. According to him the state was not 'withering away' in the process of perfection, but would be scattered into smaller units. He wrote *in Harjan* in 1948 to the people of independent India: "True democracy cannot be worked by twenty men sitting at the Center. It has to be worked from below by the people of every village."24 Modern democracy is highly centralized; it is hierarchical in nature and its power is concentrated in the hands of a top few in the hierarchy who are unwilling to share power with others. This defeats the purpose of democracy as the individual has no voice whatsoever in shaping the policies of the government. This is election-centered, party-dominated, power-conscious and complicated.

The swadeshi spirit of Gandhi helped him to discover an indigenous alternative to modern democracy in the village *swaraj* of the *panchayats.* Since a village was a small unit, all its members could share and contribute to the village in a significant manner. They could influence the planning of their village; and the advantages of the community could be used for the welfare of all. In a village *swaraj,* individual persons could be the architects of their own government. Such a small unit, endowed with socio-political and economic powers, is called *panchayat raj.* It is a non-violent, self-sufficient, economic unit with full political powers. *Panchayat raj* would enable its members to better their living conditions in all aspects.

Panchayat raj was a system which Gandhi tried to revive from the ruins of the traditional *panchayats.* The village assembly had been called *panchayat,* as it consisted of *five* village leaders chosen by the villagers. Village *panchayats* were republics vested with full powers. Later, India was conquered by different foreign rulers and changed the pattern of administration to suit their needs.

They neglected the significance of the village *panchayats,* and the powers were transferred to a centralized body. The British authorities considered the *panchayat* system as a crude and primitive socio-political system. Moreover, they found that the *panchayats* did not effectively favour the British interests. The new administration was meant for collecting resources for the British *Raj.* Gandhi very cautiously attempted to revitalize the *panchayat raj.* As the efforts of Congress to revive the old *panchayat* system were defeated if 1921, he entrusted the Provincial Congress Committee with the task of supervising the process of empowerment of the village *panchyats.* Full autonomy could not be given to the *panchayats* primarily due to the existence of British administration, but secondly because of the immaturity of the villagers. The criminal jurisdiction of the traditional *panchayats* was suspended, as not acceptable to the British judiciary. Even civil suits could not be settled unless both the parties agreed to accept the verdict of the *panchayat.* Gandhi and other village volunteers considered national independence as a favorable condition for the establishment of autonomous republics of village *swaraj.*

Gandhi and others, planned the structure of the *panchayat raj* in an ever-widening and never-ascending circular form. A *panchayat* consisted of five persons elected through adult franchise by the members of the village. The cooperation among the different *panchayats* was assured by linking the village *panchayats* with other units. Two *panchayats* could be joined together under an elected leader from among them, to form a unit. Such a leader would be a first grade leader. Fifty first grade leaders representing a hundred *panchayats* jointly form another unit and would elect a second grade leader from among them. Second grade leaders from every part of India would plan for the whole of India. They would serve the nation with due care and attention in their own respective areas. In order to regulate their function, a chief could be chosen. The *panchayat raj* system could be treated as a national network which incorporated all citizens and cultures into the national stream. Decentralizing the political system could overcome the isolation of individuals as well as the communities, for every section would be recognized in such a system.

Every *panchayat* should be able to maintain and manage its affairs by itself. The *panchayat raj* aimed at the formation of a non-violent, self-sufficient economic unit with full political power. Village workers should organize a self-contained and self-supporting village through agriculture and handicrafts. People should also be educated in sanitation and hygiene. Adequate measures should be taken to prevent ill-health and disease.

Panchayat raj was structured in the form of an 'oceanic circle' whose center was the individual who was ready to perish for the good of all. Thus the realization of the ideals of the village *swaraj* depended on the moral authority of her humble members. Under such a political system no individual or unit could compete with each others for selfish advantages. Competition would be only for excelling in their moral perfection.

Non-Violent Economic Order

In the economic sphere, the adoption of *swadeshi* was considered to be the local arrangement for providing accessibility of livelihood for all individuals in a non-violent way. Existence of this world involves a certain amount of violence; modern economic activities require a higher degree of violence. The purpose of a non-violent economy is to minimize this violence to the greatest extent possible.

Moral values are the guiding principles of the non-violent economy. It demands from all its members that they be satisfied with a minimum of basic needs. The goal of the non-violent economy is to produce the basic necessities of life and to distribute them to all. Such an economy is workable if the needs are simple, because "simplicity is the essence of universality."

The simple needs of all members could be satisfied by society and similarly the means to gratify those wants also should be simple. Righteous ways were promoted to produce food, clothing and shelter for all. It was to be a human-centered and need-based economy.

The foundation of the non-violent economy was the labourer. All the members of the society should work and earn their livelihood. Therefore, an economic structure should be planned in such a way that it be able to provide an opportunity for everybody to work. This would be possible when all would be willing to work and could also be provided with jobs. What Gandhi meant in this regard, was not to make everyone simply a wage labourer, but a manual labourer. According to him, it was a moral and spiritual demand to be a manual labourer. It is said in the Bible that one eats by the sweat of one's brow. The *Gita* considers laboring for food as *yajna.* Everybody was expected to work with his hands for his daily bread; this was known as bread labor. Gandhi explained: "The idea is that every healthy individual must labor enough for his food, and his intellectual faculties must be exercised not in order to obtain a living or amass a fortune but only in the service of mankind." Accordingly, the advantages of the able members should be shared with the weak. When we work only for the satisfaction of our basic necessities, many of the humanly created problems are reduced. A non-violent economy discourages the human tendency to amass surplus wealth and goods.

A non-violent economy should work towards promoting social justice; the welfare of all is its goal. The weak and the poor in the society should not be neglected, but should be able to meet their needs as anybody else. Gandhi expressed his wish in the following words: "I want to bring about an equalization of status. My ideal is equal distribution, but so far as I can see, it is not to be realized. I therefore work for equitable distribution." A good economic structure should be able to obstruct the possibility of unequal possession of wealth by any single individual. On the contrary, capitalism enables a few to amass wealth by destroying the integrated development of the individual and the society. Economic inequality also led to social, political and cultural inequalities in a society. The direct task of the village *swaraj* is to create economic equality so that one could uphold one's own dignity as a human being. Economic disadvantages in a society used to force an individual to accept sub-human conditions of living and it was difficult for a person to escape such an inferior position. Instead, all must have equal opportunity; everyone should be able to fulfil his or her human wants.

Any lopsided growth in society should be discouraged. Gandhi suggested a structural re-arrangement towards this end by a "leveling down of the few rich in whose hands is concentrated the bulk of the nation's wealth, on the one hand, and a levelling up of the semi-starved naked millions, on the other." Thus, the status of all could be placed more or less in the same level. A non-violent social structure could be aspired to only if the wide gap among the different members of the community could be reduced.

Gandhi opted for "Trusteeship" as a workable proposition for the village *swaraj* for the proper distribution of wealth for the welfare of all. In every village, there might be a few with many exemplary qualities and abilities. If they utilized those abilities to amass to themselves wealth and other advantages without sharing them with others they would be encouraging a violent economy. They should be satisfied with what they essentially needed. All they possessed and produced, apart from what they needed, they should be willing to use for the general welfare of the society and more specifically for the most disadvantaged people in the society. A trustee was only a guardian of wealth in a village *swaraj*. "The rich man will be left in possession of his wealth, of which he will use what he reasonably requires for his personal needs and will act as a trustee for the remainder to be used for the society." The trusteeship affirmed the social character of wealth. Some should possess the wealth to protect it, but the guardian of wealth could use from what he possessed only what was necessary for him for an honourable livelihood.

Gandhi suggested the theory of trusteeship to the nation as an alternative to the socialist program of annihilating *zamindars* and chiefs. He felt that the advantages and abilities of those gifted people should be used for building up of the village *swaraj*. He wanted those privileged members of the society to overcome their greed and come down to the level of the bread labourers.

Many in India, were not as optimistic as Gandhi about the workability of trusteeship. Critics questioned the wisdom of Gandhi in entrusting the affairs of the villages to the already ill-reputed village heads. *Zamindars* and other rich people who enjoyed power, wealth, status and recognition would not be willing to part with the privileges enjoyed by them. It was logical to conclude that they would exploit the poor members of our villages much more systematically and intensively when their possessions were legitimized. Gandhi accepted the genuineness of these arguments. But his faith in *satya* and *ahimsa* gave him a strong ground for his belief that any person, however incorrigible he might be, could be corrected. And his experience was that the villagers, even in their crude behaviour, were not as selfish as the English rulers or the city people. They were simple, and on many occasions he could guide them with the help of the Congress volunteers. Through prayer, pleading and persuasion, they could convert many village heads to be right leaders of the village. The *bhoodana* movement of Vinobabhave was an example to this effect. If these means failed, volunteers might be asked to enter into non-violent, non-cooperation and civil disobedience, so that the village heads might be convinced of their duty to the society. Gandhi admitted that trusteeship was an ideal, but if we worked towards that ideal, we could be closer to it. Because of the close and clannish relations among the villagers, trusteeship could be practiced successfully. In villages, nobody could flourish or could aspire to be great without the willing cooperation of the villagers. For example, the wealth in the villages was visibly produced, accumulated and maintained by the collective efforts of many, especially the poor, in the villages. Trusteeship was considered only an initial step in the formation of a non-violent economy. Gradually property should lose its individual character and should become the property of the entire village.

Gandhi preferred trusteeship to government ownership. As trustees were locally available persons who lived with the villagers and were aware of the regional resources and traditional technology, they would be the right planners for the *swadeshi* economy. Moreover, social wealth could easily be decentralized and distributed to all the members through them. Gandhi observed that under trusteeship, there might be a tendency for the privatization of ownership due to selfishness. Yet he opted for trusteeship in preference to state ownership, as the violence of private ownership would be less injurious to people than the violence of the state. The state was coercive in nature, and represented violence in a concentrated and organized manner. According to him, the state was a soulless machine. However evil an individual might be, as he had a soul, he could be corrected. Thus, through non-violent means, true trusteeship could be established.

Gandhi was of the opinion that mechanization and industrialization obstructed the realization of the village *swaraj*. Industrialization could endure only by large-scale consumption. The goods to be produced were not chosen on the basis of the needs of the people but were profit motivated. Therefore, it was the market mechanism that decided production in the economy. Industrialists flooded the market with various consumer articles and imposed them on the people through fair or foul means. One of the great disadvantages of mechanization was that it aggravated the unemployment problem. Gandhi pointed out that the advanced countries even in their glory struggled hard to find jobs for their people. In order to gain more profits capitalists introduced labor saving technology. If agriculture was also to be mechanized in the same manner, more and more people would be alienated from their traditional means of livelihood.

As an alternative, Gandhi urged reviving the traditional village production processes which were labor intensive and need based. He encouraged the development of technology which could serve the interests of all and welcomed the improvement of the cottage machines that could reduce the hardships of the manual labourers.

CULTURAL DIFFUSION AND *SWADESHI*

Gandhi had closely observed the different living traditions in India and had discovered the richness of her heritage. It was one of the richest living cultures among the countries of the world. He exhorted the people of India to make it still more meritorious by removing from it all its demerits and eliminating the negative elements from our culture. The lost or faded glory of the tradition had to be rediscovered and enriched before drawing from alien cultures. Yet, Gandhi did not appreciate a clannish seclusion from other societies by avoiding all possible meetings with outsiders. A temporary separation from other cultures was encouraged by him in order to create a proper environment for self-analysis. He felt that this would help us to realize ourselves and relate with others with self-dignity. Gandhi wrote in *Young India* in 1921: "I do respectfully contend that an appreciation of other cultures can follow, never precede, an appreciation and assimilation of our *own*. It is my firm opinion that no culture has treasures so rich as ours. We have not known it, we have been made even to deprecate its study and depreciate its value. We have almost ceased to live it."

A healthy meeting with other cultures should be based on mutual respect. He encouraged a healthy mingling of our culture with other cultures, but not at the cost of losing one's own culture. Incorporation of other traditions with ours should not destroy the healthy, social and moral order of our culture: "I do not want my house to be walled in on all sides and my windows to be stuffed.

I want the cultures of all lands to be blown about my house as freely as possible. But I refuse to be blown off my feet by any." We should be open to others and enrich our tradition by receiving from the great treasures of other groups. The inventions which have taken place in this world should be treated as the wealth of every community. For example, Gandhi entertained the idea of training a few scholars in foreign languages so that they could translate the classical works in those languages into various regional languages for the advantage of all, but he felt that it should not destroy the social and moral heritage of India. Similarly no particular culture should be imposed on anybody or any group of people. Instead, the elements of an alien culture could be accepted voluntarily by any community who found them useful and acceptable and it would be ideal if the receiver could also give something back to the giver.

Gandhi upheld similar views regarding the *swadeshi* economy. It did not mean that there should be mutual exclusion among the societies. The *swadeshi* concept was not against receiving essential services or goods from foreigners when they could not be produced by immediate neighbours; similarly we could also extend the benefit of our service to the people of nearby places. The motivation behind the principle of self-dependency and self-sufficiency was not against interdependency; rational animals are social in nature, and an ideal social order requires that all the people work together as brothers. But Gandhi emphasized the point that dependency should be mutual, and it should not pave the way for oppression and exploitation. Therefore, it should be a fraternal cooperation where the relationship should not be hegemonic or businesslike, but between equals.

PRAYER AND FASTING

In Western Medicine there is a phenomenon known as the "placebo effect." Even when an unsuspecting patient is prescribed sugar pills instead of medicine, still the patient sometimes reports that symptoms improve. In other words, the mere belief that the pills — made of sugar that has no pharmacological value — will help leads to an improvement in the condition of the individual. This is a remarkable phenomenon whose full significance has until recently not been fully appreciated by the medical community. Stripped to its essentials, it suggests that *faith can heal.* Traditionally, in Western Medicine, this effect was considered a nuisance whose effect had to be subtracted from clinical drug tests. Hence to this day "double blind" tests are conducted in which neither patient nor doctor can distinguish the patients prescribed the real drugs apart from those given the placebos. Fortunately, even secular society is slowly opening up to the use of meditation, prayer, etc. A very encouraging development is that recently, the medical community has begun to realize the relevance of an individual's beliefs to health. For example, a research team at Harvard Medical School conducted tests to study the effects of prayer on the health of patients.

Why study prayer, and what does the placebo effect have to do with it? When people supplicate God for health, they are implicitly placing their faith — trusting their beliefs — in the power of prayer. Indeed, prayer is a potent means of accessing and altering our innermost beliefs. Fasting has similarly been used for tens of thousands of years as a complement to prayer. Moreover, prayer and fasting can lead to slightly altered states of consciousness in which the material world becomes less important, thereby opening our minds to the subtler — more spiritual — aspects of our existence. The power of prayer is not limited to matters of health, however. Through mechanisms as yet not properly understood by science, prayer and fasting seem to be able to release disproportionately large forces. Priests, shamans, politicians, healers and spiritualists of all ages have made liberal use of prayer and fasting for thousands of years. Basically, prayer and fasting are two of the most basic tools of the "art" and "science" of spiritual transformation.

In our age, prayer and fasting have become less important, even empty rituals in some sad cases. But if we sincerely aspire to build a new kind of civilization based on collective security, nonviolence, and spiritual values, then it would be unconscionable to neglect the value of prayer, meditation, deep contemplation, and fasting. Ultimately, we need to change people's hearts, so every attempt to build a better, nonviolent civilization will fail if matters of the heart and of the spirit are neglected.

This chapter examines prayer and fasting as understood by Gandhi and by the Bahá'ís. Gandhi made effective use of prayer and fasting — indeed, his fasts attained worldwide fame. Prayer and fasting are also integral aspects of the life-pattern in the Bahá'í community. Bahá'ís pray at least daily. They also fast from sunrise to sunset, abstaining from all food and drink, for a period of 19 days that ends every year with the Bahá'í New Year Festival of Naw Rúz. The Bahá'í New Year, like the ancient Persian New Year, is astronomically fixed to coincide with the March equinox (usually March 21). The Bahá'í fast is not binding on children, pregnant or nursing mothers, travelers, or on those who are too old or too weak.

Need for Prayer

Gandhi believed that Truth is God and the Bahá'í writings often refer to God as the "Sun of Truth."** As the physical sun provides nourishing energy to the physical earth, so does the Sun of Truth provide nourishment to the earth of our hearts. Gandhi considers prayer to be a form of communion with the Spirit of Truth: This God whom we seek to realize is Truth. Or to put it another way Truth is God. This Truth is not merely the truth we are expected to speak. It is that which alone is, which constitutes the stuff of which all things are made, which subsists by virtue of its own power, which is not supported by anything else but supports everything that exists. Truth alone is eternal, everything else is momentary. It need not assume shape or form. It is pure intelligence as well as pure bliss. We call it [God] because everything is regulated by Its will. It and the law it promulgates are one. Therefore it is not a blind law. It governs the entire universe. To propitiate this Truth is [prayer] which in effect means an earnest desire to be filled with the spirit of Truth. This desire should be present all the twenty-four hours. But our souls are too dull to have this awareness day and night. Therefore we offer prayers for a short time in the hope that a time will come when all our conduct will be one continuously sustained prayer.

Gandhi further explains that prayer is a means of freeing us form excessive attachment to the material world: I agree that, if man could practice the presence of God all the twenty-four hours, there would be no need for a separate time for prayer. But most people find this impossible. The sordid everyday world is too much with them. For them the practice of complete withdrawal of the mind from all outward things, even though it might be only for a few minutes everyday, will be found to be of infinite use. Silent communion will help them to experience an undisturbed peace in the midst of turmoil, to curb anger and cultivate patience.

Not only is it a means to become more detached from the trappings of this world, but people also crave closeness to the True Beloved of their hearts. Hence, prayer serves not only to make us more detached, but also to bind us more tightly to the Source of our spiritual life. Prayer is the language of love. 'Abdu'l-Bahá explains: If one friend loves another, is it not natural that he should wish to say so? Though he knows that friend is aware of his love, does he still not wish to tell him of it?... It is true that God knows the wishes of all hearts; but the impulse to pray is a natural one, springing from man's love to God... Prayer need not be in words, but rather in thought and action. But if this love and this desire are lacking, it is useless to try to force them. Words without love mean nothing. If a person talks to you as an unpleasant duty, finding neither love nor enjoyment in the meeting, do you wish to converse with him?

As the above passages suggest, the human mind is intrinsically attracted to truth and beauty. It can be argued that human beings are instinctively drawn to prayer. From this point of view, prayer is as necessary for our spiritual health as food is necessary for the body. Gandhi explains concisely: As food is necessary for the body, prayer is necessary for the soul.

Bahá'u'lláh echoes this theme in a prayer: O my Lord! Make Thy beauty to be my food, and Thy presence my drink...

Conversation with God

According to 'Abdu'l-Bahá, prayer is "conversation with God." He explains further: We must strive to attain to that condition by being separated from all things and from the people of the world and by turning to God alone. It will take some effort on the part of man to attain to that condition, but he must work for it, strive for it. We can attain to it by thinking and caring less for material things and more for the spiritual. The further we go from the one, the nearer we are to the other. The choice is ours. Our spiritual perception, our inward sight must be opened, so that we can see the signs and traces of God's spirit in everything. Everything can reflect to us the light of the Spirit.

Gandhi held similar views on prayer. He explains the devotional attitude as follows: True meditation consists in closing the eyes and ears of the mind to all else, except the object of one's devotion.

In heartfelt prayer the worshipper's attention is concentrated on the object of worship so much so that he is not conscious of anything else besides. The worshipper has well been compared to a lover. The lover forgets the whole world and even himself in the presence of the beloved. The identification of the worshipper with God should be closer still...

Power of Prayer

Neither Gandhi nor the Bahá'ís underestimate the power of prayer. Gandhi believed that the power of prayer is very great indeed:

Supplication, worship, prayer are no superstition; they are acts more real than the acts of eating, drinking, sitting or walking. It is no exaggeration to say that they alone are real, all else is unreal.

God answers prayer in His own way, not ours. His ways are different from the ways of mortals. Hence they are inscrutable. Prayer presupposes faith. No prayer goes in vain. Prayer is like any other action. It bears fruit whether we see it or not, and the fruit of heart prayer [sic] is far more potent than action so-called.

Bahá'ís believe that the power of prayer is very great because the source of the power is none other than God. Esslemont explains concisely:

If a magnet be held over some iron filings the latter will fly upwards and cling to it, but this involves no interference with the law of gravitation. The force of gravity continues to act on the filings just as before. What has happened is that a superior force has been brought into play — another force whose action is just as regular and calculable as that of gravity. The Bahá'í view is that prayer brings into action higher forces, as yet comparatively little known; but there seems no reason to believe that these forces are more arbitrary in their action than the physical forces. The difference is that they have not yet been fully studied and experimentally investigated, and their action appears mysterious and incalculable because of our ignorance... A small force, when applied to the sluice gate of a reservoir, may release and regulate an enormous flow of water-power, or, when applied to the steering gear of an ocean liner, may control the course of the huge vessel. In the Bahá'í view, the power that brings about answers to prayer is the inexhaustible Power of God. The part of the suppliant is only to exert the feeble force necessary to release the flow or determine the course of the Divine Bounty, which is ever ready to serve those who have learned how to draw upon it.

Nature of Fasting

According to both Gandhi and the Bahá'í Faith, the purpose of fasting is to bring us closer to God. 'Abdu'l-Bahá explains:

Fasting is a symbol. Fasting signifies abstinence from lust. Physical fasting is a symbol of that abstinence, and is a reminder; that is, just as a person abstains from physical appetites, he is to abstain from self-appetites and self-desires. But mere abstention from food has no effect on the spirit. It is only a symbol, a reminder. Otherwise it is of no importance. Fasting for this purpose does not mean entire abstinence from food. The golden rule as to food is, do not take too much or too little. Moderation is necessary. There is a sect in India who practice extreme abstinence, and gradually reduce their food until they exist on almost nothing. But their intelligence suffers. A man is not fit to do service for God with brain or body if he is weakened by lack of food. He cannot see clearly. Some of these ideas can also be found in the writings of Gandhi: A genuine fast cleanses the body, mind and soul. It crucifies the flesh and to that extent sets the soul free. A sincere prayer can work wonders. It is an intense longing of the soul for its even greater purity. Purity thus gained, when it is utilized for a noble purpose, becomes prayer.

I believe that there is no prayer without fasting, and there is no real fast without prayer.

I know that the mental attitude is everything. Just as prayer may be merely a mechanical intonation as of a bird, so may a fast be a mere mechanical torture of the flesh... Neither will touch the soul.

CULTURE—THE MEANING OF CULTURE

The term 'culture' is translated as an equivalent of *samskara* in many Indian languages. It is considered as a moral quality to be achieved through a process of purification. Many Indian thinkers have used the words 'culture' and 'civilization' as analogous, but they are not the same. The term *nagarikatha*, which stands for 'civilization,' denotes the social and material progress of a particular period or of a people belonging to a particular race or community, etc. The two words were used as similar because of the presence in both the words of the act of refinement. Their adjectival forms such as 'cultured', 'civilized', etc., indicate the sense of 'cultivated', 'refined', etc. For example, one who is refined is said to be a cultured or civilized person. The refinement will not be complete without moral purification. An individual or social stage would not be referred to as cultured or civilized unless the individual or the society was guided morally.

The members of a morally oriented society should consciously eliminate the evils and bring the society closer to goodness. Mahatma Gandhi advocated such a concept of culture.

Theory of Cultural Change

Gandhi did not develop any systematic theory as such on social or cultural transformation. But we may be able to draw out of his teachings what was implicit in his thoughts. According to him, human life progresses towards goodness by overcoming evils. There are elements of good and evil in every person. Similarly, society too consists of both *himsa* and *ahimsa.* Humanity should progress towards goodness by being non-violent. Therefore, the essence of human progress should be moral progress. He also observed that humanity was advancing morally. He argued that the existence of society is itself a sign of the presence of *ahimsa* in society, for social life would be impossible if *himsa* prevailed over the goodness that still remains with human beings. We can maintain a level of mutual trust and social order because of the non-violent life style of many.

Gandhi described human history as a movement from *himsa to ahimsa.* He called it the great law of history. But the law was considered not natural, but moral and spiritual. The historical role of man, according to Gandhi, was to participate in the creation of a non-violent society with non-violent love.

At the same time, progress towards *ahimsa* was often obstructed by our violent activities. Some people satisfies their selfish interests without fulfilling their social responsibilities. They used their social placement for the promotion of their own goals, and were motivated by brute force. Gandhi developed *satyagraha* as a method to eliminate such brute force from among the people. *Satyagraha* could help us derive the force that could transform a society by insistence on truth and love.

Satyagraha as a method is aimed at the elimination of evil from society. The intention of *satyagraha* was to annihilate only the evil, not the evil doer.

Therefore, we should not use evil means to eliminate evil, lest evil accumulate. *Satyagraha* could transform society by making of the evil doer as an activist of *ahimsa.* Only a fully convinced and a well-trained person could seek the conversion of the enemy. *Satyagraha* was not an emotional outburst against the evil doer, but the determination of the volunteers to act in the best way possible for the welfare of all. The *Satyagraha* campaign should be a program developed gradually towards a non-violent social order. It should be planned to function step by step, so that the deviations or the degradations could be effectively checked.

According to Gandhi, most persons consciously or unconsciously are used to practicing *satyagraha.* Many members of our families voluntarily accept suffering for the sake of each other, without any ill will against them. We serve others without considering how much others have contributed to our welfare. Similarly, in our families, we correct each other in many ways, even to the extent of causing pain or disturbance to each other. But we do not do it with any evil intention or ill will towards them. What we desire is for the best in life for all the members of family.

Many of our families enjoy great peace and prosperity because of the self-suffering love of the members of those families. But many are not aware that they have been practicing non-violence. If they awakened to their abilities and social roles, they would work for a non-violent society. We need such education, which can bring out the talents and willingness of the students for the creation of an orderly society. In such a society, all would consciously and consistently work for the welfare of all. But some may not be happy with a non-violent society. They may prefer to live in a violent society, where they can pursue their personal goals, which would be against the collective interest. In such a situation of violence, the non-violent members have to sacrifice themselves for the conversion of such evil doers. Selfless love of the *satyagraha* volunteers can win over evil doers to the service of society. Until then the non-violent struggle should be continued. The *satyagrahis* are those who are optimistic about the final victory of goodness.

BASIC PRINCIPLES OF NON-VIOLENT CULTURAL ORDER

A cultured society would become a reality only when it is based on and maintained through the tools of truth and non-violence. According to Gandhi, *swaraj* could not be achieved through untruth or by violent means. He considered *satya and ahimsa* as the basic foundations of a non-violent social order.

Satya is usually considered a virtue. But the Gandhian concept of *satya* should be understood not in its moral sense, but in its metaphysical sense.

Sat, the Real is 'one,' and Gandhi believed in the Oneness of Reality. As that Reality pervades all, Gandhi affirmed the essential unity of everything in Reality. Though called by different names by different people, this Supreme Absolute was seen by Gandhi as the beginning and as the end of everything.

Gandhi considered the Reality as both immanent and transcendent. He is within everything; the things of the world change and perish, but He remains as the underlying principle behind all these changes. The Reality transcends the changing and perishable phenomena of the world; it is the Supreme Essence and the Primordial Being. Gandhi, like the Upanishadic thinkers, held that the highest possible, positive description of the Reality was *Satchitananda,* i.e. Truth, Consciousness and Bliss. As the Truth stands for the ontological reality that 'embraces all and everything;' he described God as Truth. But he felt the necessity of modifying this definition when he was exposed more to the different metaphysical positions. His belief that `God is Truth' might not be accepted by all, especially by the atheists. Therefore, he looked for a better explanation for the all-embracing Reality, which could be acceptable to all. This attempt is found in Romain Rolland's narration of his conversations with Gandhi in December 1931. Romain Rolland described Gandhi's views on God as follows: He was asked at Lausanne to define what he understood by God. He explained how, among the noblest attributes which the Hindu Scriptures ascribed to God, he had in his youth chosen the word *truth* as most truly defining the essential element. He had then said, *'God is Truth.'* But he added, two years ago I advanced another step. I now say, *Truth is God.* For even the atheists do not doubt the necessity for the power of truth. In their passion for discovering the truth, the atheists have not hesitated to deny the existence of God and from their point of view, they are right.

When Gandhi defined Truth as God, his intention was to transcend the limitations of the different concepts of God which were held by the various religions and atheists, because such concepts divide people in the name of the doctrines in which they believe. However, Gandhi's concept would be acceptable to all, as it was not against the belief of anyone. In this way, he invited both believers and non-believers in God to pursue the Truth, and through that process make the world a little more non-violent.

God, who is within us, is our final end. *Satyagraha* is an unending urge for the Truth. In *The Message of the Gita,* Gandhi says: "Man is not at peace with himself till he has become like unto God. The endeavour to reach this state is the supreme, the only ambition worth having. And this is self-realization. This self-realization is the subject of the *Gita,* as it is of all scriptures." The *Gita* showed the most excellent way for self-realization, namely, was *Nishkama karma.* In normal life *karma* is unavoidable. "There must be action where there is body. Not one phenomenon for man is embodied being is exempted from labor." A human being is placed in the world in a way that he or she can neither avoid work nor run away from work. But as actions bear their results, human beings, as actors, are bound by *karmaphala*. Hence, the *Gita* suggested *nishkama karma* or renunciation of the fruits of action as the means of liberation from bondage.

A nishkama karmin should not give up action, because the *Gita* teaches that the one who gives up action falls, and the one who gives up only the reward rises. This is *karma* without *kama*. The renunciation of the fruits of action does not mean that one should be indifferent to the results of action: it is not a purposeless action. The action of the *karma yogi* is to aim not at any selfish end but at the welfare of all. Gandhi quoted from the *Gita,* "No one has attained his goal without action... If even I were lazily to cease working, the world would perish. How much more necessary then for the people at large to engage in action?" Action for *loka samgraha* is unattached work: the worker should not be possessive of his work, nor of its fruits for himself. Renunciation means absence of hankering after the fruit. The worker should achieve equanimity of mind to be a selfless servant; he should be unaffected by the ups and downs of the world.

From ancient days, *ahimsa* has been considered as the first and the foremost ethical principle. Indian traditions treated it as an important moral quality of a *mumukshu* in his progress towards salvation. The literal meaning of *ahimsa* is abstinence from any form of killing. *Ahimsa* was practiced by abstaining from evil thoughts, harmful words and damaging actions. Gandhi's concept of *ahimsa* was broader in its application compared to the traditional understanding. For him "the principle of *ahimsa* is violated by every evil thought, by undue haste, by lying, by hatred, by wishing ill to anybody. It is also violated by our holding on to what the world needs". All our activities were bound by the principle of *ahimsa.*

According to Gandhi, both *satya* and *ahimsa* were closely intertwined. *Satya* is the end of *ahimsa* which is the means; they are not different, but two aspects of the same thing. Through his life and teachings, Gandhi affirmed that without *ahimsa* it was impossible to seek Truth.

At the same time, the path *of ahimsa* could be visualized by a person only if it was illuminated by the Truth itself, because the subject, the object and the way of our search would not be known unless the True Self revealed them to us. In other words, the higher human aspirations could be realized only as God's own gift. This is possible only with a living faith in God. Thus, the true practice of *ahimsa* is a blessing from God himself. It would help us not only to seek God, but to gain the courage to reveal Him to others through selfless service. *Ahimsa* is an expression of infinite love. A non-violent man involves himself in ceaseless work for the good of all. A *karma yogi,* who has given himself up for the service of society, volunteers to suffer for the sake of the happiness of the human race. The non-violent volunteer was capable of transforming the society with his selfless acts. Conversion of the hearts of others would take place by seeing his exemplary behaviour. Gandhi saw such volunteers as the corner stones of village *swaraj.*

Socio-cultural transformation takes place not only by loving cooperation, but also by self-suffering non-cooperation. When individuals or institutions believed in evil and violence without refraining from them, non-violent love could show its face through non-cooperation and civil disobedience. Gandhi suggested resistance as an effective method of protesting against injustice and the evil in society. He assumed that injustice and tyranny could not be practiced without the willing or unwilling cooperation and support of the sufferers of those evils. We could resist the evils by dissociating ourselves from the evil doers. In this way, Gandhi used the virtue of *ahimsa* as a technique for social and cultural transformation and emancipation.

Brahmacharya is one of the requisites for a volunteer of a non-violent order. Its literal meaning is conduct that moves one to be in touch with God. This requires very great concentration on Him, which may become possible only by turning away from sensual pleasures and passions. An individual self, who can control himself by keeping the senses in their proper places, can seek the Ultimate Self successfully.

A celibate life can be opted for by married people, too. But both the husband and the wife should agree voluntarily to follow the vow of celibacy in their pursuit of Truth. They should be able to grow from their love and commitments within the family to the broader aspects of universal love. They should be successful as *grahastasramins* who could do sacrifices such as *deva yajna, pitru yajna, bhuta yajna,* etc. That way, the family which could carry out selfless duties could gradually extend its love and service to others. They should behave as if they were unmarried and think of each other as brother and sister. While making themselves available for universal service. Thus, their love would be free from the impurity of lust and attachment.

Non-stealing and non-possession are the other two important virtues to be followed in a cultured society. They are similar in many ways. The usual understanding of the word 'stealing' was the wrongful attempt by one to take the property of others.

But Gandhi perceived *asteya* in a wider social sense. Relating it to the satisfaction of basic human needs, to possess what one does not need is an act of stealing: "We are not always aware of our real needs, and most of us improperly multiply our wants, and thus unconsciously make thieves of ourselves." 6 Only a person who could progressively reduce his wants could be a successfully non-violent person. Much of the disorders and miseries in the world originate from the massive breaking of the principle of *asteya.* The anxiety and worry about the future could be eliminated in us, if we followed the principle of non-stealing. A humble, simple and vigilant person could observe this principle and gradually become a non-violent person.

Gandhi's version of non-possession also was related to his concept of a contented life. A*parigraha* differs from *asteya* in that the things which were possessed by one were not taken or stolen from anybody else who was entitled to hold it. For example, the possession of an inherited property, which was surplus in relation to one's needs would be considered as a non-virtuous holding. One who pursues truth should be satisfied with the gratification of the needs of the present. Gandhi states very emphatically: "A seeker after Truth, a follower of the law of Love cannot hold anything against tomorrow. God never stores for the morrow; He never creates more than what is strictly needed for the moment.

If therefore we repose faith in His providence, we should rest assured that He will give us every day our daily bread." Therefore, those who own more than what they require should realize that the surplus they hold is not theirs, but that of others. Thus they should safe-guard the surplus wealth in order to cater to the needs and welfare of all. The votary of *satya* and *ahimsa* should uphold absolute honesty, purity of heart and self-discipline. According to Gandhi, to be honest is difficult, but not impossible. Many feel that it is imprudent to be honest and say that one can be successful in business only by using dishonest means. Gandhi was sincere to the old saying that 'honesty is the best policy.' He found that there were no inner contradictions between business and honesty; on the contrary, he felt that honesty brought prosperity to business. He advised the *satyagrahis* to be always honest.

An impure person cannot practice non-violence. As selfishness arises out of impure hearts, greed would compel one to seek the advantages of the world. Vinoba suggested internal purity or *Antah-Shuddi as* one of the qualities needed for a *sarvodaya* worker. He should activate *Shuddha Vyavahara* or a pure and honest life, and renounce unfair ways of earning wealth or securing commodities and comforts. Purity of heart was considered as a basic requirement for a volunteer of the village non-violent culture.

THE VILLAGE AS THE BEDROCK OF CULTURE

According to Gandhi, the possibility of moral and spiritual life was the criterion of an ideal culture. He could learn it from the way of life of the villagers who were leading a contented life. His experience with villagers helped him to derive the idea of simplicity as the essential feature of a contented life. Most villagers, even in their poverty, try to be self-satisfied and self-dependent. He observed that the greatest heritage that we receive from our fore-fathers was the religious spirit. "The innate culture that the villages of India show, the art which one sees in the homes of the poor, the restraint with which the villagers conduct themselves, are surely due to the religion that has bound them together from time immemorial." He feared that this great religious heritage would decay completely through the influence of modern civilization, leading gradually to irreligion. Gandhi recognized that many hated religious values due to the evils meted out in the name of religion. If ignorant and fanatic votaries of a particular religion became intolerant of other religions, society would lose its harmony and peace in the name of religion. But though such discouraging elements were associated with religious practices, we should not give up religion and lose its good values. Instead of repudiating religions, we should purify them by overcoming imperfect beliefs. Then religions would help to establish harmony both within the person and in society.

Similarly, Gandhi considered morality as an essential feature of a cultured society. He supported his argument by explaining the Gujarati equivalent of the term civilization as good conduct. According to him, "Civilization is that mode of conduct which points out to man the path of duty." Civilization was primarily concerned with the moral life of individuals in a particular society. A moral person could gain self-satisfaction by controlling his passions and desires, which would help everybody to live in peace and contentment. We must work towards a social system where we can lead a good moral life. Our ancestors opted for a kind of social structure where the members could seek real happiness by avoiding all luxuries. Dissuaded from aggression and greediness, their culture was relatively stable. They feared that any rapid change would break the social and moral fibers. Gandhi appreciated their choice of an economic structure where everyone would be satisfied with the satisfaction of basic needs.

CRITIQUE OF INDUSTRIAL CULTURE

According to Gandhi, the existence and the continuity of humanity heavily depended on the presence of *ahimsa* in the society. Humanity has been evolving toward perfection by eliminating the elements of *himsa* from the society. But modern civilization has obstructed this process and intruded a kind of violence in industrial societies which destroyed traditional values and the ancient cultures of Europe. Gandhi feared the spread of the violent industrial culture to the other parts of the world. He warned of such an invasion and suggested the means by which India and other traditional communities could withstand such a cultural invasion. He opposed the industrial culture on the following grounds.

Competition and Exploitation

The traditional, need-based and hand-made production methods of the various societies could produce all the essential goods required by them. To a certain extent they were self-sufficient. Yet, these societies also experienced many crises, such as famines due to natural calamities, traumatic death due to contagious diseases, feelings of insecurity due to war, etc. Human attempts to create a self-sufficient society without any misery were the reason for the onset of industrial culture. Unfortunately, industrialization converted the self-sufficient economies into dependent economies. With the industrial revolution, powerful machines entered into the various production processes. Those machines could produce in abundance and made the commodities better and cheaper.

Massive production required the expansion of markets for raw materials. New market mechanisms were developed to bring more and more people into the consumer network. The products entered into the local as well as the distant markets and eliminated the traditional producers from their production processes. Seeing the unending greediness of the industrialists, Gandhi expressed, "Industrialism is, I am afraid, going to be a curse for mankind. Industrialism depends entirely on your capacity to exploit, on foreign markets being open to you, and on the absence of competitors." The industrialized countries sent expeditions to the non-industrialized states and established their colonies, they exploited other nations systematically. The exploited nations initially appreciated the presence of industrially advanced states, considered this a blessing and allowed themselves to be exploited. Gradually this paved the way for imperialism.

The material ambition of the capitalists often transgressed the limits of their markets and led to a brutal war for markets among nations. Gandhi observed: "What is the cause of the present chaos? It is exploitation, I will not say, of the weaker nations by the stronger, but of sister nations by sister nations. And my fundamental objection to machinery rests on the fact that it is machinery that has enabled these nations to exploit others." He traced the cause for the degradation of culture among nations to the adoption of mechanization. With the entry of powerful machines in the production sector, man lost control over his tools and, on the contrary, machines began to regulate human behaviour. Thus, we were moved to work against our own brothers by competing and exploiting within ourselves.

The main goal of the capitalist was making profit. When more and more people entered into the fray for earning profit, the fear of incurring loss was also in the minds of everybody. Therefore, they were forced to engage in a ruthless fight among themselves for their own survival. Accordingly, "in trade and manufacture there is oppressive competition, which results in fraud, chicanery and theft." Every capitalist believed that more profit could be extracted only by exploitation. They tried to get more work from the workers by offering lesser pay and by getting more money from the consumers by over-charging. Capitalists never worried about the miserable living conditions of the workers, either in their factories or in their houses. Gandhi had a direct personal knowledge of the poor living conditions of the mill workers in Bombay where they worked like slaves. The condition of the women workers in the mills was shocking. Such a production process could never be considered friendly to humanity.

Industrialization was based on the unscrupulous exploitation of the natural resources. According to Gandhi, it was human duty to protect all that belonged to the subhuman world. Human willingness to be the custodian of the universe was one of the most wonderful phenomena in human evolution. But by using machines, we exploited nature to satisfy more and more of our greed. Therefore, industrialization was against the peaceful coexistence of man with nature.

Due to competition and exploitation, humanity lost its dignity. It was unethical to continue with a social structure that was regulated by warring competition aimed at the elimination of one's own co-producers and co-workers. It was immoral to promote a system which was based on the exploitation of one's own fellow beings. Gandhi had no second thoughts about condemning such a culture, "Indeed, the West has had a surfeit of industrialism and exploitation. The fact is that this industrial civilization is a disease because it is all evil." Gandhi criticized the competitive and rapid mechanization because of its immoral nature and failure to establish a peaceful society.

The Problem of Unemployment

Work was an essential feature of all human beings. Man was a self-reflective actor who should earn his livelihood through his labor. Gandhi insisted on producing the essential goods required for everyone by one's own toil. He observed that the mechanization was gradually dislodging the necessary human labor from the workers. The majority of the people could not continue with their traditional work. Only a few were incorporated in the new productive methods. For example, the Indian handicraft had been destroyed by the cloth mills of Manchester. Thus, they were deprived of their livelihood. Gandhi pointed out such a danger: "If by some chance, one man could plough up by some mechanical invention of his the whole of the land of India, and control all the agricultural produce and if the millions had no other occupation, they would starve, and being idle, they would become dunces, as many have already become." The introduction of labor-saving machines was a criminal act, according to him. By eliminating human labor, the human character as a self-reflective actor was destroyed.

The machine was highly admired as an instrument which could liberate humankind from the hardships of tiresome and strenuous labor. But the capitalists mechanized the production processes with developed techniques with a view to save on labor. No capitalist used the machine to liberate the labourer from the tediousness of hard work, but only to reduce the work force for earning more profit. Even though human relations should be built on the basis of love, in reality they were based on greed. Gandhi was not blindly opposed to the use of the machines. He appreciated the use of those types of machinery which could serve the interests of all. He was for a decentralized and labor intensive type of machinery which could eliminate pauperism and idleness among the workers.

Mechanization, initially, displaced the traditional workers from their means of livelihood. Of course, a few got better employment opportunities initially but due to the excess of competition leading towards monopoly even those workers gradually lost their jobs and unemployment was mounting. Thus, Gandhi was against mechanization for India. With a smaller population and in better circumstances, even England could not overcome its economic crisis. In other advanced countries, too, the problems of unemployment could not be solved. If India should dislodge its people from their traditional fields of work, Gandhi wondered where they could be accommodated.

Centralization and Concentration

Machines, of course, eased the production process. Machinery produced a larger quantity of goods within a short period of time with a minimum number of wage labourers. The traditional producers could not compete with this type of mechanized production. Therefore, thousands of traditional producers were forced to leave the field so that production became centralized in the hands of a few. Factory civilization had its base on the centralized economic system. The commodities were produced in the centralized factories and distributed to the various markets at distant places through a well-developed transport system. There was no direct personal link between the producers and the consumers.

As huge investments were required for industrialization, the traditional producers could not mechanize their production techniques, because the traditionalists were not working for the accumulation of wealth but for earning their livelihood. Therefore, only those who had already accumulated wealth through some other means established factories and monopolized the production of commodities.

No individual will undertake the risks of such a huge investment unless he could get the money back with very high returns. His intention was a high level of profit. Every capitalist aimed at the elimination of his competitors and wanted to become a monopolist in the supply of goods to the market. In this way, wealth became concentrated in the hands of a few. Gandhi opposed this phenomenon in every way, "I want the concentration of wealth, not in the hands of a few, but in the hands of all. Today machinery merely helps a few to ride on the backs of millions." The most unequal kind of society in the history of the world has been created by industrialization. Greater inequalities between the rich and the poor became a feature of the industrial culture. The rich were the symbol of power, status, privilege and luxury; the poor remained powerless, under privileged and destitute, with the gap between the rich and the poor increasing day by day.

The centralization of the economy and the concentration of wealth could not be protected without the help of the police. A good portion of the wealth was spent on maintaining the army and the police forces. The economy could be centralized only by adopting violent means, which was inconsistent with the non-violent structure of a society.

Urbanization

Centralization of an economy led to the concentration of the population in the industrial areas, producing an urban civilization. Centralization of the economy was due to the mechanization of the production processes. Huge machines and large scale production could not be decentralized due to such factors as the availability of raw materials, power supply, skilled labourers, technicians, managerial hands, etc. Cities provided the necessary conditions which could bring together the infrastructure and other necessary facilities. Thus, cities became the focus for facilities, accessibility, capabilities, and so on. Urban civilization itself was considered the symbol of progress.

More and more people moved to the cities attracted by job opportunities, decent salaries and huge profits. Gradually, cities became overpopulated and living conditions in urban areas became miserable. Gandhi considered urbanization a snare, where all the vices grew.

Urbanization depended on its capacity to exploit the village economy. It destroyed the village handicrafts which were the backbone of the rural culture. Cities could survive only by sucking the blood of the villagers. Cities lived on the farm products produced in the villages but taken to the cities because of their higher purchasing capacity. Consequently, villagers "produce the food and go hungry. They produce milk, and their children have to go without it." The modern economic structure failed to satisfy the basic needs of a vast section of the people who were really producing goods for the fulfilment of the basic needs of humanity. Gandhi was of the strong opinion that life in cities was based on the exploitation of the labor of the villagers. He asserted, "We must not be deceived by the wealth to be seen in the cities of India. It does not come from England or America. It comes from the blood of the poorest." At the same time, the luxuries provided by the urban civilization were beyond the reach of the villagers.

Value Crises

Like many other thinkers, Gandhi also subscribed to the view that modern civilization, which was the creation of modern science and technology, was a disease. Industrial culture provided facilities by which we could do many good things for the advantage of humanity, but it could not move us beyond the perpetuation of the unredeemable evils in the universe.

Modern culture rested on a bundle of paradoxes. We have machines which could reduce the hardships of labourers, but modern production techniques converted millions of workers into beasts. Modern culture promoted bodily ease, but did so by risking the lives of millions in dangerous occupations: millions sacrificed their life for the sake of millionaires. Imbalance had crept into society and every walk of life. There was abject poverty in the midst of plenty. The problem of unemployment rose with the rise in the number of new production centres, for the growth of production techniques many lost their means of livelihood. The health conditions of the people deteriorated. There were new diseases which were unknown to us earlier. More and more scientists and doctors were engaged in researches to discover remedies, but with no avail. A good number of people survived longer, but with prolonged ailments.

The social organism to use affected by disease and Gandhi accused modern civilization for the degradation of morality. Industrial culture made religion less important, which modern science compartmentalized knowledge into sharp specializations. This influenced the moral and religious pursuits of learning, too, relegating them to the concerns only of those who were specializing in those subjects, while others remained indifferent to them. In this way, Europe became a land of agnostics and atheists. The impetus of commerce rendered religion purposeless as modern civilization substituted God with money. All the great religions of the world have taught against the very ambition which is characteristic of modern civilization. They advised refraining from worldly pursuits and turning to godly pursuits.

Bibliography

Andrews, C. F.: *The Gandhian Thought: Social & Political Development*, Akashdeep Pub. House, Delhi, 1990.

Arun, B. : *Gandhian Protest,* New Delhi, Rawat Pub., 2008.

Bakshi, S.R. : *Gandhian Satyagraha and His Technique (1920-1928),* New Delhi, Commonwealth, 2005.

Clayton, A.C.: *Gangai's Pilgrimage and Other Stories,* Culley, London, 1909.

Dalton, Dennis : *Gandhi's Power : Nonviolence in Action*, New Delhi, OUP, 2001.

Das, Ratan : *Gandhi and Mao*, New Delhi, Sarup & Sons, 2004.

Dayal, Parmeshwari : *Gandhian Theory of Social Reconstruction,* New Delhi, Atlantic, 2006.

Deshpande, Vasant: *The Mhaisal Untouchables*, Dastane Ramchandra & Co., Pune, 1983.

Dhanagre, D N: *Agrarian Movements and Gandhian Politics*, Agra University, Agra, 1975.

Dipty Moyee : *Gandhi's Doctrine of Truth and Non-Violence : A Critical Study*, New Delhi, Dominant Pub., 2008.

Dutta, Anil : *Challenges of 21 Century : Gandhian Alternatives*, New Delhi, Mittal Pub., 2003.

Eaton, Jeanette: *Gandhi, Fighter Without a Sword*, Morrow, New York, 1950.

Gangal, Anurag : *Contemporary Global Problems : A Gandhian Perspective*, Jammu, Vinod, 1995.

Gaur, V. P.: *Mahatma Gandhi: a Study of his Message of Non-Violence*, Sterling Publishers, New Delhi, 1977.

George, Davis : *Dynamics of Power : The Gandhian Perspective*, New Delhi, Frank Bros. & Co., 2000.

Gorhe, Neelam: *Social Development and Dalit Women*, Gyan Pub. House, New Delhi, 1995.

Green, Martin: *The Challenge of the Mahatmas*, Basic Books, New York, 1978.

Guha, Ramachandra : *India After Gandhi : The History of the World's Largest Democracy*, New Delhi, Picador, 2007.

Guha, Samar: *The Mahatma and the Netaji: Two men of Destiny of India*, Sterling Publishers, New Delhi, 1986.

Gupta, Manmath Nath: *Gandhi and his Times*, Lipi Prakashan, New Delhi, 1982.

Jain, Vidya: *M.K. Gandhi, Leader of the Masses*, Deep & Deep Publications, New Delhi, 1995.

John, S.J. : *Gandhi and Gutierrez : Two Paradigms of Liberative Transformation*, New Delhi, Decent Books, 2004.

Kshirsagar, R. K.: *Dalit Movement in India and Its Leaders (1857-1956)*, MD Pub. Pvt. Ltd., New Delhi, 1994.

Kumar, S.B. : *Environmental Problems and Gandhian Solutions : The Only Ray of Hope to the Present Ailing World*, New Delhi, Deep & Deep, 2002.

Lewis, Martin Deming: *Gandhi: Maker of Modern India?*, Heath, Boston, 1965.

Maharajan, M. : *Mahatma Gandhi and the New Millennium*, New Delhi, Discovery Publishing, 2001.

Makkuni, Ranjit : *Eternal Gandhi : Design of the Multimedia Museum*, Mumbai, Aditya Birla Group, 2007.

Malik, Saroj: *Gandhian Satyagraha and Contemporary World, Rohtak*, Manthan Publications, Delhi, 1985.

McDonough, Sheila : *Gandhi's Responses to Islam*, New Delhi, D.K. Printworld, 1994.

Mehendale, M. S.: *Gandhi Looks at Leprosy*, Bharatiya Vidya Bhavan, Bombay, 1971.

Moon, Penderel: *Gandhi and Modern India*, Norton, New York, 1969.

Munshi, Kanaiyalal Maneklal: *Gandhi: the Master*, Rajkamal Publications, Delhi, 1948.

Nauriya, Anil : *The African Element in Gandhi*, New Delhi, Gyan Pub., 2006.

Rani, Asha : *Gandhian Non-Violence and India's Freedom Struggle*, Shree Pub. House, Delhi, 1981.

Rao, K. L. Seshagiri: *Mahatma Gandhi and Comparative Religion*, Motilal Banarsidass, New Delhi, 1978.

Rothermund, Dietmar: *Mahatma Gandhi, an Essay in Political Biography*, Manohar Publications, New Delhi, 1991.

Ruhela, S.P. : *Gandhian Ideas on Education—Their Relevance in the 21 Century*, Delhi, Indian Publishers, 2002.

Sankhdher, M. M.: *Gandhi, Gandhism and the Partition of India*, Deep & Deep Publications, New Delhi, 1982.

Sharma, A.K. : *Gandhian Perspectives on Population and Development*, New Delhi, Concept, 1996.

Singh, Shankar Dayal: *Gandhi's First Step: Champaran Movement*, B.R. Pub. Corp., Delhi, 1994.

Uppal J. N.: *Gandhi, Ordained in South Africa*, Ministry of Information and Broadcasting, Govt. of India, New Delhi, 1995.

Wolfenstein, E. Victor: *The Revolutionary Personality: Lenin, Trotsky, Gandhi, Princeton*, Princeton University Press, N. J., 1967.

Wolpert, Stanley : *Gandhi's Passion : The Life and Legacy of Mahatma Gandhi*, Delhi, Oxford University Press, 2001.

Index

❑❑❑